Road Passenger Transport Management

Road Passenger Transport Management

Planning and coordinating
passenger transport operations

Edited by
Tony Francis &
David Hurdle

KoganPage

Publisher's note

Every possible effort has been made to ensure that the information contained in this book is accurate at the time of going to press, and the publisher and authors cannot accept responsibility for any errors or omissions, however caused. No responsibility for loss or damage occasioned to any person acting, or refraining from action, as a result of the material in this publication can be accepted by the editor, the publisher or the authors.

First published in Great Britain and the United States in 2020 by Kogan Page Limited

2nd Floor, 45 Gee Street	122 W 27th St, 10th Floor	4737/23 Ansari Road
London	New York, NY 10001	Daryaganj
EC1V 3RS	USA	New Delhi 110002
United Kingdom		India

www.koganpage.com

Kogan Page books are printed on paper from sustainable forests.

ISBNs

Hardback	978 1 78966 047 0
Paperback	978 0 7494 9701 9
eBook	978 0 7494 9702 6

British Library Cataloguing-in-Publication Data

A CIP record for this book is available from the British Library.

Library of Congress Cataloging-in-Publication Data

Names: Francis, Tony (Transportation consultant), editor. | Hurdle, David, editor.
Title: Road passenger transport management : planning and coordinating passenger transport operations / [edited by] Tony Francis, David Hurdle.
Description: London, United Kingdom ; New York, NY : Kogan Page, 2020. | Includes bibliographical references and index. |
Identifiers: LCCN 2020013941 (print) | LCCN 2020013942 (ebook) | ISBN 9780749497019 (paperback) | ISBN 9781789660470 (hardback) | ISBN 9780749497026 (ebook)
Subjects: LCSH: Bus lines–Great Britain–Management. | Transportation–Passenger traffic–Planning.
Classification: LCC HE5663.A6 R655 2020 (print) | LCC HE5663.A6 (ebook) | DDC 388.3/22068–dc23

Typeset by Integra Software Services, Pondicherry
Print production managed by Jellyfish
Printed and bound by CPI Group (UK) Ltd, Croydon CR0 4YY

CONTENTS

ABOUT THE EDITORS

Tony Francis

Tony Francis FCIT first became involved with public transport when he joined London Transport in 1963 and subsequently worked for subsidiaries of the National Bus Company, including supporting the establishment of the present National Express network. He moved to local government and with Kent County Council became Head of Passenger Transport, developing and implementing polices for the enhancement of bus and rail services.

He subsequently moved to the Strategic Rail Authority, working with passenger transport executives on the improvement of local public transport networks, then moved to the Department for Transport on capital investment projects including the West Coast and Great Western Main Lines. Such activity required working with numerous stakeholders in the public transport business to ensure maximum return on capital investment and to the wider community.

He is also Secretary of the Omnibus Society and the Bus Archive and supports the examination work of the Chartered Institute of Logistics and Transport as well as authoring articles on various current and historic aspects of passenger transport.

David Hurdle

David Hurdle DipTP, MA, MRTPI, FCILT began his career with London Transport in 1964 in various aspects of bus operation. He qualified as a Transport Planner, then moved to the Greater London Council where he secured bus priority measures and sought good access for buses in highway, traffic, town centre schemes and new residential areas, and became a Town Planner.

In the last 20 years, as a transport consultant, he has prepared, or advised on, over 90 Travel Plans. He has published *Little Bus Stories* for 4–7 year olds to establish early interest in the industry, and writes a regular public transport column in a monthly magazine in his home town of Sheringham, Norfolk.

LIST OF CONTRIBUTORS

The editors express their utmost gratitude to those who have contributed to this book. They have spent much time researching and writing to ensure the reader can have a good and comprehensive understanding of the bus and coach business.

Ian Barlex

Ian Barlex is a specialist in road and rail passenger and freight transport, vehicle operations and fleet management, with 47 years' experience: 17 years in industry, and subsequently 30 years as a consultant. He left KPMG, where he was Director of the Transport Advisory Group, in 2007, to start his own consulting practice.

He is a Fellow of the Institute of Consulting, a Certified Management Consultant, and a Member of the Institute of Transport Administration. In addition to his consulting activities, Ian advises the Transport Benevolent Fund, the UK Passenger Transport Industry charity, in the capacity of external Development Director.

John Birtwistle

John Birtwistle started his road public transport career in the last years of the regulated regime, working on ticketing, information and marketing initiatives. Since then he has worked for operators, authorities and (briefly) manufacturers before many years in general transport consultancy, joining FirstGroup in 2001.

He currently leads initiatives on a variety of subjects, including domestic and European policy and legislation, local authority partnerships, business opportunities, concessionary travel, vehicle technology, legal and compliance issues, ticketing schemes and information. He has advised on the implementation of bus rapid transit in the UK and USA. John regularly represents First, and the UK bus industry, on governmental and industry committees.

He was the 2016 President of the Confederation of Passenger Transport, the UK bus and coach trade association, and is the current President of the European Passenger Transport Operators Association.

Gavin Booth

Gavin Booth was born in Edinburgh and joined the Scottish Bus Group in 1961 as a management trainee. He was Group Marketing Manager when he left the group at the time of privatization in 1988. Since that time he has been a self-employed consultant and has written extensively on transport matters, with more than 70 published books under his name.

More recently he was Chair of Bus Users UK and was latterly Scottish Director for Bus Users, working on behalf of bus passengers.

Stuart Cole

Professor Stuart Cole CBE is Emeritus Professor of Transport at the University of South Wales where he established the Wales Transport Research Centre in 2001 and became its first Director. He entered transport professionally in 1974 as Cheshire County Council's Economic Advisor – Transportation. In 1979 he went into academia at the Polytechnic of North London (subsequently the University of North London and London Metropolitan University) as a Senior Lecturer then Principal Lecturer in Transport, and was the first Director of TRaC (Transport Research and Consultancy).

Stuart's main research interests are in public transport (bus, rail and coach) highways management, economics, policy and planning. He has authored over 150 articles as well as the *Applied Transport Economics* textbook. In transport management practice he is a member of, and adviser to, the Board of TrawsCymru, the Welsh Government's long distance bus/coach operation, which he set up in 2012 having researched its base, together with the Bwcabus demand-responsive bus system in west Wales. He is currently on the Great Western Railway advisory board and is President of the Heart of Wales Line Travellers Association. Stuart is a member of the Technical Committee of Eisteddfod Genedlaethol Cymru (which deals with parking, bus and people logistics).

He chaired the Welsh Government's Active Travel Board (2012–15) and has sat on the Welsh Government's Air Quality Commission since 2018. Stuart has produced reports/advice/evidence for the Senedd (formerly the National Assembly for Wales), the Welsh Government, the UK Wales Office, the European Commission, the European Parliament, the Silk Commission, the House of Commons, 10 Downing Street's Policy Unit, and the Federation of Small Businesses.

Between 1984 and 2010 Stuart was Transport Specialist Adviser for the House of Commons Select Committee on Welsh Affairs on 15 inquiries. He has 45 years' experience on relevant and practical solutions to transport and planning policy. He has worked on transport projects in Wales, UK, Europe, North America, southern Africa, China, India, Russia, Ukraine, Georgia and widely in European Union member states including Estonia, Latvia, Lithuania, Poland, Czech Republic, France, The Netherlands, Greece, Italy, Germany, Spain and Portugal for the European Commission.

He is acknowledged by parliaments and governments and the transport industry as one of Wales', UK's and Europe's leading experts in transport economics and policy. Stuart is a regular broadcaster on BBC Cymru Wales radio and television, S4C, and on occasion BBC Radio 4, BBC News Channel and ITV Cymru Wales. He has a monthly transport column in the *Western Mail* and a fortnightly podcast (Transport Talk) on Business News Wales. Stuart is a Fellow of the Chartered Institute of Logistics and Transport and a Fellow of the Institution of Civil Engineers.

He was awarded the CBE in the Queen's Birthday Honours in June 2012 for services to transport in Wales.

Ben Colson

Ben Colson MBE, BA(Hons), FCILT joined the state-owned National Bus Company (NBC) after completing a Business Studies degree course, and held a number of posts in different locations, including senior management positions at Taunton and Northampton. The privatization of the bus industry saw the Northampton-based part of NBC bought by Stagecoach in 1987, the third and final operator it bought directly from the State. Two years later, Stagecoach transferred Ben to Stagecoach North West, covering an area from Greater Manchester to Hadrian's Wall – a mix of metropolitan, regional town and deep rural operation.

In January 1996, with a colleague from the bus industry, Ben bought the Norfolk Green bus company, with just three buses based in rural West Norfolk. A few months later Stagecoach requested that he also take the role of Commercial Director of the newly acquired Stagecoach Manchester operation, and a few months after that the fallout from the IRA bomb in the city brought him face to face with the politics of local transport.

Meanwhile, Norfolk Green grew in size and stature, peaking at just over 80 vehicles and covering a wide area of North Cambridgeshire, South Lincolnshire, and North and West Norfolk. In 2010 it was judged the Bus Operator of the Year in the annual UK Bus Awards, the only SME operator to be so acclaimed.

Norfolk Green was sold in late 2013 due to health issues. Since then Ben spent two and a half years as Chairman of ALBUM, the organization representing the interests of smaller operators, and is now Chair of Bus Users UK, the charity committed to improving bus users' experience and advocating for the bus as a means of reducing social isolation.

Roger French

Roger French began his career in the bus industry in 1970 with holiday jobs, including bus conducting in London and working at London Transport's head office at '55 Broadway'. After university he worked with bus companies in West Yorkshire, Kent and South Wales before moving to Brighton in 1982, staying at the helm of that city's buses for 31 years until retirement in 2013.

He was part of the management buy-out team of the Brighton & Hove Bus Company in 1987 and remained involved after its subsequent sale to the Go-Ahead Group six years later, continuing as Managing Director of the company.

During his long career in Brighton he became active in the community, being involved in many committees, forums, partnerships and charities. He was awarded an OBE for services to public transport in 2005, an Honorary MA by the University of Brighton in 2007, a Deputy Lord Lieutenant for East Sussex in 2007 and was awarded the Freedom of the City of Brighton & Hove in 2013.

Since retiring, he travels extensively around the UK commenting on public transport matters online and in trade magazines. He is a Patron of the Young Bus Managers' Network and a Trustee of the Foundation for Integrated Transport.

Claire Haigh

Claire Haigh is Chief Executive of Greener Journeys, a coalition of the UK's major public transport organizations committed to encouraging people to make more sustainable travel choices.

She also chairs the Delivery & Impacts Independent Review Panel for the Government's Joint Air Quality Unit (DfT/Defra), is the Executive Director of the Transport Knowledge Hub and is a Director of the Low Carbon Vehicle Partnership. She has previously been an adviser and board member of Transport for Greater Manchester.

Steve Harris

Steve Harris started his career with London Transport in 1986 as a driver, gaining promotion after 15 months to a supervisory position. At that time, one could only commence employment as a graduate or start at the bottom.

The mid-1990s saw him managing Cricklewood and then Willesden garages for Metroline, followed by Edgware. He left Metroline in 2001 to work with Steve Telling and Bill Hiron after they had been successful in gaining work from the London bus tendering market.

Steve was asked by the then-Managing Director to re-join Metroline in 2004 as a business manager. There then followed an appointment as Operations Director in 2011, followed by Managing Director in 2018. He studied for the Chartered Institute of Logistics and Transport corporate qualifications in the mid-1990s under Professor Stuart Cole, and became a Fellow of the Institute in 2016. Metroline has 15 garages and over 2,000 buses operating over 100 Transport for London routes.

Kevin Hawkins

Kevin Hawkins is an experienced professional in the bus industry. He was with Arriva and its predecessors for over 35 years, with roles in bus service planning, management of depots as a General Manager and, ultimately, as Regional Commercial Director.

He is now with a specialist consultancy, undertaking work for both local authorities and bus operators on a wide range of tasks, including bus operations, fares, network reviews and ticket machine data. He is married with two very grown up children and lives in West Sussex.

David Jenkins

David Jenkins BSc (Hons) CMILT is a graduate of the renowned Aston University transport course, and had it not been for privatization, would have been among the last senior management trainees recruited by the National Bus Company. Instead he carried out the same role with Southern Vectis, on the Isle of Wight and at their fledgling mainland operations.

Subsequently he held management positions with National Welsh and Crosville Wales, where he introduced joint bus and rail ticketing in Ceredigion. He then moved to Kent County Council, where he carried out much integration of school travel with the local bus network, then became involved with infrastructure and Local Transport Plans.

After a brief interlude as Project Manager for what became the RV1 central London bus route, he returned to transport planning posts at Kent County Council, bringing a more pro-public transport aspect to its work.

Since 2009 he has been an independent consultant, working with others to provide advice to most of the major bus groups, as well as long-standing work assisting a council public transport team, and occasionally working with developers. He writes in the trade and enthusiast press, and has a wide range of contacts within the industry.

Stephen Joseph

Stephen Joseph OBE is a transport policy consultant and visiting professor at the University of Hertfordshire. He chairs the editorial board of Bauer Media's *Smart Transport* programme, and is a trustee of the Foundation for Integrated Transport. He stepped down in 2018 as Chief Executive of the Campaign for Better Transport, having been in that role since 1988.

Stephen was a member of the Commission for Integrated Transport from 1999 to 2005, having been one of the panel of external advisers on the *Transport White Paper 1997–98*, and was a member of the Standing Advisory Committee on Trunk Road Assessment (SACTRA) during its inquiry into transport and the economy. He was also on the steering group for the Government's road user charging feasibility study 2003–04, and was a member of challenge panels or advisory groups for Government plans on high-speed rail, eco-towns, transport appraisal and the Local Sustainable Transport Fund.

He was awarded the OBE (Order of the British Empire) in 1996 for services to transport and the environment, and received an honorary doctorate from the University of Hertfordshire in November 2010.

G Nigel King

G Nigel King is a chartered Civil Engineer specializing in traffic and transportation, with almost 60 years' experience in the sector. A Civil Engineering BSc graduate from Imperial College, London, followed by graduate training with British Railways GW and a post-graduate qualification in Traffic and Transportation from Newcastle University, he has concentrated his expertise in Greater London and has held roles as Head of Traffic and Safety Division at the Greater London Council, Assistant Director (Transportation and Traffic Management) at Royal Borough of Kensington and Chelsea and latterly, Head of the Bus Priority and Traffic Unit (BPTU) and the London Bus Initiative (LBI) for London Transport, as well as consulting for Oscar Faber.

With a comprehensive knowledge of traffic management systems as well as selective traffic management (bus priority), he offers a clear overview of transportation in Greater London as well as nationwide. King has chaired and presented at numerous committees, public enquires and seminars.

King has focused his expertise on the 'people moving' capacity of roads, as opposed to the standard 'vehicle moving', with the particular emphasis on the need to protect buses from the effects of traffic congestion in order to 'keep buses moving'.

Cyril McIntyre

Cyril McIntyre BA, BSc (Econ), CMILT is a Transport Consultant and Editor of *Omnibus Magazine*, the official journal of the Omnibus Society of which he has been a member since 1966. He retired from the position of Fleet Planning & Control Manager at Bus Éireann in 2006, after a transport career which spanned 45 years.

During that period, he worked in a variety of roles in Córas Iompair Éireann (the Irish state transport organization) and its subsidiary Bus Éireann, gaining a wide range of experience across several sectors – railway operations, rail and road freight services, bus operations, computer systems and media relations.

Tim Pharoah

Tim Pharoah is a transport and planning consultant working independently. He has more than 50 years' experience of transport and land use planning, urban regeneration and public realm design, in local authorities, private consultancies, and the academic sector. He is a keen advocate of planning for vibrant urban communities through integrated accessibility, public realm design and speed management.

He was the lead author of *Buses in Urban Developments*, the Chartered Institution of Highways and Transportation's good practice guide, published in 2018.

Susannah Rosenfeld-King

Susannah Rosenfeld-King is a lecturer and practising artist with a BA from Central Saint Martins, a PGCE from the Institute for Education and a Masters from Middlesex University, where she works as a visiting lecturer. Rosenfeld-King has worked in the academic and educative fields for over 25 years with 20 of these spent living in London.

During her time in London, Rosenfeld-King also worked at the Royal Borough of Kensington and Chelsea in their Town Planning department as well as at the London Bus Initiative (LBI). In 2019 Rosenfeld-King collaborated with G Nigel King on site visits to survey specific bus priority measures in London.

David Sidebottom

David Sidebottom started his current role as Transport Focus's Director in June 2011. He initially started working at Transport Focus in January 2006 as a Passenger Link Manager, before being promoted to the post of Bus

Passenger Director in January 2010. David was responsible for the planning and delivery of Transport Focus's then-new bus, coach and tram passenger representation duties.

Prior to this, he spent over 11 years representing the needs and interests of energy consumers in the north west of England where he was regional director of Energywatch, the former gas and electricity consumer council.

Ray Stenning

As the founder and head of the specialist design, marketing and advertising agency Best Impressions, Ray Stenning has possibly done more than anyone else over the past 40 years to change how public transport is perceived, presented and sold through projects and schemes big and small in the bus, coach and rail sectors. As an example, he has probably designed more commanding liveries than anyone else in the world.

Ray is committed and passionate about the role that public transport should play in a progressive society and not only practices what he preaches, he also preaches what he practices as a conference speaker and writer in trade magazines on his pet subjects of design, marketing and customer care. He has been described as colourful, and is certainly unconventional.

He is considered a bit outrageous to some, courageous to others, but under that threatening exterior he has a heart the size of a planet and just wants to create desire and get public transport to be seen as the most desirable way to travel.

Peter White

Peter White joined the University of Westminster (then known as the Polytechnic of Central London) in 1971, as a Lecturer in Public Transport Systems, subsequently being promoted to Professor. He retired from his teaching role in 2015, but continues to be active as an Emeritus Professor in public transport research, especially bus, express coach and rail systems.

He is the author of the textbook *Public Transport: Its planning, management and operation* (6th edition published December 2016), and many published papers. Research interests over many years have included factors affecting the demand for public transport, its market composition, and efficiency of operation. He is the author of a rapid evidence review on the role of the UK public road passenger transport system for the Government Office for Science, available on the GOV.UK website.

His experience includes acting as an adviser to five enquiries on transport-related matters by Parliamentary Select Committees in Britain. He is a Fellow of the Chartered Institute of Logistics and Transport (FCILT).

FOREWORD

Buses are the most used form of transport in the United Kingdom, whilst coaches have valuable roles both in long distance and local transport. Governments increasingly recognize that buses and coaches not only provide connectivity, but they contribute to reducing environmental pollution, tackling climate change and improving life quality. Considerable investment is planned for new services, fleets of all electric buses and more extensive priority measures. A career in buses and coaches offers rewarding opportunities both at a personal level and in contributing to solutions to problems that are increasingly more urgent in 21st-century communities.

The aim of this book is to provide an insight into the workings of the road passenger transport industry, to help those keen to make a career in that business and to assist others who may have to deal with it from the outside (for example in local government), but not necessarily having had the opportunity to understand how it all works.

Although this book seeks to describe the key planning, operating and overall environment aspects in which both buses and coaches function, it is hoped that the reader will be encouraged to explore further, especially in the area where they work and live. Bus services must be designed and provided to meet the requirements of the locality in which they function, but equally there are national standards and disciplines, especially ensuring safety and reliability, that must be observed.

Those working in the bus and coach business have varied skills across many professional backgrounds. Everyone, regardless of different backgrounds and skills, must come together to work as a single team focusing on the provision of quality services. These teams may involve multi-organizational working, particularly with highway and planning departments in local authorities. All should be proud of their part in developing and delivering quality passenger transport.

The editors and contributors to this book are to be congratulated on assembling a guide to the state of the art in UK road passenger transport. The various chapters are written by eminent and busy people, all of whom have gathered enormous experience and understanding of the workings of the humble bus, which is increasingly recognized as having the potential to contribute far more to a sustainable lifestyle, for both rural and urban communities.

We hope you enjoy using this book as an essential companion to study in the art and science of successful road passenger transport management. For the courses run by the Chartered Institute of Logistics and Transport, this book should become an invaluable companion, as it will among the publications and learning resources of the various professional institutes on whose disciplines road passenger transport managers directly or indirectly rely.

Austin Birks (Chairman) and John Carr (Policy Co-ordinator),
Bus and Coach Forum,
The Chartered Institute of Logistics and Transport

PREFACE
Tony Francis and David Hurdle

It is important to begin by explaining the current context, trends and issues facing both the bus industry and those associated with it such as local authorities, and to highlight some key messages for the future.

Buses have never been as important in their 200-year-and-more history as now: 50 per cent of all public transport passenger journeys in England are by bus. There are 33,900 buses, with London accounting for 29 per cent of them, and 51 per cent of all bus passenger journeys. (All the following information applies to England, and is taken from the Department for Transport's annual bus statistics for 2018/19 (Department for Transport, 2019).)

Trends

The overall trend in bus travel, that of decline, is clearly a major concern given the role that buses can play in encouraging more sustainable travel. Passenger journeys have fallen by 7 per cent from 1982 to 2018–19. Although there have been upward trends, eg during 2004–08, there has been a downward trend since 2008. In London, bus use increased each year between 1998/99 and 2012/13, since when it has declined each year; albeit still higher, 22 per cent, in 2018/19 than in 2004/05.

Real-term increases in the cost of bus travel continue to contribute to the unattractiveness of using buses. In the year to March 2019, bus fares increased by 3.3 per cent, faster than the annual all items Consumer Prices Index rate of inflation of 1.9 per cent. Between March 2005 and March 2019, inflation rose 38 per cent, but bus fares rose 71 per cent.

Another worrying trend is that central and local government support for local bus services has been declining since 2009, putting further pressure on bus operations. Support consists of three elements:

1 Payments for supported services. Bus mileage outside London has declined by 14 per cent since 2004/05. This has been driven by a 50 per cent decrease in local authority supported mileage.

2 The Bus Service Operators Grant (BSOG). This has decreased by 46 per cent in real terms between 2004/05 and 2018/19.

3 Concessionary travel reimbursement. This comprises 47 per cent of total support. Concessionary travel (for older and disabled people, and young people where local authority schemes exist) makes up 34 per cent of bus passenger journeys.

There are huge variations in bus travel around England. Outside London the local authorities with the lowest bus passenger journeys per head are Rutland and Windsor and Maidenhead, with just 9 per year. Compare this with the highest – Brighton and Hove with 172, and Nottingham with 150. The average is 45. Out of the 88 authorities outside London, 70 saw a decrease from 2009/10 to 2018/19.

Issues

The debates on climate change and air pollution alone require urgent action and different policies. Quite simply, roads are used to over-capacity, and how we travel needs to change. Buses, with their efficient use of road space, contribute to an immediate and quality solution. But their role is often misunderstood; with some justification, people have poor perceptions of them. They are sometimes unreliable, uncomfortable, and turn up late or not at all.

In 2018/19, 83 per cent of non-frequent services ran on time; 'on time' is defined as between one minute early and 5 minutes and 59 seconds late. This means that nearly one in five did not. There was also a large variation in punctuality between authorities, ranging from 63 per cent to 97 per cent. But this can change.

A key aspect of operating buses is that they use public roads that are owned and maintained by a variety of national, regional and local authorities, unlike railways that have their own right of way. Roads are used by many other vehicles, and this can result in congestion, slow speeds and unpredictable delays to buses. Highway authorities should be fully appreciative of this and of the ways that they can each assist efficient bus operation. They have an enormous influence in enabling efficient bus operation, and reliable and attractive services.

Furthermore, planning authorities can ensure that new developments such as housing, business and commercial centres build in and accommodate efficient bus operation. Employers should also be encouraging their staff to travel more sustainably. Despite declining bus use throughout the United Kingdom, there have been some excellent examples of passenger growth. It can be achieved given the will.

And the role that buses can play in the future looks promising. The industry is embracing new fuels and new technology. The vast majority of buses, 92 per cent, have CCTV, 98 per cent have an Automatic Vehicle Location device, 74 per cent are enabled for payment by contactless bank card, and 31 per cent have free wi-fi.

A factor often not recognized is that bus travel is six times safer than car travel, and the safest of any form of travel; the fatality rates per billion passenger miles being 0.3 and 1.8 respectively.

Messages

First we need to understand the bus industry and the essential assistance it needs. This book's purpose is to do that. It is a manual aimed at:

- people joining the industry;
- those within it and progressing their careers, who could benefit from learning about good practice elsewhere (through case studies), and about greater co-operation with local authorities and other partners;
- crucially, local authorities at all levels, and how they can assist bus operation and increase patronage.

Therefore, all aspects of bus operation are covered.

Part One of the book explains how the bus business works, from the legal framework to planning services, fares and revenue, and staffing. Part Two then covers wider engagement. It stresses the importance of operators working in partnership with other organizations, be they local authorities, employers, developers. It examines the market for public transport, planning new housing to ensure efficient bus operation and maximum use, bus priority measures to ensure efficient operation, the particular challenge of providing rural bus services, Travel Planning with employers to reduce 'drive-alone' car use and maximize sustainable travel, buses' social role, the all-important need to promote bus services and not just publicize them, and finally their future role in a rapidly-changing environmental context.

Although in decline, bus travel remains an important, and safe, form of travel. Yet as well as suffering from declining use, it is also witnessing less financial support from central and local government and having to implement above-inflation fare rises.

The role of bus services needs to be far better appreciated and supported. Yet a key finding from preparing this book is the inconsistency throughout the country in supporting the bus industry. If ever there was a need for an effective national strategy, it is now. Buses can play a major short-term role in tackling climate change, which by its very nature requires urgent, and different, action now. As at 21 October 2019, 65 per cent of the UK's councils had declared a climate change emergency (Climate Emergency UK, 2019). But bus operation needs the support of central and local government to do its job properly and efficiently, and to ensure all services are attractive to use.

The book has drawn upon the expertise and experience of many well-respected professionals in, and close to, the industry. Each chapter leaves messages. These need to be acted upon to ensure that the industry contributes to more sustainable travel by being both efficient to operate and attractive to use. Operators working in partnership with other bodies is key.

A final message. Bus operators are not in business to run buses; they are in business to carry people, with a full understanding of their individual and collective needs.

References

Climate Emergency UK (2019) [accessed 16 January 2020] List of Councils who have declared a Climate Emergency, *Climate Emergency UK* [online] www.climateemergency.uk/blog/list-of-councils/ (archived at https://perma.cc/3QHF-R4Z7)

Department for Transport (2019) [accessed 14 January 2020] Annual bus statistics: England 2018/19, *GOV.UK* [online] https://assets.publishing.service.gov.uk/government/uploads/system/uploads/attachment_data/file/852652/annual-bus-statistics-2019.pdf (archived at https://perma.cc/L646-GD4B)

PREFACE
COVID-19 update

Two major issues directly affecting bus and coach operation arose in early 2020:

- The COVID-19 global pandemic – this had an *immediate* impact on the industry.
- The publication of the Department for Transport's (DfT's) 'Decarbonising Transport, Setting the Challenge' (Department for Transport, 2020a) – this will have a *long-term* impact but nevertheless needs to start to be addressed urgently. This consultation document could not have arrived at a more timely moment as 'pandemic actions' help the aims of decarbonizing transport.

COVID-19: Operators' responses

If nothing else the outbreak has shown how public transport can respond quickly and flexibly when it needs to. Operators rose to the challenge and emergency timetables were introduced at very short notice. They maintained necessary services, eg to hospitals. There were examples of:

- free travel for NHS workers;
- bus drivers doing deliveries in remote areas;
- making space in depots for storing new and recommissioned ambulances;
- operating NHS shuttle services;
- social distancing and additional cleaning on buses;
- bus, and coach, operators providing additional services to key distribution and food manufacturing sites; and
- coach operators delivering food parcels to vulnerable people.

COVID-19: Government support

The Government provided emergency funding to the industry (Department for Transport, 2020b):

- The COVID-19 Bus Services Support Grant (CBSSG) funded operators' reduced bus networks and also local authority revenue shortfalls on supported services.
- Bus Service Operators Grant was still paid based on pre-virus service levels.
- The DfT requested councils to continue to pay bus and coach operators for tendered services, concessionary fare reimbursement and home-to-school transport at pre-virus levels.
- Traffic Commissioners issued emergency guidance for short notice applications to change timetables.

The Future

The above raise many questions that, as at May 2020, are impossible to answer yet:

- Will patronage return to what it was if more commuters work from home? Instead of having maybe every Friday off, or working at home then, might people work at home two or more days a week, or for two hours then go to work late morning when fares may be lower?
- What about off-peak travel? Online shopping has been rising for years and has now had a further boost. Given this trend and more shops closing will off-peak shopping trips reduce?
- Some people may have tried alternative ways to travel such as cycling, walking and car sharing. Will this continue or revert?
- 'Social distancing' on public transport may well add significantly to operators' costs.
- Will people be wary of using public transport?
- Although operators may face reduced custom will they be able to reduce the number of buses and staff to match lower demand? Having some resources only for use for a few hours per day, at peak times, has always been expensive and inefficient.
- Will less traffic and so less congestion, also less cash-handling, speed up services, improving efficiency? Or will more people use cars instead of public transport?

- If the industry shrinks some operators may be the victims. For instance, the express coach network in England and Wales, though not Scotland, as at April 2020, virtually disappeared, preceded by excursion, tour and hire work.

- There are several imponderables – government interventions, including more Clean Air Zones and Road User Charges to increase taxes; how the country's deepest economic recession ever will affect travel; how might businesses adapt and people's lifestyles change?

But there *are* several 'positives' such as less air pollution and carbon dioxide emissions, and the industry's proven ability and flexibility to adapt quickly to new demands. Although the aftermath of the virus pandemic on bus and coach services is at present very uncertain, and the future impossible to predict, their environmental role is *clear cut*. As the first sentence of the DfT's document on decarbonizing transport reads, 'Climate change is the most pressing environmental challenge of our time'; and a key point made is – 'Public transport and active (cycling and walking) travel will be the natural first choice for our daily activities. We will use our cars less and be able to rely on a convenient, cost-effective and coherent public transport network'.

Following the DfT's consultation, a Transport Decarbonization Plan will follow, as will a National Bus Strategy. So, to sum up:

There are many questions about the future that cannot be answered yet.

However, the bus and coach industry has ably demonstrated it can respond to an extremely challenging situation, *and* its environmental role is crucial in tackling the Climate Change Emergency. Quite simply, many of the drastic measures implemented during the COVID-19 pandemic about travelling less are in fact versions of the shifts we will *need* to make to achieve net zero carbon emissions.

Working in partnership with other stakeholders, both in the public and private sectors, will be essential to, for example, help identify new markets for bus and coach travel.

References

Department for Transport (2020a) Decarbonising Transport, Setting the Challenge
Department for Transport (2020b) COVID-19 – Supporting the bus sector and its passengers, letter to Confederation of Passenger Transport UK, 25 March 2020

LIST OF ABBREVIATIONS

ABT	Account Based Ticketing
APTA	American Public Transportation Association
AQP	Advanced Quality Partnership
AVL	Automatic Vehicle Location
BCR	benefit/cost ratio
BET	British Electric Traction [Company]
BPTU	Bus Priority and Traffic Unit
BRT	bus rapid transit
BSOG	Bus Service Operators Grant
BSSG	Bus Service Support Group
Btec	Business and Technology Education Council
C&G	City & Guilds
CCTV	closed-circuit television
CIÉ	Córas Iompair Éireann
CILT	Chartered Institute of Logistics and Transport
CMA	Competition and Markets Authority
COIF	Certificate of Initial Fitness
CPC	Certificate of Professional Competence
CPT	Confederation of Passenger Transport
DCPC	Drivers' Certificate of Professional Competence
DfES	Department for Education and Skills
DfI	Department for Infrastructure [Northern Ireland]
DfT	Department for Transport
DiPTAC	Disabled Person's Transport Advisory Committee
DoT	Department of Transport
DR	demand-responsive
DRT	demand responsive travel
DVA	Driver and Vehicle Agency [Northern Ireland]
DVLA	Driver and Vehicle Licensing Agency
DVSA	Driver and Vehicle Standards Agency
EISC	Economic, Infrastructure and Skills Committee
EMA	Europay, Mastercard, Visa
EP	Enhanced Partnership
EQV	Equality Quality Verifier

EU	European Union
FDR	Fuel Duty Rebate
FSB	Federation of Small Business
GDA	Greater Dublin Area
GDPR	General Data Protection Regulation
GLA	Greater London Authority
GPS	Global Positioning Satellite
GNR(I)	Great Northern Railway (Ireland)
HE	Highways England
HGV	heavy goods vehicle
HR	Human Resources
IPCC	Intergovernmental Panel on Climate Change
IPP	incentive per passenger
IQV	Internal Quality Verifier
JAUPT	Joint Approvals Unit for Periodic Training
JTA	Joint Transport Authority
LAEI	London Atmospheric Emissions Inventory
LBI	London Bus Initiative
LCO	Legislative Competence Order
LEA	local education authority
LSP	London Service Permit
LTA	local transport authority
LTB	Local Transport Body
LTP	Local Transport Plan
MaaS	Mobility-as-a-Service
mpg	miles per gallon
MTC	multi-operator travelcard
NBC	National Bus Company
NHS	National Health Service
NITHC	Northern Ireland Transport Holding Company
NOx	nitrogen oxide
NPPF	National Planning Policy Framework
NTA	National Transport Authority
NTS	National Travel Survey
NXWM	National Express West Midlands
O	Operator
OCRS	Operator Compliance Risk Score
OFT	Office of Fair Trading
OMO	one-man-operation

P&R	Park and Ride
pcu	passenger car unit
PGCE	Postgraduate Certificate in Education
PHV	private hire vehicle
PLC	public limited company
PPG13	Planning Policy Guidance Transport
PPK	pence per km
PSV	Public Service Vehicle
PTA	Passenger Transport Authority
PTR	Public Transport Regulations
PVR	Peak Vehicle Requirements
QCS	Quality Contract Scheme
RSA	Road Safety Authority
SACTRA	Standing Advisory Committee on Trunk Road Assessment
SME	small and medium-sized
SQBC	statutory quality bus contract
SQBP	statutory quality bus partnership
SVD	selective vehicle detection
TC	Traffic Commissioner
TCA	Travel Concession Authority
TEBPP	TransportEnergy Best Practice Programme
TFI	Transport for Ireland
TfL	Transport for London
TfN	Transport for the North
TfW	Transport for Wales
TIM	Ticket Issuing Machine
TRL	Transport Research Laboratory
TUPE	Transfer of Undertakings (Protection of Employment)
VCA	Vehicle Certification Agency
VOSA	Vehicle and Operator Services Agency

PART ONE
How the bus
business works

Definition of road passenger transport

01

PETER WHITE

Introduction

The main emphasis of this chapter is on bus and coach services, but reference is also made to the taxi and private hire vehicle (PHV) sector. The focus is on this topic in the United Kingdom of Great Britain and Northern Ireland, together with reference to international services. Selected examples are used from other countries to illustrate developments in specific service types.

The major service types are described, with discussion of the typical patterns of provision. Substantial differences between the 'deregulated' parts of Britain, and where deregulation did not apply – London and Northern Ireland – are identified. Specific market segments, such as those for education travel, Park and Ride (P&R) services, bus rapid transit (BRT), interurban, demand-responsive and express services, are described. The roles of community transport, and taxis and PHVs, are also examined.

The chapter concludes by looking at current and future developments.

Principal types of bus service

Under legislation applicable in mainland Britain, the main distinction between the types of services is between 'local' and 'other'. 'Local' broadly corresponds to a bus as generally understood, ie a service operating on public highways with frequent kerbside stops. In general, a fixed route and timetable are specified, but 'demand-responsive' services may also be operated, defined by an area of coverage and time period. Services operate at separate fares, which comprise not only payments in cash but also passenger journeys validated by smartcard, contactless bank card, concessionary passes, travelcard, etc.

Outside London, operators are free to register the services they wish to operate (subject to a required period of notice), specifying route and timetable. Fares are not generally subject to regulation, although may be specified under individual contract arrangements, such as those that apply to some P&R services. This situation has applied since the Transport Act of 1985, in force since October 1986. More detailed information on the registration process, role of the Traffic Commissioners, and the operator licence system is given in Chapter 3.

A typical pattern of a local bus service would be operation on at least six days per week (Monday to Saturday inclusive), with many services in urban areas also operating on Sundays. Weekday services typically start about 06.30 and run between about 08.00 and 18.00 at a similar frequency throughout that period, as confirmed in data published by the Department for Transport (DfT) based on aggregating data from service registrations (DfT, 2014); these data also show that evening and Sunday service frequencies outside London, are, in aggregate, about one-third of weekday daytime levels.

Many services continue into the evening, especially in urban areas, albeit at reduced frequencies. Peak demand for journeys to/from work and places of education is balanced by inter-peak demand for purposes such as shopping, stimulated by free concessionary travel for older people. This pattern supports good vehicle utilization, and reasonably efficient scheduling of driver shifts, in contrast with a much more 'peaked' pattern of service provision found in the 1970s, and still to be seen in other countries such as the USA. However, some additional vehicles may be needed at peak times, even if the service does not operate more frequently, simply to allow for greater running times due to traffic congestion.

Under the system within mainland Britain outside London, operators determine which services they are prepared to operate 'commercially', ie where all costs (including a profit margin) are covered from passenger revenue, compensation for free concessionary travel and the Bus Service Operators Grant (BSOG). The last is a grant paid directly to the operator for commercially-registered services (for tendered services this is paid to the contracting body), which partly offsets fuel duty otherwise paid, but also has incentives for low-carbon vehicles and smartcard ticketing.

Hence, the likely density of demand will determine both the routes covered and periods of the day and week. For lower density services, the daytime Monday–Saturday pattern above might represent the entire commercial registration, with early morning, evening and Sunday journeys provided only under contract with the local transport authority. Local authorities (principally counties, and unitaries) have discretionary powers to secure 'socially necessary' services additional to those registered commercially, but are under no obligation to do so. However, as activity patterns have changed (Sunday now being a busy day for shopping, for example) some operators have sought to provide more comprehensive services commercially. Growing flexibility in working patterns also supports this.

It is highly desirable that where separate commercial and contracted services are provided at different time periods over the same route (which are not necessarily run by the same operator) that comprehensive passenger information and integrated ticketing is provided, since many passengers may be making return trips which may involve, for example, travelling into a centre during the daytime commercial period and returning in the evening, possibly with a different operator.

A disadvantage of the current regulatory structure is the difficulty of adding extra services such as higher frequencies, a longer operating day or more comprehensive network coverage, without going out to contract. The 'de minimis' provision in the legislation allows this to happen only to a very limited extent. The gradual introduction of Partnership Agreements is enabling the incidence of comprehensively planned and coordinated services to expand.

London and Northern Ireland

The great majority of bus services within Greater London are operated on contract to Transport for London (TfL). Contracts are usually issued on a route-by-route basis, covering the whole week. Fares are set by TfL, resulting in a simple fare structure over the whole network. Cash fares are no longer collected on-bus. As elsewhere in Britain, a similar frequency is provided through the Monday to Saturday daytime period, but a substantially higher level of evening and Sunday service is operated (about two-thirds of weekday daytime levels), together with many all-night services. About twenty operators provide services for TfL, both UK-owned and those from other countries such as RATP Dev of Paris, and Tower Transit of Australia.

Within London, services carrying local traffic, other than those operated on behalf of TfL, are regulated under the 'London Service Permit' (LSP) system, managed by TfL. Operators apply for permits, typically specifying route and timetable. These may include services at separate fares operating wholly within London (such as to a private school), those for tourists (such as 'hop on/hop off' open-toppers), and sections of longer routes (local cross-boundary services, commuter coaches and longer-distance express services carrying local passengers within London). Such services are not part of the TfL fares system.

Northern Ireland retains a system closer to that of mainland Britain prior to deregulation in the 1980s (see Chapter 3), the great majority of services being provided by the state-owned Translink organization through its subsidiaries. Even within the express sector, it is difficult for other operators to secure consent to compete with Translink.

Variations within the local bus market

Education demand and service provision

In addition to the typical service pattern described above, education travel demand forms a substantial component, often accounting for much of the demand at peak periods, in addition to adult journeys between home and work.

In respect of school travel, there is a statutory obligation on local education authorities (LEAs) to provide free travel for pupils up to the age of 16 inclusive, where they live above a certain distance from the nearest appropriate school, two miles up to age of eight, three miles above that age (discretion to offer more generous provision has generally declined due to spending constraints). In many areas, separate services are provided under contract for these pupils, and where no passengers at separate fares are carried, registration as a local service does not apply. In most cases, these services form an important source of work for local bus and coach operators, especially in rural areas. The LEA may also ensure such provision through vehicles it owns directly, or by purchasing season tickets for travel on scheduled local services.

In many areas, a substantial demand also arises from 'non statutory' school travel, ie that below the free statutory distances, the pupils paying separate fares on registered local services. In general, such traffic is not commercially worthwhile if extra peak capacity has to be provided (or separate routes) and operators may only be willing to provide this on a contracted service basis. Traditionally, lower fares (such as half the adult rate) have been charged, but there is no consistent pattern. A recent phenomenon is the extension by a few operators of 'child' fares to higher age groups, eg to 18, or to all students (in a few cases with no age limit) and young people. A generous provision applies in London, where entirely free travel is provided up to the age of 17 inclusive.

The growth of education and training up to the age of 18, often through further education colleges, has also created additional demand, as has the expansion of universities. Likewise, such demand may be handled either by use of the general public network or specific services. In the case of some universities, networks initially developed to serve out-of-centre campuses have expanded to provide general public services throughout the year, notably 'Uno' in Hertfordshire and Northampton, 'Unilink' in Southampton and 'Your Bus', a First Group/University partnership in York.

Park and Ride services

Growing car congestion in the centres of urban areas may not always be resolved by provision of additional parking spaces and/or road capacity. Indeed, in historic cities such as Oxford or York, much of their character might be destroyed by such measures, quite apart from the capital cost incurred. Since about 1980, extensive bus-based Park and Ride (P&R) provision has developed (typically in cities of this size rather than larger conurbations).

P&R sites on the fringe of the built-up area (such as Thornhill on the east of Oxford) intercept car traffic for the city centre, which is then handled usually by dedicated P&R buses registered as local services. Site provision is normally the responsibility of the local authority, and may be charged separately. In the case of large schemes, demand is sufficient to justify commercially-registered bus operation, such as in Cambridge and York. In Scotland, there is comprehensive P&R bus service provision across the Forth between Fife and Edinburgh. Patronage may be assisted by off-peak demand from shopping and tourist activity; a largely peak-based service is unlikely to be commercially viable due to poor vehicle utilization.

This development of bus-based P&R is rarely found in other countries, where P&R is normally rail-based (as it mostly is in the larger conurbations of Britain). A criticism made is that in many cases the total volume of car-kilometres is actually increased, as a number of additional trips are made from the rural or suburban catchment areas to the P&R sites (for example, those who formerly used a rural bus service, driving to the P&R site instead). However, it should be borne in mind that these additional car-km are often on relatively uncongested rural roads, whereas removal of those on congested urban roads between the P&R site and the centre will provide much greater benefits (Mills and White, 2018).

P&R services may be particularly attractive where combined with bus rapid transit, since much faster journeys can be provided into the urban centre, for example from the large sites located on the Cambridgeshire busway.

Interurban services

Whilst most local bus journeys are very short (the average passenger trip is around 8km outside London), the role of 'interurban' services caters for somewhat longer trips. These are still services registered as 'local' (as distinct from 'express'), connecting smaller urban areas with larger regional cities. Intermediate local traffic from villages is still also carried, but routeing has often been made more direct in recent years. Examples include Transdev's service 36 (Ripon–Harrogate–Leeds), the Yorkshire Coastliner network, with its associated fast Leeds–York 'City Zap' service, and First's Peterborough–Wisbech–King's Lynn–Dereham–Norwich cross-Norfolk service. These often fill gaps in the rail network dating from the 'Beeching' cuts of the 1960s, and in some cases may offer through ticketing with rail (Luke, Steer and White, 2018).

Traditionally, bus operators made little effort to distinguish such services from other local operations, but in recent years have realized the benefits of distinctive marketing, higher frequency, and improved vehicle quality. Strong demand growth has often been reported, and operations are generally commercially viable.

Another significant example is the Express City Connect network of Stagecoach in Scotland, principally linking towns and cities of Fife with Edinburgh and Glasgow via the Forth Bridge, also serving two large P&R hubs. Within Wales, the publicly-funded TrawsCymru network provides extensive interurban links which fill gaps in the rail network.

At the time of writing (early 2020), political pressures to reopen rural railways can be seen in a number of areas, but their economic justification is often very dubious, and strengthened interurban bus services may provide much better value.

Other 'passenger carrying' services

As well as education services, an area usually has minibuses carrying people to social care day centres and non-emergency patient transport to hospitals and clinics. There may also be superstore and hotel courtesy buses, and minibuses owned by clubs and societies. Some of these are referred to later in this chapter in association with 'total transport' trials of coordinating education, social and health transport. A previous, and interesting, attempt at coordination in the UK, in this instance Royal Mail operating postbuses that combined a public bus service with mail delivery and collection, has now ceased. It operated for 50 years from 1967 until 2017 in remote rural areas. Such services had been common in some European countries, such as Austria and Finland, for decades.

Bus priorities and bus rapid transit

A feature of local bus services running on all-purpose streets is that average speeds may be low, especially where frequent junctions are found, and general congestion slows down traffic, in addition to the effect of bus passenger stops as such. Since buses use road space much more efficiently than private cars, overall road user time savings may be produced by giving buses priority over cars (ie the aggregate time savings to bus users exceed the time losses to car users).

For the purposes of calculating road capacity, a private car is normally given a passenger car unit (pcu) value of 1, and a bus of 2.5. For example, if at peak times a car carries 1.2 occupants and a bus carries 25, occupants per pcu are 1.2 for the car, and 10 for the bus. For a fully-loaded double decker with 75 passengers, this value would be 30. At off-peak times, this ratio may be less favourable since car occupancies are higher (eg for shopping trips), and bus loads lower. Over the day as a whole, buses in London have an average load of about 17, and buses elsewhere about 10 (White, 2015).

The most common form of bus priority is the with-flow nearside bus lane approaching a junction, enabling buses to get close enough to the stop line for the next available green phase at traffic lights. In some cases, the signals are activated to change to green by the approaching bus, either in conjunction with a bus lane, or as an alternative to it. Other examples include contra-flow lanes where buses are able to operate in both directions on what are otherwise one-way streets, and bus-only streets, for example in shopping areas. 'Bus gates' are pieces of traffic engineering that allow buses to bypass traffic queues (eg on city radial approaches) or to enter areas prohibited to other vehicles, such as city-centre shopping districts. 'Bus gates' may be activated by traffic signals, carefully designed approach lanes, or by rising bollards that only lower on the approach of an appropriately-coded vehicle. Bus priority is considered in detail in Chapter 11.

Rail tends to offer substantial time savings over buses, due to operating on a reserved track throughout (for 'heavy' rail) or a mix of segregated and street track ('light rail', as in Manchester or Nottingham, for example). However, passenger door-to-door time savings may be less substantial, especially where rail stations are poorly located or widely spaced. Capital costs may be very high, and service frequencies low.

Bus rapid transit (BRT) effectively enables buses to match some of the characteristics of rail, by running on a segregated track. In most cases, this is a simple two-lane conventional road surface (for example, the pioneering UK busway in Runcorn). In others, a form of guidance may be used, such as 'Kerb Guided Busway' in which a small vertical strip at each side enables the bus to follow a slightly narrower alignment. Forms of track more akin to railway (which deters use by other forms of traffic) may be found, with both features seen in the Luton and Cambridgeshire bus systems. However, the critical feature is segregation from other traffic.

A further advantage over rail is that busways can be constructed on an incremental basis, bypassing the most congested sections of existing road networks, rather than a substantial length being needed for a new operation to be worthwhile (as is the case with light rail). Through running beyond the busway section enables better penetration of urban centres, and into low-density catchment areas. However, it should be noted that these will themselves often depend on on-street bus priorities to offer sufficient speed and reliability (for example, the extensive with-flow lanes on the East Lancashire Road, linked with the fully-segregated busway section of the Leigh to Manchester scheme).

In some countries very high flows may be handled by busways, akin to those of 'heavy' urban rail (about 20,000 passengers per hour or more, notably in South American cities and Brisbane, Australia). In Britain, existing rail coverage means that such capacity is not needed. Nonetheless, even modest flows may produce very good benefit/cost ratios (BCRs) on the existing criteria used in Britain.

The most substantial scheme in Britain is that in Cambridgeshire, from St Ives through central Cambridge (on-street) to Trumpington, with through running beyond in rural areas. Two schemes producing very good BCRs are the South Hampshire route (over a former rail alignment between Fareham and Gosport), and the Fastway scheme in Gatwick/Crawley, although this includes very few long busway sections, and comprises mainly sections approaching junctions.

The higher average speeds on busways will provide substantial operating cost savings and bus user benefits, in addition to which benefits are gained from diversion of car users, often about 20 per cent of all busway users (eg for Leigh to Manchester and Fastrack in North Kent), or higher in the case of Cambridgeshire.

Demand-responsive services

Demand-responsive (DR) services for the general public play a limited role in Britain at present, but may expand in future. Typically, minibuses of between eight and 20 seats may be used, usually at the smaller end of this scale. Area and times of operation are set, along with fares, but the route taken on each vehicular trip varies according to passenger demands. In the past, users normally had to make advance telephone requests, but developments in scheduling and routeing software now mean that requests can be made (usually via a website or mobile phone app) only a few minutes before the service is required. The user is then notified of the likely pick-up time. In-vehicle journey time will vary according to the number and range of other user demands met on the same journey.

This type of service enables low-density rural areas to be covered that would otherwise require very poorly used fixed-route services. The most extensive example in Britain is the 'Call Connect' service covering most of the county of Lincolnshire. DR services also meet some types of demand within urban areas, such as orbital movements not catered for by the major radial routes. They may enable passenger access within a shorter walking distance than stops on fixed routes (for the latter, access within a 400 metre walk is a typical standard, whereas DR pick-ups may be within about 200 metres of users). These 'virtual stops' thus enable better accessibility, without the need for additional infrastructure.

Note that public DR services should not be confused with 'dial-a-ride' services geared to the needs of older and disabled people who are unable to travel independently to bus stops, and thus need a door-to-door service. These are restricted to specified user groups and usually involve very high public expenditure per trip provided.

Some theoretical studies, notably those for the International Transport Forum, of Lisbon and Dublin, have examined the scope for DR service comprehensively replacing fixed-route bus services over large urban areas, which might also prove much more attractive to those now using cars. However, a large-scale trial has yet to take place. It is also the case that DR services are not always more convenient for the user – for example, on a frequent fixed-route service, the user simply turns up and waits a short time at the stop, without the need to pre-book either outward or return journeys, and in-vehicle time is more predictable.

Experiments are now taking place in Britain of DR services within urban areas, with a view to commercial viability, notably the 'Click' services of Arriva in Liverpool, and the 'PickMeUp' service operated by the Oxford Bus Company, complementing its fixed-route network in that city. However, it was not possible to attain commercial viability for a 'Click' operation in Sittingbourne, and that service has reverted to fixed-route operation.

'Non-local' services

These are public services offered by bus and coach operators which do not require service registration, and for which no separate statistics (other than some aggregate totals) are published. However, operators must hold Operator ('O') licences, meeting strict quality standards. They include the following.

Express services

Generally speaking, these are fixed-route, fixed-timetable services, running over longer distances. Extensive use may be made of motorways, but many minor settlements are also served, providing very useful through links (for example, to points in the West Country). Passengers pay separate fares, generally by pre-booking, although payment on vehicle is also accepted. Standing passengers are not carried.

They are distinguished from 'local' services by the fact that all passengers must travel a distance of at least 15 miles (about 24km) measured in a straight line. Where shorter-distance passengers are carried, registration as a 'local' service is required – in some cases this means that a through route from, say, London to a rural area might run as 'express' over the motorway section, then as 'local' within the rural area. Local service registration also provides eligibility for BSOG, but constrains operator freedom to change services due to the 70 day notice period (for purely 'express' services, changes can be made literally overnight).

The deregulation of express services dates from the Transport Act 1980, and has since been followed by other European countries which had severely restricted express coaches competing with rail, such as France and Germany. Strong ridership growth has been reported. However, in contrast to earlier expectations that many smaller operators would participate in this market, it has come to be dominated by a few major network operators (National Express and Megabus in England and Wales, and Flixbus within Germany and many other countries).

A recent development in Britain has been the 'Snap' product, which operates in response to user demand (in some respects analogous to local DR services), running directly between points requested when sufficient demand exists. Journeys are provided by vehicles hired-in from established operators. Currently, it is confined mainly to two corridors, and is thus very small compared to the other operators discussed above.

Excursions and tours

These are services operated from one or more pick-up points to destinations such as a seaside resort or stately home, charging each customer separately. Services are advertised in advance, but the operator retains the right not to run them on all advertised days if demand is insufficient.

An excursion is typically completed within a day, a tour involves overnight accommodation. In both cases, the operator may also include meals, admission charges etc., within the overall price to the customer. As in the case of express services, where passengers travel less than 15 miles, registration as a local service is needed – for example, some sightseeing tours within cities. This applies in any case to 'hop-on/hop-off' services where a fixed schedule and intermediate stops are provided.

Private hire

These are services where the entire vehicle is hired by an organization, and no charge is made by the operator to individual passengers. 'Private hire' takes the form of one-off trips such as those by a sports club or voluntary organization.

'Contract' services are those where a regular operation is carried out, such as to a place of employment or education. Another example is that of free services to shops (typically an out-of-town superstore, paid for by the store) usually on a fixed schedule. The first – the 'works bus' of past generations – is now rare, as employment patterns have changed, and employers place responsibility for travel arrangements on individual workers (although Silicon Valley IT companies appear to be re-inventing the concept in California), but school contract work remains extensive, especially in rural areas, primarily to meet statutory requirements for free travel for pupils living above certain distances from school.

Vehicles provided for such services are run by O-licence holders, meeting full quality standards, and this work often forms a substantial part of such firms' turnover. Interworking with private hire, excursions and scheduled local services helps to improve vehicle utilization. In some cases, school services may also carry other fare-paying passengers, such as pupils below the statutory free travel distance, or the general public in rural areas. For these, registration as a local service is required. Registration is also needed where a separate fare is deemed to be paid, even if not collected on the vehicle, such as a works service where a deduction is made from wages, or a hotel courtesy service where a charge is made as part of the customer's bill.

The overall scale of 'non-local' or 'other' operations is currently very difficult to quantify as virtually no data are published currently. However, in 2004/05, 69 per cent of all bus and coach passenger revenue (including concessionary travel compensation) came from 'local' services, and 31 per cent from 'other'; in terms of vehicle-km run, 'other' represented a slightly higher share, at 35 per cent (DfT, 2006).

International services

International services in the British context are mainly long-distance operations, analogous to express, tours etc. as defined above. Local services crossing the border between Northern Ireland and the Republic of Ireland can also be seen as 'international'. Whereas express and tour services within mainland Britain do not require service registration, such registrations are made with the Driver and Vehicle Standards Agency (DVSA) for international operations.

Within the EU, the principal service types are:

- Regular: Services on a fixed schedule at separate fares, similar to express and registered local services within Britain. They incorporate the previously separate category of 'Shuttle' services (operations between two fixed points, such as one within Britain and an overseas resort).

- Occasional: Services broadly equivalent to excursions, tours and private hire, run according to passenger demand. These include 'closed-door tours' where the same party of passengers undertakes the full return trip.

An important feature of EU international regular services is that 'cabotage' traffic can be carried, ie trips within a member state other than that within which the operator is based. Other agreements, such as Interbus, provide broadly equivalent conditions, but without cabotage rights.

International coach traffic between Britain and the rest of Europe peaked some years ago, vehicle movements by sea and the Channel Tunnel falling from 278,000 in 1999 to 165,000 in 2012 (DfT, 2019a), as traffic has been lost to faster and often lower-cost air services, although some growth has come from workers from other EU countries normally resident in Britain but making home visits (notably to Poland).

Community transport

This term is used to cover a wide range of services supplementing those of conventional bus and coach operations, often provided by voluntary, non-profit-making organizations (in some cases these have expanded to become fully-licensed operations, notably the HCT Group – running extensively in London and some other areas – but retaining their non-profit-making status). In most cases, minibuses are used. Staffing may be largely by volunteers, with some paid supervisory and management staff.

The legal basis of such services was regularized under the Transport Act 1985:

- Section 19 services are those provided for a specific group of users, such as members of an old persons' organization or a youth club, and not open to the general public. There is no requirement to offer concessionary travel.

- Section 22 services are open to the general public, and are required to offer concessionary travel (older people often forming the great majority of their users).

In both cases, vehicle and driver licensing requirements are less strict than for fully O-licensed services. Minibuses operate under a permit system, rather than being solely regulated by the Traffic Commissioners: a total of 9,570 'standard' (minibus) permits were issued in 2018–19, plus 99 'large bus' permits and 118 community bus permits (Traffic Commissioners for Great Britain, 2019). However, many organizations do voluntarily submit their drivers to stricter training requirements. In some cases, local authorities have made contributions, for example by funding new vehicles.

These services generally fill gaps in the public network, often in rural areas where finding either commercial services or even operators willing to bid for contracts may be difficult. However, the question has been raised of the extent to which 'unfair' competition may arise with fully-licensed operators, especially in bidding for tendered services. These have resulted in guidance from the DfT, restricting some aspects of community transport operations, and disputes continue at the time of writing (early 2020).

The extent to which community transport operators fill gaps may also be constrained by the availability of a pool of volunteer drivers (often those in the early phase of retirement), which may vary from area to area. Whilst these services play a useful role, their overall share of bus travel is very modest, about 5 million passengers per year, also including DR services (DfT, 2019b), equivalent to 0.4 per cent of all bus trips outside London and the metropolitan areas.

Taxi and private hire vehicle services

This mode has both a complementary and competing role with respect to bus services. It forms part of the public transport system in the sense of a service available to the public on demand, albeit dependent on willingness and ability to pay higher fares.

A 'taxi' is defined as a vehicle operating on a fixed fare scale, usually via a meter, which is regulated by the licensing body (usually a lower-tier local authority, but TfL in the case of London). It may 'ply for hire', picking up at the kerbside or designated ranks. A private hire vehicle (PHV) – also known as a minicab in Britain – is not subject to price controls, the fare being agreed in advance between passenger and operator; and cannot ply for hire. In London there is a very marked distinction between the two, but elsewhere this is less sharp, as most trips are pre-booked. The National Travel Survey (NTS) combines trips on both as a single mode. Both taxi and PHV vehicles are defined by a maximum seating capacity of 8, but often less in practice.

The percentage of all person trips by taxi/PHV is very small, about 0.9 per cent, compared with bus at 5.5 per cent (DfT, 2017). However, in terms of user expenditure it is more significant, given the much higher payment per trip made. There is a marked peak in demand late evening on Fridays and Saturdays. To a large extent, taxi/PHV use comes from lower income groups who are also dependent on buses.

Recent years have seen a sharp increase in the supply of licenced taxis/PHVs and drivers, although this does not necessarily indicate a pro rata increase in vehicle-hours offered to users. For example, the combined total of taxis and PHVs in England rose from 184,000 in 2005 to 285,000 in 2018 (DfT, 2018a). However, NTS data for England shows a peak of use per head of 12 trips in 2002 and 2003, with a drop to 10 in 2018, perhaps suggesting that much of the diversion to newer variants such as Uber (licensed as PHVs in Britain) may be within the taxi/PHV market rather than from buses (DfT, 2018b).

The regulatory framework for taxis and PHVs is very complex, not having been subject to systematic reform. The Transport Act of 1985, in addition to deregulating local buses, encouraged the removal of quantity limits by local authorities (although about one-third outside London still do so). It also permitted sharing of vehicles, initiated by the driver, with a separate fare charged to each passenger, although the extent of this appears very limited to date. Taxibus operations (running a service using a taxi rather than a bus) were also permitted, but likewise with limited impact.

Whilst one might expect taxis/PHVs to be more extensive in rural and lower density areas where greater gaps exist in the bus network, this is not the case. In March 2018, the number of taxis and PHVs per 1,000 population in England averaged 5.1, highest in Greater London (at 12.3) falling to about 4 in other urban areas and only 2.6 in 'mainly rural districts' (DfT, 2018b). The likely reason is that there is a much higher probability of securing a sequence of bookings during a driver shift in areas of higher density demand.

Taxis and PHVs can be seen as a competitor to buses, both for passenger custom, and in terms of fairness (for example, lack of controls on drivers' hours of work), but also a complementary role (to cover areas and/or times of low demand density, for example). The shared taxi and taxibus modes might be a suitable planned substitute for buses on some rural routes, and in evenings in urban areas, but the size limitation of eight reduces scope for coping with fluctuations in demand.

Types of bus and coach operator

Apart from community transport services (see above), all operators are required to meet operator licence conditions (see Chapter 3). Subject to these conditions, an operator can run any fleet size from one upward. Business organizations thus range from sole traders to private limited companies, and public limited companies (PLCs) whose shares may be traded.

In 2017–18, some 8,756 operator licences were on issue, of which 3,885 were 'restricted'; total vehicle discs on issue were 95,634 (ie an average of about 11 vehicles per operator) (Traffic Commissioners for Great Britain, 2019). A total of 20,591 service registrations were 'live', but only a minority of O-licence operators run registered local services. A separate DfT estimate indicates that about 34,500 buses were run by operators of local services in England in 2017–18 (DfT, 2019b).

Although evidence for economies of scale in operations is limited, the period after deregulation and privatization saw a marked re-consolidation of most former public sector operators into five large groups which now account for about 70 per cent of the local bus market in Britain (Stagecoach, First, Go-Ahead, Arriva and National Express), although Arriva is no longer listed on the stock exchange following its acquisition by Deutsche Bahn.

The skewed nature of the industry running local services was also indicated by the distribution of O-licence discs in 2005/06. Operators with one to six discs each accounted for only 0.2 per cent of local bus passenger journeys, but 29 per cent of all 'other' vehicle-km run, whereas those with 31 or more discs each accounted for 97.6 per cent of local passengers (DfT, 2006).

Current developments and policy issues

The Bus Services Act 2017, applicable in England (similar powers have been enacted in Scotland, and are proposed for Wales) makes a number of changes, reducing the emphasis on competition as a policy aim, as found in the 1985 Transport Act, to one on partnership and co-operation. In particular, Enhanced Partnerships (EPs) would enable much greater inter-operator coordination than found at present, and a wider role for public authorities, including taking local service registration procedures from the Traffic Commissioners. 'Franchising' (ie contracting on the London model) would also be made easier. The extent to which these powers may be taken up is not yet clear.

Within rural areas in particular, there may be a wasteful overlap in functions performed by transport operators and public authorities. For example, a village might be served by a dedicated school bus, a poorly-loaded local bus service, specialist transport from social services, and non-emergency ambulance services (for example, to take day patients to clinics). Bringing all of these together under the 'total transport' concept could enable better use of resources, and perhaps improved services. However, institutional factors make this process very slow at present.

Growing interest is being shown in the 'Mobility-as-a-Service' (MaaS) concept, under which a single organization might provide purchase of all types of public transport service purchase (including bus, trams, rail and taxis/PHVs) through a single portal perhaps also including car and cycle hire. As yet, progress is limited.

Organized car-sharing is of growing importance. It is commonly an ingredient in Travel Plans whereby employers try to minimize single occupancy use – see Chapter 13. 'Car clubs' are also gaining popularity, whereby users have the benefit of car use without having to own one. In cities well-served by conventional public transport, occasional trips by car club members enable activities to be reached that are otherwise not accessible, whilst avoiding the need for car purchase.

It is important to distinguish between car sharing in 'sequential' form (different hirers successively hiring the same car) and in 'parallel' (a driver and passengers sharing for the same trip). The latter has developed to only a limited degree in Britain, but is noteworthy in France, especially for long-distance travel offered by BlaBlaCar – indeed, that company has taken over one of the main express coach operators there.

Acknowledgement

Helpful comments were provided on an earlier version of this chapter by Martin Higginson.

References

DfT (2006) *Public Transport Statistics Bulletin GB*, London

DfT (2014) *Bus Statistics England 2014*, London

DfT (2017) [accessed 26 February 2020] Transport Statistics Great Britain 2017, *GOV.UK* [online] https://assets.publishing.service.gov.uk/government/uploads/system/uploads/attachment_data/file/661933/tsgb-2017-report-summaries.pdf (archived at https://perma.cc/P578-7CR4)

DfT (2018a) [accessed 14 February 2020] TAXI0101: Taxis, Private Hire Vehicles (PHVs) and their drivers: England and Wales, *GOV.UK* [online] https://assets.publishing.service.gov.uk/government/uploads/system/uploads/attachment_data/file/833573/taxi0101.ods (archived at https://perma.cc/9F68-22AE)

DfT (2018b) [accessed 14 February 2020] Taxis and Private Hire Vehicles per 1,000 people by licensing area and rural–urban classification: England and Wales, *GOV.UK* [online] https://assets.publishing.service.gov.uk/government/uploads/system/uploads/attachment_data/file/833577/taxi0105.ods (archived at https://perma.cc/DC53-HDDH)

DfT (2019a) [accessed 14 February 2020] Department for Transport Sea Passenger Statistics Table, *GOV.UK* [online] https://assets.publishing.service.gov.uk/government/uploads/system/uploads/attachment_data/file/566154/spas0402.ods (archived at https://perma.cc/2C58-J83L)

DfT (2019b) *Annual bus statistics: England 2017/18*, London

Luke, D, Steer, J and White, P (2018) [accessed 31 March 2019] Interurban Bus: Time to raise the profile, *Greengauge 21* [online] www.greengauge21.net/wp-content/uploads/GG21_IBR_A4P_WEB.pdf (archived at https://perma.cc/7A4G-4A55)

Mills, G and White, P (2018) Evaluating the long-term impacts of bus-based park and ride, *Research in Transportation Economics*, **69**, pp 536–43

Traffic Commissioners for Great Britain (2019) *Annual Report to the Secretary of State 2018–19*, London

White, P (2015) *Impacts of Bus Priorities and Busways on Energy Efficiency and Emissions*, Greener Journeys, London

Further reading

DfT (2018) [accessed 14 February 2020] National Travel Survey: 2018 tables, *GOV.UK* [online] https://assets.publishing.service.gov.uk/government/uploads/system/uploads/attachment_data/file/822145/national-travel-survey-2018.zip (archived at https://perma.cc/334S-FJX2)

DfT (2019) [accessed 14 February 2020] NTS0303: Average number of trips, stages, miles and time spent travelling by main mode: England, *GOV.UK* [online] https://assets.publishing.service.gov.uk/government/uploads/system/uploads/attachment_data/file/821414/nts0303.ods (archived at https://perma.cc/2LMZ-M94F)

History, heritage, current challenges

TONY FRANCIS AND STEPHEN JOSEPH

The start

Public transport, by road, in the United Kingdom has existed for many centuries. However, predominantly transport resources were concentrated on the movement of goods, livestock and food. For example, extensive pack horse operations existed to move finished goods carrying the occasional passenger.

The foundations of today's network of bus and coach services can be found in the extensive horse-drawn stage coach services. These provided timetabled, interurban links across much of the country, facilitated considerably by the better upkeep of highways following the widespread applications of toll roads in the 18th century. These reached a peak just prior to the start of the industrial revolution, after the end of the Napoleonic Wars in 1815. The rivers and seas surrounding the country also offered waterborne transport for people and importantly goods.

Village carrier services transported both passengers and goods, linking many rural communities with the appropriate market town. These were normally horse-drawn, but bullocks and other animals were also used, being a significant forerunner of the present local bus network.

Urban development

During the 19th century in urban areas, local, horse-drawn services developed as the populations grew and distances between home, work and recreation increased. However, initially these were only affordable for the middle and upper classes. Many workers in the newly industrial towns had no option but to walk. In London, the first recognized service upon which the present bus network originated was that offered by a George Shillibeer, who commenced a horse bus service between Paddington and The Bank via the Angel on 4 July 1829. The concept of a regular, timetabled service was established, and during the remainder of the 19th century significant local networks appeared and expanded. Alongside this, the long distance stage carriage operations virtually disappeared as the railway network, offering far faster, more comfortable and safer services, expanded rapidly across the country.

Enterprises such as the London General Omnibus Company, whose origins can be traced back to Paris, developed considerably and became a significant forerunner to the present Transport for London (TfL).

Whilst railways benefited by the application of the latest technical developments during the 19th century, including advances in steam propulsion and the electric telegraph, travel by road remained with the horse. Experiments took place using steam-driven passenger carrying vehicles, but the weight of machinery and fuel made them expensive and impractical. Gas and compressed air (even clockwork!) were also applied, with limited success.

Rail came to the road by way of the tram (or light rail as it is more recently called), initially horse-drawn and later with steam and finally powered by electricity. Indeed, by the end of this century, the electric tram became a foundation of local urban travel, offering mass transport for all classes of the community. The trams needed power generation and as these were often funded and managed by the local authority, they also modernized the towns providing electric power to factories and many homes.

Horse to motor

The end of the 19th century saw the application of the petrol-fuelled, internal combustion engine. This offered an enormous advantage over horse traction. To provide an all-day service, a horse-drawn bus had a maximum capacity of some 26 passengers, requiring 10 horses (plus feed, stabling and vet costs) working in rotation, plus two spares covering 80 miles at most. A 1905 built double deck motor bus, whilst incurring a higher initial cost, carried 34 passengers and could cover 120 miles a day.

By 1911 regular horse bus operation in London had ceased in favour of conventional, petrol-fuelled vehicles or petrol electric ones. In the latter case, the engine powered a generator and propulsion was through an electric motor. This was effectively a forerunner of today's hybrid engine.

The First World War, whilst creating enormous human tragedy, advanced the capabilities of motorized transport, both in quality and quantity. Buses and trams continued, albeit on reduced services (the military commandeered many buses, especially from London) and women were employed in many operating and engineering roles. The end of this conflict provided the country with a much enhanced vehicle manufacturing base and numerous trained drivers, along with administrative skills and resources to plan and operate motorized transport. This was the real start of the extensive networks of local bus and coach services that exist today.

Rapid development – the Roaring Twenties

This period represented not only a significant growth in bus and coach services throughout the country, but a revolution in technology. This transformed the bus from a solid-tyre, open-top petrol-engined vehicle, with the driver exposed to the elements, to something akin to today's buses. Pneumatic tyres, covered tops and enclosed driving cabs, powered by the more efficient and economical diesel engines, became normal by the end of the decade.

Urban and rural communities were rapidly linked by bus, and the beginnings of the long distance coach network appeared. There was no uniform licensing or quality control of services and vehicles. This was left to individual local authorities, who applied varying standards or even no standards at all.

As with any industrial expansion, major players entered the scene, in this case conglomerates such the British Electric Traction (BET) Company and the Tilling Group. They agreed areas of operation. This avoided direct competition and allowed them to develop their business without interference. The railway companies began to show an interest in this competitive road-based business, and took financial interest in the area companies that the groups had established. However, little was done to integrate bus and rail services; the separate undertakings continued as such, although some inter-availability of ticketing eventually occurred.

Towards the end of this decade, government concluded that better control of this whole business was desirable. The Road Traffic Act 1930 established the Traffic Commissioners (TCs), who not only imposed quality controls (as now) but also issued licences for individual services. Initially most operators gained approval for the existing network, but new services were subject to objections from other operators and local authorities. The TCs' task was to determine approval of applications from the weight of evidence given by both applicant and objectors. This system was retained until the Transport Act 1985.

The lead toward conflict

The industry continued to grow and consolidate during the 1930s, with area companies owned by the major groups of the time dominating the scene. The smaller undertakings operating in largely rural areas continued to be acquired by these companies, but others remained untouched. Tramways, mostly owned by local authorities, were reaching the end of their useful life and were being converted to motor bus operation.

However, the shadow of the Second World War grew, and from 1939 totally overshadowed all decision making. Car ownership, although growing, was still small by today's levels and thus the bus played a very significant role in everyone's life.

The industry had to face new challenges. Those included the loss of staff and vehicles being taken on by HM Forces, imposition of fuel rationing and increased use of services, especially in connection with factories making war equipment and those serving military bases. Women were encouraged to join the industry once more in a variety of roles, and government agreed to the manufacture of basic 'utility' designed buses to help meet demand.

With the conflict ending in 1945 and the election of a Labour Government, application of public ownership was paramount. In 1948, the rail companies were nationalized and their bus interests followed similarly. However, other parts of the industry, eg the BET Company with its subsidiary units such as the East Kent Road Car Company (now part of Stagecoach plc), continued untouched.

The earlier Education Act of 1944 contained within it a requirement to provided free travel for pupils living over prescribed distances from their nearest appropriate school. This continues today, and meeting this is the backbone of many local bus services, especially in rural areas. At this time buses held some 40 per cent of the domestic travel market, cycling 10 per cent, private transport around 30 per cent, and the remainder by rail.

It took until the mid-1950s for the country to recover from the effects of the total war which it had experienced. Car ownership remained low; a new car, if affordable, might take up to two years from ordering to delivery.

Thus the bus industry continued to flourish and grow, gradually replacing older and worn-out vehicles with new equipment. One revolutionary output of the bus industry in postwar Britain was the introduction of the underfloor engine vehicle allowing a flat floor throughout the length of the bus or coach. Unfortunately this represented a high floor, not compatible with to-day's accessibility requirements.

This was the period when coach operations were also playing an important part. Before low-cost airlines and their reach of distant resorts, demand was high for coach links between major population areas and domestic seaside resorts. Operators such as Grey Green Coaches, A. Timpson and Sons and others provided substantial express services from east and south east London to coastal resorts in Essex, Kent and Sussex.

You've never had it so good, and thereafter

The Suez Crisis of 1956, when Great Britain and France with assistance from Israel unsuccessfully attempted to regain control of the Suez Canal, possibly marked the end of austerity and the start of rising living standards and thus car ownership growth. The country concentrated more on domestic needs, but this impacted negatively on the bus business. Year-on-year total passenger carryings declined as affordable motor cars became available.

All was not lost as, for example, the planning of new towns (for example those around London) took account of the provision of bus services, ensuring that these aligned with housing development. That was perhaps a little straightforward as a significant proportion of the population were employed in adjoining industrial estates.

Towards the end of this decade, the first elements of the motorway network were being designed and opened. The Preston bypass was the first in 1958, but others quickly followed, allowing faster, interurban express coach services to be offered. At a time when parts of the railway network were still in need of modernization, this gave road-based services something of an advantage.

However, overall, growing congestion, dwindling patronage and a staff shortage (the manufacturing industry could offer more attractive wages than many neighbouring bus undertakings) presented, for a time, an unmanageable crisis.

Once more the matter of public ownership arose.

After the darkness followed the dawn

The election of a Labour Government in 1968 generated a review of transport, especially in addressing the deterioration of the bus business. Under the then-Transport Minister Barbara Castle, it was felt that regional transport authorities should be established, out of which, in due course, came the Passenger Transport Authorities (PTAs), such as those covering the West Midlands and Merseyside. They also absorbed the various local authority bus undertakings in their jurisdictions.

The publicly-owned regional bus companies, along with the private sector BET business, came together in 1969 as part of the state-owned National Bus Company (NBC). Although much of the industry was either central or local government-owned, the challenge remained as to how to stem the continual loss of passengers. NBC took the then-radical step of researching its customers' needs through surveys, establishing precisely where people were travelling from and to where. This 'Market Research Project' or MAP resulted in many routes being changed to reflect the traffic habits of the time and not those from formative days. This took place in near-parallel with successful experiments using minibuses, offering more frequent services, and thus did not require reference to a timetable; very much 'a turn up and go' offer to intending passengers.

This was also the period when one-person operation was being applied, eliminating the fare collecting conductor. Whilst this reduced costs, it often extended journey times and thus represented a disincentive to use public transport. Nevertheless, overall attempts were being made to make buses more relevant to current needs.

This was also aided by the new role of local authorities, with the power to subsidize (initially rural) services through the Local Government Act 1972. That led to closer cooperation between county councils and operators to ensure a relevant bus network for the community.

The free market and to new horizons

Buses have been frequently influenced by government thinking, and never more so than the administration led by Margaret Thatcher, Prime Minister from 1979. Privatization of British industry including the NBC followed, but equally, if not more, importantly, the ending of the TCs' decision making on service provision. The Transport Act 1985 allowed bus operators to determine what commercial services they wished to provide, and no other operator or authorities could oppose. It was designed to encourage competition 'on the road'.

Coach services had already been deregulated in 1980, and this generated new services, in particular commuter links between communities outside London and the centre of the capital itself. These represented an alternative to rail travel, especially where housing was distant from a rail system.

Some local authorities opposed such a free market move for buses, preferring instead competition 'off the road' through a franchising system. They did not succeed. The 1985 Act permitted authorities to secure bus services deemed by them as socially necessary, but not offered commercially by any operator. Operators had to determine what to provide commercially, and furthermore they could not work collaboratively for fear of infringing competition legislation. Not only were the various regional bus undertakings sold to the private sector, but many local authority owned businesses (including those which passed to the PTAs) also passed that way.

The national system for concessionary travel on local bus services for elderly and disabled people was implemented in 2008. This, as with free travel for certain school children, influences the frequency and extent of many services. The need for all those with an interest in public transport – operators, local authorities, user groups and local businesses – to work together has been recognized throughout the history of the bus industry. This continues through more recent legislation described elsewhere in this book.

This is the situation in which the current bus business functions.

Challenges

The bus industry now faces multiple challenges, but the overwhelming one is declining usage in aggregate. Some of the main drivers of bus use – notably shopping trips in towns – have been declining as retail moves online and high streets empty. There is also limited public funding for buses and limited Government engagement (especially compared with roads and railways). Alongside these, new technology and new mobility providers have appeared, especially Uber, which offers on-demand transport at low prices. Beside this, and the lure of autonomous cars, buses look old fashioned. They are also expensive when fuel duty has been frozen and car parking is free/cheap.

As a result, while current bus users are loyal and value their services – Transport Focus surveys consistently show very high levels of satisfaction among bus users (Transport Focus, 2019) – a lot of people will not use buses and need to be attracted to them. There is also the challenge of air quality, with many cities targeting buses in their clean air zones, and of new development in locations and in layouts that are difficult to serve with bus services.

However, there are ways out of this. The bus is not dead, but it does need fresh thinking and the role of local authorities and national government is going to be more important in its survival. There are examples of good practice around the country that show what can be done. The Bus Services Act 2017 provides some helpful tools for the industry and local authorities. The Government has produced guidance on the Act (Department for Transport, 2017); and there is also useful information in the Campaign for Better Transport's guide *Three Steps to Better Bus Services* (Campaign for Better Transport, 2018).

Partnerships

There is now a long history of partnerships between operators and local authorities; the Act gives new opportunities and some authorities and operators are working on ways of taking them up. This can apply in rural as well as urban areas. There are many examples – here are just some.

The Liverpool City Region Bus Alliance has been successful in growing bus use in the city. The Alliance – in legal terms a voluntary partnership – started with Merseytravel, the transport authority, and the main operators Arriva and Stagecoach in it, but smaller operators have joined recently. The headline target was to increase fare-paying passengers by 20 per cent by 2020, and growth from 2014 to 2018 was an encouraging 16 per cent; however the COVID-19 pandemic in 2020 will now have had a significant impact.

The above growth was driven largely by young people's ridership, with an innovative 'MyTicket' offer for 5–18 year olds of a £2.20 flat fare per day across the whole city region. This has seen bus ridership by young people rise by 168 per cent in three years. The Alliance has a joint investment plan with performance measures including on-bus cleaning and customer service training.

Other features of the Alliance include:

- a commitment from operators to provide modern bus fleets with an average age of no more than seven years;
- introduction of contactless payment and smart ticketing;

- network reviews, with a detailed two-stage public consultation process in each city region district to agree changes to the bus network in each area;
- a protocol for consultation by operators on individual route changes;
- a marketing campaign – Better by Bus (Better by Bus, 2019).

Alongside the Alliance, Merseytravel has reviewed and reformed its tendered service arrangements to bring tendered services up to the standards specified in the Alliance (Liverpool City Region Bus Alliance, 2019).

The Alliance has succeeded despite the removal of bus lanes by the Liverpool City mayor. In fact, there has been investment in different kinds of bus priority as part of the Alliance (Liverpool City Region Local Enterprise Partnership, 2019), and there are plans being worked up for five 'green routes' as part of the city region's Transforming Cities Fund programme.

There are other bus partnerships and alliances, including the West Midlands Bus Alliance (Transport for West Midlands, 2019). This has also seen a wide range of measures introduced including a fleet of new buses, low fare zones, network development plans, contactless ticketing, a 'safer travel partnership' and these have now been developed into a set of '50 Deliverables' (West Midlands Bus Alliance, 2019). The Alliance is complemented by advanced quality partnerships covering Birmingham and Wolverhampton city centres and Solihull.

There are partnerships in more rural areas. Cornwall has a partnership as part of implementing its 'one public transport network for Cornwall' (Cornwall County Council, 2019a). An interesting feature about this is that it is data-driven – its showcase corridors are based around data on population, potential fare-paying passengers, travel to work trips and new housing targets for each settlement (Cornwall County Council, 2019b).

Another long-standing county partnership is in Hertfordshire, which has since 2000 had one focused on information and joint ticketing. This partnership, marketed as Intalink, pools funding from bus and train operators and from the district councils to provide high-quality information. The information now encompasses stop-specific timetables, real-time information linked to the council's traffic management system, and investment in transport hubs at many of the county's town centres and railway stations. Bus stop management and maintenance is also included, as well as joint tickets and now a mobile ticketing app. The Intalink brand is used on all the bus stops and information points, and on many of the buses operated in the county (Hertfordshire County Council, 2019).

There are many other partnerships and alliances around the country; some are comprehensive and include detailed provision for bus services, while others are more general. Previous legislation defined partnerships quite prescriptively: operators would contribute new vehicles and services, while local authorities contributed bus infrastructure and sometimes bus priority schemes.

The Bus Services Act's Enhanced Partnership provision creates new opportunities for more creative partnerships. Wider local authority policies like parking controls and charges can now be included, and by agreement authorities can take over service registration from the TCs.

Franchising

The Bus Services Act also allows local authorities the option of franchising of bus services. In this case, a contract for services would be let by the local transport authority. Franchising is strongly opposed by many in the industry, who see it as a means of stifling growth and innovation, likely to result in under-investment. In general, in public debate operators identify franchising solely with the system used by TfL. TfL franchises are gross cost (TfL take all revenue) and include very detailed service specifications.

However, franchising can be very different: in Jersey, where the Government has franchising powers, a new contract let in 2013 was won by Libertybus, a subsidiary of HCT Group. In this franchise, revenue risk lies with the operators, who design the network themselves within broad parameters and objectives. Although the Government set out its specification, non-compliant bids were actively encouraged. Since the new contract began, passenger numbers are up by a third, five new routes have been added, frequencies have improved, passenger satisfaction is up by 5 per cent and subsidy levels are down by £800,000. The Government and the operator put this down to the way the contract incentivizes the operator to grow passenger numbers (HCT Group, 2016).

This suggests that the distinction between franchising and partnerships could be more blurred than some argument suggests. As the Campaign for Better Transport guide suggests:

> For example, a local authority might wish to franchise a small section of its bus network, perhaps only one important route. Or in areas struggling to maintain unprofitable routes which are nevertheless socially necessary, a local authority might create a franchise bundle, inviting tenders for exclusive rights to a highly profitable route, on the condition that the winning bidder also took on the socially necessary routes. So, for example, the tender might link together a heavily used central town route together with a handful of feeder routes connecting outlying villages or suburbs to the centre of town. (Campaign for Better Transport, 2018)

In particular, the Jersey example suggests that franchising arrangements could leave the financial risk largely with the operator, thereby reducing the financial exposure of the local authority. Another case might be with new housing development, where a franchise arrangement might allow bus operators to grow patronage over time, free from concern that on-road low-quality competition might arise once the development is occupied and the market is more mature, and thus undermine all the previous investment.

Franchising can therefore be an opportunity as well as a threat to the industry. It should be thought of as one way of tackling the overriding issue of decline in patronage. To address this, the bus industry in the future needs to be outward-focused, innovative and creative, and seek partnerships and alliances with all kinds of groups. A good example of the role of these wider groups in growing the bus market is in Sevenoaks, where the very active Town Council has developed two new bus services – a vintage bus linking the railway station with the National Trust property at Knole Park, and a new service linking new housing developments around the town. These came from the council's public consultation on its neighbourhood plan, and the new service for housing estates was initially subsidized by Kent County Council but is now commercial.

The council won the Transport Planning Society 'People's Award' in 2018 for these services (Transport Planning Society, 2018).

Conclusions

Generally, the bus industry needs to find ways to ally with groups wanting to clean up cities and cut air pollution. At present, there is a tendency for clean air zone plans to target buses and avoid tackling cars. Buses need to be seen as part of the solution to air pollution and congestion, rather than part of the problem, but politicians are going to need support in promoting buses and giving them priority.

At present, there is no incentive for councillors to support buses: a growing bus market in their area does not give them increased revenue, whereas car users contribute parking fees. So a creative approach might, for example, involve operators offering to share with local authorities any uplift in bus revenue from traffic restraint like bus priority schemes, parking restraints or clean air zone charges. In fact, some of the city plans to tackle air pollution do include pro-bus investment – both Leeds and Liverpool have a programme of 'green routes' giving continuous bus priority into the city centre, but are facing local resistance to these. Broad alliances with groups concerned about health and the environment and with businesses concerned about congestion and pollution blighting their trade can help persuade politicians to support measures that help buses prosper.

This all suggests some key principles in planning bus networks in the future:

- Look at networks, not just routes, in rural and urban areas. Interconnect in Lincolnshire is a good example of demand-responsive 'call connect' services feeding into commercial fixed route services on main corridors.

- Simple ticketing, covering all operators (and all public transport where appropriate), like the Merseytravel MyTicket scheme.

- Better interchange and interconnections, between different buses and between bus and other modes, as is being developed in Cornwall.

The death of the bus, foretold by some technology advocates, has been greatly exaggerated (even Uber is now offering public transport options in the USA, and Uber and Lyft both offer shared travel in larger vehicles on semi-fixed routes). But buses will need to change, and be part of door-to-door seamless travel, with high-quality vehicles and stops that look more like railway stations.

'Mobility-as-a-Service' is a glib catchphrase, but it is an opportunity for the bus industry, not just a threat. Some operators are experimenting with new services: Arriva has ArrivaClick, operating in various places under contract (Arriva, 2019). Go-Ahead launched the PickMeUp demand responsive service in Oxford, linked to local businesses (Go-Ahead, 2018). However, none of these are commercial businesses, so they will demand new financial models, possibly allied with other transport contracts.

Wider Government policy is slowly becoming more supportive. There is now to be a national strategy for buses, bringing them into line with other modes of transport in England, and some new funding for buses is coming forward. However, there is limited or no integration: taxis and buses are rigidly divided in law, and rail and bus are treated entirely separately. But the industry, with allies, can change this. The national bus strategy came about from united pressure and there is interest in more holistic transport provision, through 'total transport' schemes bringing together the commissioning of different public sector transport contracts. Bus management in the future will be about seeking allies to support buses, and coming up with creative ways of getting people to use them.

References

Arriva (2019) [accessed 25 June 2019] Arriva in the UK, bringing you ArrivaClick, *Arriva* [online] www.arrivabus.co.uk/arrivaclick/ (archived at https://perma.cc/H8AF-PVNK)

Better by Bus (2019) [accessed 25 June 2019] Making buses even better, *Better by Bus* [online] https://betterbybus.org/about/ (archived at https://perma.cc/SHV4-MLAU)

Campaign for Better Transport (2018) [accessed 25 June 2019] Three stages to better bus services using the Bus Services Act, *Campaign for Better Transport* [online] https://bettertransport.org.uk/sites/default/files/research-files/bus-services-act-guidance.pdf (archived at https://perma.cc/V6LA-K5SZ)

Cornwall County Council (2019a) [accessed 25 June 2019] Ongoing developments, *Cornwall County Council* [online] www.cornwall.gov.uk/transport-and-streets/public-transport/ongoing-developments/ (archived at https://perma.cc/5SLX-KXJS)

Cornwall County Council (2019b) [accessed 25 June 2019] Growth Deal 3 Transport Graphic, *Cornwall County Council* [online] www.cornwall.gov.uk/media/30207693/growth-deal-3-transport-graphic-nov17-mapo-only.pdf (archived at https://perma.cc/Q3T7-Q25N)

Department for Transport (2017) [accessed 25 June 2019] The Bus Services Act 2017 New powers and opportunities, *GOV.UK* [online] https://assets.publishing.service.gov.uk/government/uploads/system/uploads/attachment_data/file/664318/bus-services-act-2017-new-powers-and-opportunities.pdf (archived at https://perma.cc/DJ8F-YFUG)

Go-Ahead (2018) [accessed 25 June 2019] Go-Ahead enters ridesharing market with UK's most ambitious on-demand bus service in Oxford, *Go-Ahead* [online] www.go-ahead.com/media/press-releases/go-ahead-enters-ridesharing-market-uks-most-ambitious-demand-bus-service-oxford (archived at https://perma.cc/H687-3683)

HCT Group (2016) [accessed 25 June 2019] Practical bus franchising the Jersey model, *HCT Group* [online] http://hctgroup.org/uploaded/Practical%20bus%20franchising%20-%20the%20Jersey%20model.pdf (archived at https://perma.cc/95JN-GELU)

Hertfordshire County Council (2019) [accessed 25 June 2019] Intalink, *Intalink* [online] www.intalink.org.uk/ (archived at https://perma.cc/97B5-H4ZG)

Liverpool City Region Bus Alliance (2019) [accessed 25 June 2019] How we're making a difference..., *Liverpool City Region Bus Alliance* [online] www.buspartnership.com/_uploads/voluntary/Liverpool%20CR%20top%2010%20achievements%20-%20year%20one.pdf (archived at https://perma.cc/EB58-9TLJ)

Liverpool City Region Local Enterprise Partnership (2019) [accessed 25 February 2020] Liverpool City Region bus users amongst the first to benefit from traffic light technology to improve journeys, *Liverpool City Region Local Enterprise Partnership* [online] www.liverpoollep.org/news/liverpool-city-region-bus-users-amongst-the-first-to-benefit-from-traffic-light-technology-to-improve-journeys/ (archived at https://perma.cc/2ZMV-F3Q4)

Transport Focus (2019) [accessed 26 June 2019] Bus Passenger Survey – Autumn 2018 report, *Transport Focus* [online] www.transportfocus.org.uk/research-publications/publications/bus-passenger-survey-autumn-2018-report/ (archived at https://perma.cc/KMF7-YLGT)

Transport for West Midlands (2019) [accessed 25 June 2019] Bus Alliance, *Transport for West Midlands* [online] www.tfwm.org.uk/operations/bus-alliance/ (archived at https://perma.cc/VN82-C2ZK)

Transport Planning Society (2018) [accessed 25 June 2019] Transport Planning Day People's Award 2018, *Transport Planning Society* [online] https://tps.org.uk/tp-day-2020-announced/planning-campaign/tp-day (archived at https://perma.cc/3EJ6-D6DW)

West Midlands Bus Alliance (2019) [accessed 25 June 2019] 50 deliverables for Bus Alliance, *Transport for West Midlands* [online] www.tfwm.org.uk/media/38960/bus-alliance-50-deliverables.pdf (archived at https://perma.cc/E6Q7-EQJP)

Further reading

Barker, T C and Robbins, M (2006) *A History of London Transport*, Routledge, London

Bates, A (1836) *Directory of Stage Coach Services*, David & Charles

Bus Archive [online] www.busarchive.org.uk/ (archived at https://perma.cc/RC3B-95QM)

Klapper, C F (1984) *Golden Age of Buses*, Routledge & Kegan Paul

Omnibus Society [online] www.omnibus-society.org/ (archived at https://perma.cc/3EKV-XLTT)

Parke, J F and Francis, A J (1983) *Halcyon Days of Buses*, Ian Allan Limited, Shepperton

Strong, L A G (1956) *The Rolling Road*, Hutchinson, London

The legal and regulatory framework

03

IAN BARLEX

Introduction

This chapter outlines the bus industry's legal and regulatory frameworks. It sets out the relevant legislation under which it functions and the relationships with central and local government.

The legal framework

Background

The law as applicable to road passenger transport businesses and their operations throughout the constituent parts of the UK is enshrined in numerous primary and secondary statutes. Primary legislation comprises Acts of Parliament. Secondary legislation is created by ministers under delegated powers granted by the Acts, and is normally in the form of statutory instruments.

The individual Acts and statutory instruments are far too numerous to list here, and it frequently applies that the older the legislation, the more likely that significant component elements of it will in any case have been revoked or superseded by subsequent statutes. Highways and transport legislation follows this pattern; in some cases, very limited provisions of once major Acts remain in force. The principal source of information concerning all UK legislation is www.legislation.gov.uk, which contains the full text of all primary and secondary legislation, often accompanied by helpful explanatory notes, and with changes brought about by subsequent statutes highlighted.

Legislation particularly relevant to the evolution and operation of the road transport industry includes the following.

Transport legislation

Transport legislation includes:

- successive Transport Acts (1968, 1978, 1980, 1981, 1982, 1983, 1985, 2000);
- the Public Passenger Vehicles Act 1981;
- the Local Transport Act 2008;
- the Bus Services Act 2017.

Highways legislation

This includes the following:

- the Road Traffic Regulation Act 1984;
- the Road Traffic Acts (1988, 1991);
- the Traffic Management Act 2004;
- the Road Safety Act 2006.

Other legislation

Numerous other statutes have impacted on the industry's operations. Some key examples are referred to below.

Principal transport legislation

Transport Acts

Transport Acts have generally been wide-ranging and multi-modal, extending to the likes of road and rail passenger and freight transport, docks, harbours and waterways, air travel, and many road traffic and highways issues. Much of the content of the earlier Acts has been revoked or superseded. The principal remaining relevant element of the 1968 Transport Act concerns domestic drivers' hours, which themselves have been the subject of subsequent amending regulations. The Acts between 1978 and 1983 contain little or no current legislation affecting road passenger transport. Many of the relevant provisions of 1968, 1978 and 1980 were later consolidated in the Public Passenger Vehicles Act 1981.

The 1985 Transport Act oversaw the major restructuring of the industry and its regulatory framework, providing the basis for the system in operation today. Key features were the deregulation of local bus service operation outside London and Northern Ireland, the transfer of the hitherto publicly owned National Bus Company subsidiaries to the private sector, and the formation of companies to run the municipally-owned bus undertakings. Associated sections address the financing of local transport services, the functions of local authorities and the Passenger Transport Authorities, and their powers and duties to support unremunerative services; and concessionary fares schemes.

The 1985 Transport Act introduced section 19 and 21 permits, which provide for the operation of buses for community benefit by local organizations, and set out the rules related to the carriage of passengers by taxis and private hire cars at separate fares.

The Transport Act 2000 was an important piece of legislation incorporating extensive coverage of air, rail and road issues as well as local public transport. Large sections of the 2000 Act have been amended or superseded by subsequent legislation, including the Local Transport Act 2008 and the Bus Services Act 2017. Significant features included:

- the introduction of Quality Partnerships and Quality Contracts;
- the introduction of area ticketing schemes (all later superseded in England by the new mechanisms introduced by the Bus Services Act 2017);
- provisions on mandatory concessionary fares schemes (later superseded by the Concessionary Bus Travel Act 2007);
- new tendering criteria, and the introduction of the competition test;
- the replacement of fuel duty rebate by the Bus Service Operators Grant (BSOG);
- provisions related to road user charging and workplace parking levies.

Public Passenger Vehicles Act 1981

The Public Passenger Vehicles Act 1981 brought together public service vehicle (PSV)-related legislation that had appeared in a number of earlier statutes, including the Transport Acts referred to above. While various sections were subsequently repealed and superseded by the 1985 Act, large tracts of this Act are still applicable, covering areas such as the definition of PSVs, PSV operator and driver licensing, PSV fitness, vehicle inspections and prohibitions, traffic areas and Traffic Commissioners (TCs), and the regulations governing the conduct of operating staff (drivers, inspectors and conductors).

Local Transport Act 2008

The Local Transport Act 2008 was a significant Act with extensive clauses related to public passenger transport, its avowed aim being to tackle the problems caused by deteriorating traffic conditions and to improve local bus services. Its sections included provisions related to local transport authorities, their constitution, duties and responsibilities (including the introduction of Integrated Transport Authorities); revisions to quality partnership and quality contract structures (later superseded in England by the Bus Services Act 2017), and powers for the introduction of road user charging schemes.

It also revisited the provision of local bus services by means other than conventional large buses – permit and community bus operation, and the use of taxis and private hire vehicles (PHVs) to provide local services.

Bus Services Act 2017

The Bus Services Act 2017 was a major piece of legislation which altered the regulatory landscape for local bus services within England. It took effect by amending, replacing, or inserting new sections into a number of earlier statutes, notably the Transport Acts of 1985 and 2000; also the Equality Act 2010 in respect of the provision of passenger information by operators.

The Act introduced three new mechanisms:

- Advanced Quality Partnerships (AQPs) (Department for Transport, 2018), which are statutory schemes replacing the previous quality partnership mechanism in the 2000 Act. AQPs introduce a number of new features, including the option for a Local Transport Authority to introduce 'measures' (such as reduced parking provision or higher parking charges) alongside or instead of facilities and infrastructure as its contribution to the partnership. Provision is made for operators to submit admissible objections to a scheme if the standards of service demanded of them are not practicable or commercially viable, or if they would be disproportionate to the contribution the authority is making by way of facilities and/or measures.

- Enhanced Partnerships (Department for Transport, 2017a), which are agreements between authorities and operators to work together to deliver improvements to services. These partnerships comprise two parts; a plan, which sets out the vision, and one or more schemes, which set out the planned actions. An enhanced partnership is a legally binding agreement which can only be established ('made') with the formal agreement of a defined proportion of the affected operators. If an operator does not deliver services which meet the standards set out in the agreement, it may be the subject of disciplinary action by the TC. If an authority does not deliver on its commitments, the operator(s) may take legal action.

- Franchising (Department for Transport, 2017b), a similar mechanism to that used by Transport for London (TfL) to procure local services within the capital, and a replacement for the previous Quality Contract regime. Franchising schemes are statutory schemes to which access is only automatically available to Mayoral Combined Authorities. Other authorities may obtain the powers but only with the consent of the Secretary of State and after the appropriate regulations have been issued.

Note that each of the three mechanisms described above are available for use in England only. For the time being, the previous regime of Quality Partnerships and Quality Contracts remains on the statute for Wales by virtue of the Transport Act 2000. In Scotland, the Transport (Scotland) Act 2019 provides for new mechanisms to operate there.

The Bus Services Act 2017 incorporated further new legislation in addition to the three mechanisms described above. Again in England, it introduced the concept of Advanced Ticketing Systems to replace the previous ticketing scheme powers in the Transport Act 2000. It also empowered the Secretary of State to issue new regulations related to improved on-board information on buses, by inserting new sections into the Transport Act 2000 and the Equality Act 2010, and requiring operators to provide open data on timetables, service information and fares. The on-board information measures are applicable throughout Great Britain. Open data is confined to England, the initial stage of its implementation is required to be complete by 31 December 2020, following a transitional period.

Principal highways legislation

Alongside the statutes directly concerned with bus and coach operation, highways legislation is of great significance because it establishes the rules for the use of the road network. The Road Traffic Regulation Act of 1984 brought together much of the earlier legislation concerned with the likes of traffic regulation, parking, speed limits, control and enforcement. The Road Traffic Acts of 1988 and 1991 (the latter Act widely amended and supplemented the former) provide the basis of much of today's road traffic law, although there have been numerous amendments in the 30 years or so since they were passed. Among the significant areas that they address are driving licences and driving instruction, vehicle testing and the condition of vehicles used on the road, insurance, and police powers, driving offences and penalties.

The Road Safety Act 2006 was particularly concerned with driving standards and contraventions. It created a number of new offences, and realigned the system of penalties to reflect then current thinking on the severity of offences. It also addressed co-operation with foreign authorities in relation to some driving matters – the licensing of drivers and the registration of vehicles.

Other relevant legislation

The workings of the transport industry are, of course, affected and influenced by a myriad of other legislation which reflects Government programmes and the development of society as a whole. This would be too extensive to list fully here, but some particularly relevant examples are:

- The Disability Discrimination Acts of 1995 and 2005, and the Public Service Vehicle Accessibility Regulations of 2000, which established the regime for accessibility of vehicles used to provide local services, developed by the work of the Disabled Persons Transport Advisory Committee (DiPTAC). This legislation evolved further in the Equality Act 2010, which itself had extra sections inserted by the Bus Services Act 2017, concerned with the provision of information (such as announcements and displays) to ease travelling for disabled people.

- The Safeguarding Vulnerable Groups Act 2006, which established the safeguarding regime now operated by the Disclosure and Barring Service (which combined the functions of the Independent Safeguarding Authority and the Criminal Records Bureau). The legislation, later amended by the Protection of Freedoms Act 2012, establishes it as an offence for barred individuals to work with children or vulnerable adults in numerous roles, including bus and coach driving. It also places responsibilities on employers to report to the authorities instances where an individual may have caused harm, or may pose a risk of harm, and imposes criminal sanctions if an employer knowingly employs a barred individual.

- The Deregulation Act 2015, which was designed to reduce the legislative burden on businesses, organizations and individuals. It extends over a very wide area, which includes some road traffic and parking issues, taxi and PHV licensing and motor insurance.

- The Consumer Rights Act 2015, which is concerned with the consolidation of swathes of consumer legislation and also addresses digital contracts. Its relevance to passenger transport lies in its application to service contracts, thus providing statutory rights and remedies to customers, in this case passengers.

- The Cities and Local Government Devolution Act 2016, which relates to the powers of Combined Authorities and the election of their Mayors, but also empowers the Secretary of State to establish sub-national transport bodies in England outside London, the first of which has commenced as Transport for the North (TfN).

- The Data Protection Act 2018, which implements the EU General Data Protection Regulation (GDPR), and affects all businesses in respect of how they hold and process data, and the rights of individuals over data which is held relating to them.

Legislative devolution

Many elements of GB domestic legislation do not apply in Northern Ireland, where separate statutes operate. In recent years, the pace of devolution of functions to the Scottish Parliament and the National Assembly for Wales in respect of transport and highways legislation has accelerated, with further major enactments under active consideration. Some key features of legislation specific to Scotland, Wales and Northern Ireland are summarized below.

Scotland

The Scotland Act 1998 established the Scottish Parliament; subsequent legislation has progressively transferred powers in many areas, including transport and highways, to that body.

The Transport (Scotland) Act 1989 provided for the transfer of the Scottish Transport Group bus operating subsidiaries to the private sector, in line with the privatization programme introduced in England and Wales by the Transport Act 1985.

Further Transport (Scotland) Acts were passed in 2001 and 2005. The 2005 Act introduced a number of the features of the Transport Act 2000 to Scotland, including Quality Partnerships; Quality Contracts; ticketing schemes; and road user charging. These provisions have largely been super-seded by the Transport (Scotland) Act 2019. The 2005 Act was concerned with the establishment of the Scottish Regional Transport Partnerships and regional transport strategies. It was also concerned with numerous roads, highways and traffic issues.

In 2017, the Scottish Parliament passed the Seat Belts on School Transport (Scotland) Act 2017, a statute requiring seat belts to be fitted to all vehicles used on dedicated school transport services.

The Transport (Scotland) Act 2019 is a wide-ranging Act which signifi-cantly progresses the devolution of transport legislation related to Scotland. It requires Scottish Ministers to prepare a National Transport Strategy, after a process of consultation. It introduces significant new powers related to local bus services, which provide for the implementation of Bus Improvement Partnership Plans and Schemes, and also franchising. It gives local transport authorities powers to operate local bus services using vehicles requiring a PSV operator's licence, and puts various requirements upon operators re-lated to the provision of service information.

It contains clauses relating to ticketing schemes and new ticketing tech-nology, and travel concessions. The 2019 Act is also concerned with the implementation of low emission zones; parking regulations; and workplace parking schemes.

Wales

The National Assembly of Wales was established by the Government of Wales Act 1998, and, in common with Scotland, subsequent legislation has progres-sively devolved more functions to the Welsh Assembly and Government.

The Government of Wales Act 2006 provided for a referendum to be held to establish whether the Assembly should have full law-making powers in a wide range of areas, one of which was transport and highways. The referen-dum produced a positive result, and the Wales Act 2017 was an enabling Act which formally established the new legislative competence of the Assembly.

Devolution has seen divergence in operational legislation in a number of areas, for example the BSOG, which has been replaced in the principality by the Bus Services Support Grant, which is paid subject to operators meeting the conditions of the Voluntary Welsh Bus Quality Standard (Welsh Government, 2017). The basic regulatory mechanisms remain common with those implemented by the Transport Act 2000, including Quality Partnerships and Quality Contracts, but in late 2018 and early 2019, the Welsh Government undertook a major consultation on the potential reform of the planning and delivery of local bus services and taxi and PHV licensing. A Bus Services (Wales) Bill has now been introduced.

Northern Ireland

Key legislation in respect of road passenger transport operation in Northern Ireland comprises the Transport Act (Northern Ireland) 1967 and the subsequent Transport Act (Northern Ireland) 2011. The first of these, a major Act passed by the old Northern Ireland Parliament, establishes the regulatory system governing the carriage of both passengers and goods by road; the construction and operation of railways; and the establishment of the Northern Ireland Transport Holding Company (NITHC). The NITHC is a public corporation which holds and manages transport property assets and controls the subsidiary operating companies collectively known as Translink – Ulsterbus, Metro (Citybus) and Northern Ireland Railways.

The 2011 Act reformed the system of service delivery to support a new regional transportation strategy, to encourage greater use of public transport, and to comply with the EU Regulation concerned with regulated competition in public transport. The decision had been made after consultation to retain a regulated bus network rather than to opt for deregulation, as had been implemented in Great Britain. A service permit system operates whereby operators apply for commercial service permits, as described later in this chapter.

Regulation

Regulation within the road passenger transport industry is exercised over many elements of its constituent businesses and their operations – the entities, the individuals involved (owners, managers, staff), the operations, and the vehicles. Elements of these processes are sometimes referred to as 'quality' and 'quantity' licensing, although use of the latter term reduced with the progressive deregulation of lines of business – excursions and tours, express services, local bus services, etc.

Forms of regulation

Regulation of entities

Regulation of entities is exercised through the PSV operator licensing system (Vehicle and Operator Services Agency, 2011a). There is no restriction on entry to the market per se, but operators must meet the necessary quality and safety standards.

It is necessary to hold a PSV operator's licence (O-licence) to operate any vehicle that can carry nine passengers or more for hire or reward (which encompasses both direct payment and payment in kind, whether collected or not, and whether or not a profit is made). If a smaller vehicle is used to carry passengers at separate fares, then an O-licence is also required; other smaller vehicles operating for hire or reward will normally be licensed as taxis or PHVs.

There are four categories of O-licence:

1 a standard licence confined to national operations within Great Britain;

2 a standard licence for national and international operations;

3 a restricted licence for limited operation of one or two vehicles up to eight passengers, or up to 16 passengers if not being operated as part of a passenger transport business, for example as a sideline rather than a main occupation;

4 a special restricted licence, confined to licensed taxi and PHV operators, which enables them to use such vehicles to operate local services.

It is also possible for organizations which provide transport on a 'not for profit' basis to apply for permits issued under Sections 19 or 22 of the Transport Act 1985 (Department for Transport, 2019), which will enable them to operate services for hire or reward without a full PSV O-licence. However, it is important to note that the regulations applicable to permit operations are subject to change following legal challenges and review by the authorities.

The operation of stretched limousines falls within the operator licensing regime when these vehicles are operated by a business for hire or reward (Vehicle and Operator Services Agency, 2011b). Vehicles with nine seats or more will generally be licensed as PSVs. Most limousines with eight seats or less will be licensed as PHVs, but some may fall into the PSV category.

In order to be granted a standard licence, an entity must be able to demonstrate that it:

- Is of good repute (see under *Regulation of individuals*, below).

- Meets the requirement for financial standing. The entity must have adequate funds available to run the business properly. The requirement as at 1 January 2019 for standard licences is for capital and reserves of at least £8,000 for the first vehicle operated, and £4,250 for each subsequent vehicle. These figures are reviewed annually. Financial standing requirements for restricted licences are lower, at £3,100 and £1,700 respectively, at 1 January 2019. These have been unchanged for some years, but are subject to review.

- Has in place adequate facilities or arrangements for the safe operation and maintenance of the vehicles. It is not compulsory for operators to maintain their own vehicles – this may be contracted out to another operator or an external supplier; but if such an arrangement is made, the TC will need to be satisfied with the maintenance agreement or contract. Operators must also inform the TC of their proposed frequency for safety inspections of their vehicles, which must take place at least every 13 weeks, and must provide copies of the key forms which will be used for safety inspection and driver defect reporting.

- Has in place adequate systems to ensure compliance with key standards, including driver licensing arrangements, drivers' hours regulations, the taxation and insurance of the fleet, and the quality of operation of local bus services.

- Is professionally competent (see under *Regulation of individuals*, below).

- Has a stable establishment within Great Britain – an address at which the entity keeps its key documents and records, including those applicable to compliance with driving and maintenance regulations.

The first four requirements listed above must also be met by entities seeking to obtain a restricted licence.

Applications for PSV O-licences are considered by the TCs, who will examine any objections received from the police or local authorities on grounds of repute, financial standing, professional competence, or adequacy of maintenance arrangements. A TC may attach conditions to a licence when granting it, or subsequently. An entity whose application is refused may appeal to the Upper Tribunal; entities may also appeal against conditions attached to a licence.

Regulation of individuals

All applicants for standard and restricted licences must be of good repute. In considering repute, the TC will examine relevant convictions, fixed penalties and serious infringements incurred by any relevant person – this will include the applicant, a partner in a partnership, a company or any of its officers, a nominated transport manager, or an employee or agent of the applicant.

An entity applying for a standard national or international licence must have at least one transport manager who meets the requirement for professional competence. This may be an owner, director or partner; it may be an employee (known as an internal transport manager) or an external transport manager working under contract. Limitations are placed upon the number of operators, and their fleet sizes, for whom the same external transport manager may act. The essential feature of the role is that the transport manager must have the necessary qualifications, be of good repute, and must take continuous and effective responsibility for the management of the transport operations.

Drivers of PSVs with more than nine seats are required to hold the appropriate vocational driving entitlement and a Driver's Certificate of Professional Competence (DCPC), and they must comply with the requirement for periodic training during each five-year cycle.

The Public Passenger Vehicles Act and the Public Service Vehicles Conduct Regulations regulate the conduct of PSV staff – drivers, conductors and inspectors. This includes taking the necessary care and precautions when operating in service. Operating staff have particular responsibilities towards wheelchair users and disabled persons.

Regulation of operations

Local bus service operations outside London are regulated through the road service licensing system. See Chapter 1 for what constitutes a local bus service; registration is not required for other operations if they do not carry passengers for short distances at separate fares – express services, excursions and tours, private hires and contracts, etc.

Any entity which has a PSV O-licence may, on giving the requisite notice, register a local bus service with the TC and commence its operation. Services may also be registered by organizations holding a Section 22 Community Bus Permit, and by local education authorities.

Registrations may be submitted electronically or by paper form. Notice periods for new registrations, variations to services, and withdrawals and notification requirements involving other parties (authorities) vary in

England, Scotland and Wales. Since 2018, the local bus service registration period in England has been 70 days in all, comprising a 28-day period of pre-notification to affected local transport authorities and a 42-day service registration period.

In certain circumstances, the TC may exercise their discretion and accept registrations at short notice, for example if a service is a direct replacement for a very similar one, or for minor timetable adjustments.

In England and Wales, flexible service registrations may be submitted for the various types of such services, which may have fixed sections of route but where for much of the route it may not be possible to identify all of the roads to be served in advance. In such cases, the area, any fixed stops and timings, and the days and times of operation are identified in the registration.

It should be noted that certain structures introduced by the Bus Services Act 2017, and the Transport (Scotland) Act 2019, if implemented in qualifying areas, would impose restrictions on the registration of local bus services and amend the associated processes (see the section on *Legislation*).

Once a service has been registered, an operator is obliged to run it, and to do so in accordance with the registration, and particularly the timetable. It is recognized that services may be adversely affected by difficult traffic conditions or unavoidable incidents along the route; the TCs therefore allow a window of tolerance for the punctuality of services. Ninety-five per cent of services operated are expected to operate within a six-minute window, representing up to one minute ahead and five minutes behind the scheduled departure time. If a service runs at a frequency of every 10 minutes or less, it is defined as a frequent service, and a different standard is applied. For these services, the requirement for 95 per cent of the services operated is that six or more buses should depart within any defined period of sixty minutes, and there should not be intervals between consecutive buses which exceed 15 minutes.

Regulation of vehicles

Vehicles which are used to carry nine or more passengers must meet the necessary requirements to demonstrate that they are constructed or adapted to PSV standards – this may take the form of a Type Approval Certificate, a Certificate of Initial Fitness (COIF) or a Certificate of Conformity. All such vehicles are also subject to a strict annual MOT test with effect from 12 months after they have first been registered.

Vehicles which have more than 22 seats and are employed on local or scheduled services (with limited exceptions based on age or use) must meet the PSV accessibility standards which are in place to assist disabled passengers.

Once in service, vehicles must be inspected and maintained at appropriate intervals to ensure that they are safe to operate at all times; an effective driver defect reporting system must be operated and those reports must be acted upon to ensure unfit vehicles are not put into service.

DVSA officials may carry out vehicle checks at the operator's premises, at selected points (such as termini or bus stations), or at the roadside. They are empowered to issue immediate or delayed prohibitions on the vehicle's future use in service, and in the event of an unsatisfactory record, the operator may be subject to disciplinary action by the TC.

Regulation of taxis and PHVs is fundamentally the responsibility of district councils. In London, the licensing responsibilities are discharged by TfL. If and when they are employed to operate local services, they fall under the special restricted licensing regime described earlier in this chapter; otherwise a myriad of legislation applies. Some of this is very old, and the Government has been actively reviewing taxi and hire car legislation with a view to the introduction of an updated and simplified regime. See Chapter 1 for additional detail on taxi and PHV operations.

Regulatory bodies

The regulatory processes summarized above are the responsibility of the Department for Transport (DfT) within Great Britain, and are principally exercised by certain of its executive agencies and by the TCs. Certain responsibilities have been devolved to the governments of Scotland and Wales; in Northern Ireland, the parallel responsibilities fall to the Department for Infrastructure.

The three pertinent executive agencies of the DfT are:

1 The **Driver and Vehicle Licensing Agency** (DVLA) – which manages the registration and licensing of drivers and vehicles, and is also responsible for vehicle excise duty. The DVLA issues driving licences, and manages the associated processes concerned with endorsements, disqualifications and medical conditions. It also issues tachograph cards and vehicle registration certificates. The DVLA collects and enforces vehicle excise duty and works with the police and other agencies to combat fraudulent and criminal activity in this area.

2 The **Driver and Vehicle Standards Agency** (DVSA) – which is a merger of the former Driving Standards Agency (DSA) and Vehicle and Operator Services Agency (VOSA). The DVSA manages the driving test system and

is the approval body for driving instructors, MOT test centres and staff, while undertaking testing of HGVs and PSVs itself. It is responsible for the enforcement of drivers' hours and vehicle standards, including roadside enforcement. The DVSA operates the OCRS (Operator Compliance Risk Score) system, which scores operators on their risk of non-compliance based upon their previous record, and influences decisions to stop and inspect vehicles – operators with a high score are more likely to be targeted. The agency has also introduced the Earned Recognition Scheme, which is a voluntary scheme for operators with a strong track record of compliance who employ DVSA-validated IT systems and who are prepared to share their compliance data and performance record against key indicators with the agency. Operators who are accepted into the scheme are permitted to display its marque, and they benefit from a lighter touch by the regulatory authorities, with a reduced likelihood of visits to premises and of their vehicles being stopped at the roadside for inspection. The DVSA also manages various functions in support of the TCs, including the processing of operator licence applications and bus service registrations.

3 The **Vehicle Certification Agency** (VCA) – this is the certification and type approval authority for vehicles across the UK.

Note that the responsibility for the strategic road network was formerly that of a further agency – the Highways Agency – but this was converted to an arms-length Government-owned company known as Highways England (HE) with effect from 1 April 2015. The strategic road network comprises the motorways and the all-purpose trunk roads (major A roads); the Traffic Officers employed by HE who patrol these roads have numerous powers, including stopping, directing and diverting traffic; failure to comply with their instructions is an offence.

Traffic Commissioners (TCs)

The TCs are responsible for licensing the operators of heavy goods vehicles and PSVs and the registration of local bus services outside London. They also grant the vocational licences for those who drive vehicles in these classes, and are empowered to take action against vocational licences in certain circumstances.

There are eight TCs, who head the eight traffic areas of Great Britain – Eastern, London & South East, North East, North West, West Midlands, West of England, Scotland, and Wales. Each area has a traffic area office within its boundaries, where public facilities are available and public inquiries are held, but most administration and communication is handled from the central licensing office in Leeds. Following a long period of joint jurisdiction with the West Midlands Traffic Area, a designated TC is now in place for Wales. As of 2019, the traffic area office for Wales is set to relocate from Birmingham to the principality in due course.

TCs are appointed by the Secretary of State and are statutorily independent in undertaking their functions. The roles of the TCs and in particular the statutory role of the Senior Traffic Commissioner are defined in the Local Transport Act 2008. Following this legislation, TCs are no longer tied to individual traffic areas, except in Scotland, but they remain based around the country. TCs are assisted by a number of deputies, who frequently carry out duties in respect of public inquiries.

The Senior Traffic Commissioner issues a series of 14 statutory documents which advise the TCs and their offices on how they should interpret the law and which assist the industry to understand how specific circumstances are likely to be treated by the regulatory authorities. They address issues which include repute, finance, transport managers and vocational driver conduct. These documents, together with a preface, which are updated regularly to reflect changes in the law, case law, and industry evolution, may be found on GOV.UK (Senior Traffic Commissioner, 2018).

TCs have far-reaching disciplinary powers over PSV O-licence holders. These include suspension or revocation of a licence, also the attachment of conditions to a licence which may, for example, limit the number of authorized vehicles. There are numerous grounds upon which a TC may take such action, including loss of repute or insufficient financial standing (in which cases a standard licence must be revoked), a poor prohibition record, and the failure to fulfil undertakings or the contravention of conditions attached to the licence.

Disciplinary action may also be taken in the event of the failure to operate a registered service in accordance with its timetable, or at all, or if an unregistered service is operated. In these cases, the TC is empowered to impose a financial penalty up to a maximum of £550 per vehicle authorized on the licence.

TCs are empowered to disqualify individuals whose licence has been revoked from holding an O-licence in one or more traffic areas for a defined period, or indefinitely. This may also extend to the individual's future involvement in the ownership or control of a business operating PSVs.

TCs may decide to hold a public inquiry to consider an application for a new O-licence, or variations to an existing licence, for example to increase the number of authorized vehicles, if they have received objections, or if they have any concerns related to the application. Public inquiries will also be held to consider disciplinary action of the kind outlined here, at which evidence will be heard; the operator has the right to be accompanied by a legal or professional representative.

There is right of appeal to the Upper Tribunal against the decision of a TC, for example if a licence is refused, curtailed or revoked, an individual or a business is suspended, or a financial penalty is imposed.

Regulation in London

In London, the regulatory body with control over local bus services is TfL, which is a statutory corporation (and successor to London Regional Transport) responsible for delivering the Mayor of London's transport strategy in the capital.

A local bus service with one or more stopping places in Greater London is known as a London local service; such a service may only operate if it is part of the London Bus Network, or if it has been granted a London Service Permit by TfL.

The London Bus Network is the main tendered bus network in the capital; TfL (or its subsidiaries) has powers to operate such services itself, or to contract them in from commercial operators through London Local Service Agreements. TfL retains the responsibility for service planning, routes, frequencies, specifying the vehicle types and standards to be employed and setting the fares. In adding, varying or removing services from the network, TfL is obliged to undertake a process of consultation with affected parties, including London boroughs and passenger representatives.

London Service Permits (TfL, 2019) are issued to local bus services which operate separately from the main London Bus Network in accordance with TfL's published criteria, which include the public interest and their compatibility with the mayor's transport strategy, environmental, mobility, and other standards.

Services which operate across the boundary of Greater London are treated as two different operations for regulatory purposes. Sections of such services outside Greater London must be registered with the TC in common with other provincial operations. Sections operating within Greater London must either be part of the main London Bus Network or must be issued with a London Service Permit. Some express service operators voluntarily choose to obtain London Service Permits for sections of their routes, in order to carry local traffic.

Temporary rail replacement services, private hires and unlicensed express services which have to carry fare-paying passengers for more than 15 miles do not constitute London local services.

Regulation and devolution

The progressive process of devolution (see also the section on *Legislation*) has seen some variations develop in the application of industry regulation. In Scotland, the TC has carried out additional duties in relation to taxis and parking. The requirements in relation to bus service registrations, in particular notice periods and notification arrangements, vary in Scotland and Wales.

In Northern Ireland, the licensing of bus operators is carried out by the Driver & Vehicle Agency (DVA) on behalf of the Department for Infrastructure (DfI). Similar regulatory conditions and processes apply, with some variation to the detail. There is a permit system applicable to not-for-profit operations, governed by the Transport Act (NI) 1967. Service licensing is managed by the Public Transport Services Division within the DfI. Services additional to those operated by the publicly owned Translink organization require a Commercial Bus Service Permit (Northern Ireland Government, 2019), which is applicable to a wide range of operations, including local bus, express, and sightseeing services.

Summary

As with all sectors, the bus industry has been the subject of extensive legislation over time, both directly concerned with its own operations, and reflecting wider social and political agendas. The devolutionary trend continues, with Scotland having now assumed direct responsibility for its regulatory regime, and Wales set to do so.

Control and regulation has moved cyclically over generations between a heavier and lighter touch, with the latter having been applicable to local bus services (outside London and Northern Ireland) since the 1980s, but recent legislation provides the framework for greater regulation at a local level if the responsible authorities opt to proceed on that basis.

Regulation of matters concerned with safety, conduct and accessibility has, understandably, continued to be applied at a national level to ensure consistency of approach and delivery.

References

Department for Transport (2017a) *Enhanced Partnerships Guidance*, London

Department for Transport (2017b) *Bus Franchising Guidance*, London

Department for Transport (2018) *Advanced Quality Partnership Guidance*, London

Department for Transport (2019) *Section 19 and 22 Permits and Obligations: Not for profit passenger transport*, London

Northern Ireland Government (2019) [accessed 13 September 2019] Commercial bus service permits, *Northern Ireland Government* [online] www.infrastructure-ni.gov.uk/articles/commercial-bus-service-permits (archived at https://perma.cc/C32G-WCAU)

Senior Traffic Commissioner (2018) [accessed 13 September 2019] Senior Traffic Commissioner's statutory guidance and statutory directions, *GOV.UK* [online] www.gov.uk/government/collections/senior-traffic-commissioners-statutory-guidance-and-statutory-directions (archived at https://perma.cc/K6BY-SH3H)

TfL (2019) [accessed 13 September 2019] London Service Permits, *TfL* [online] www.tfl.gov.uk/info-for/suppliers-and-contractors/london-service-permits (archived at https://perma.cc/V78H-9J57)

Vehicle and Operator Services Agency (2011a) *Public Service Vehicle Operator Licensing, Guide for Operators*, London

Vehicle and Operator Services Agency (2011b) *Guidance for operators of stretch limousines*, London

Welsh Government (2017) *Voluntary Welsh Bus Quality Standard* (2nd edn)

Planning 04

DAVID JENKINS

Introduction

This chapter explains how bus routes are planned – timing, frequency, where to serve, depot location, staffing, involving the public and local authorities, and the latter's role in assisting operation and generally securing an efficient operation that will be well used.

How do operators choose routes?

Although there are examples of new competitive services, the vast majority of routes have evolved over a period of time, with many being able to trace their origins in the UK to the 1930s or earlier.

The primary consideration is whether a route will earn more money than it costs to operate. There is a trade-off to be made between frequency offered and resources employed, with the latter constrained by the running time of a route. For example, a journey time of 25 minutes each way with a five-minute layover at each end means one bus can make a round trip in an hour. Two buses can provide a half-hourly service, three buses every 20 minutes and four buses a quarter-hourly service.

However, a journey time of 29 minutes with a one-minute layover would not result in a reliable timetable. In this instance, an operator may look to see what else has potential by extending the route for five or six minutes further, which with five minutes layover at each end gives round trip journey times of 1 hour 20 minutes. On this basis, four buses could provide a 20-minute interval service.

Conversely it may be better to curtail the service so that round trip journey times are reduced. On a rural service, this may be possible by omitting a village that necessitates a diversion off the main road. If this saved four minutes from the 29-minute journey time, costs and revenue may come into better balance.

The likely revenue from the route can be assessed by comparing its characteristics with other similar services. This can include the type and density of housing, potential destinations such as retail centres, supermarkets, health and education facilities, availability and cost of car parking, and the potential to connect or compete with other routes and transport services.

Smaller operators in particular may seek to provide services only at off-peak times, in between school journeys on weekdays. With most costs covered by guaranteed revenue from a school contract, the marginal cost of running during the off peak is small.

Relationship between revenue, costs and frequency changes

Speed and directness are generally viewed positively by passengers, while indirect routes with double-run diversions to serve cul-de-sac developments are viewed negatively. Increased running times can result from congestion, from traffic calming and other road schemes. As increasing levels of congestion and slow speeds have adverse impacts on running times, operators are faced with adding more resources to maintain the same journey patterns (likely to add costs with no additional revenue) or provide fewer journeys with the same level of resources (same costs but with reduced revenue).

There is some evidence that faster, direct routes are likely to attract more passengers than slower options, eg National Express West Midlands (NXWM). There is certainly an increasing tendency to offer simplified, straightforward routes. This lifts overall passenger numbers, but to the detriment of smaller communities, which are no longer served.

Services to new developments need to be treated differently. Remote employment areas such as business parks, and new residential areas, will take time to develop sufficient passengers to sustain a viable service. For this reason, 'Section 106' funds (secured by legal agreements when local authorities grant planning permissions) need to be made available so that services can be provided from an early date, to discourage car use, and allow time for patronage to grow. Buses serving a new residential development should be operating from when the first home is occupied. Operators are not sufficiently robust to take a risk on a such a large unknown quantity of the number of potential passengers.

Consultation

There is no formal requirement for any bus operator to consult if it wishes to make a change to its services, other than to notify the local transport authority before submitting a registration to the Traffic Commissioner.

As a result, many operators do not have a formal process to consult when making changes to services. Indeed, many do not seek any views from existing and potential customers, or even their own drivers. Instead decisions are made on little more than analysing ticket machine statistics and financial performance.

Some operators defend this approach on the basis that experience has taught them that feedback from customers can be too vague or too generic to derive any useful information. In 2018, National Express West Midlands clarified how it would deal with public comments when it put proposals out to formal consultation (NXWM, 2018).

Nevertheless, where operators are proposing to use a road that is not currently served by buses, it is worth engaging with the local transport authority and its councillors before such a proposal reaches the public domain. This will enable the operator to ascertain the degree of official support for such a move, which may be needed in the face of residents' opposition. Support may be needed from the parking authorities if a common tactic to prevent buses passing – by awkward parking – is used.

It is also common to receive complaints about passengers on double deckers being able to see into upstairs windows of private homes, though this is rarely the case. Inviting residents to travel on a bus to see for themselves can be one way of tackling this situation.

Official support will also be needed to establish any new bus stops. This can be highly contentious, with few householders wishing to see a stop located outside their premises, though occasionally the prospect of it preventing other people from parking outside their home may be welcome.

The role of the local transport authority

In England and Wales services which are not commercially viable may be planned by the local transport authority (LTA), which has a duty under section 63 of the Transport Act 1985 to 'secure the provision of such public passenger transport services as the council consider it appropriate to secure to meet any public transport requirements within the county which would not in their view be met apart from any action taken by them for that purpose' (Transport Act, 1985).

LTAs often have criteria against which they judge whether a subsidized service is appropriate. In urban areas this may focus on distance to other bus services, on frequency, or on links to community facilities. In rural areas, population size may be more important, or whether alternative transport (usually rail or community transport) is available. Journeys that meet the needs of those travelling to education or to employment will usually rank higher than journeys aimed primarily at discretional or leisure travel.

Some LTAs will also be the highway authority for the area, though this is less likely to be the case in metropolitan areas. Where this is the case, LTAs will usually have a role in establishing new bus stops, as well as maintaining and improving existing stops. Some will have formal processes for new or relocated stops, which may include public advertisements and reports to councillors. Other councils may be content with a letter addressed to affected frontagers, and deal with any issues 'behind the scenes'.

Similar procedures may be followed for shelters. In urban areas, these are usually provided under contract to the local authority, though practice varies widely as to whether this is vested in the local (district) council, the county council or the transport authority. Occasionally it may even be devolved to parish/town council level, though this is more common in rural areas.

Where bus stop clearways are desired, the highway authority can introduce these without following the complicated process needed for other parking restrictions, although good practice is that at least local consultation should take place.

The Traffic Management Act 2004 gives LTAs an important 'Network Management Duty' to keep traffic moving (Traffic Management Act, 2004). They must:

> ... manage their road network with a view to achieving, so far as may be reasonably practicable having regard to their other obligations, policies and objectives, the following objectives – (a) securing the expeditious movement of traffic on the authority's road network; and (b) facilitating the expeditious movement of traffic on road networks for which another authority is the traffic authority. The action which the authority may take in performing that duty includes, in particular, any action which they consider will contribute to securing – (a) the more efficient use of their road network; or (b) the avoidance, elimination or reduction of road congestion or other disruption to the movement of traffic on their road network or a road network for which another authority is the traffic authority.

This legislation gives operators a strong lever for securing measures to eliminate traffic congestion that affects efficient bus operation.

Public, private or community sector?

The basic principles of service planning hold good, whatever the type of ownership. If revenue from passengers does not cover the costs of operation, then funding has to be provided by a third party. The exact level of surplus of revenue over costs does vary and is mostly dependent on how the capital needed to run the business has been obtained.

Depot location and capacity

The location of a depot can affect how services are planned. While buses will leave the depot and return in the evening, drivers will need to change over during the course of the day. If the depot is located on the line of route, this can be achieved easily.

However, where it is off-route, then other ways of changing drivers need to be considered. A rest room may be acquired in a central location, which allows drivers to have breaks without returning to the depot. However, some drivers will finish and others start during the course of the day, who will need to travel to or from the depot. This can be done by travelling as a passenger on the bus route that passes the depot, or by running a bus or other vehicle (such as a car or minibus) specifically for staff. Both methods result in drivers spending less time driving, as well as adding to the cost base.

Depots which are not near routes also mean that buses will have to run out of service ('dead' or 'light' are common terms to describe this) to a point where they can pick up service. Again, this adds to the cost base, though may be quicker than following routes in service to reach an outer terminus.

A common solution, especially in rural areas, is for a small number of buses to be parked overnight at the outer end of the route. Typically known as an outstation, this arrangement is ideal for buses performing morning peak journeys towards and afternoon peak journeys from a main urban area. As an outstation usually consists of minimal facilities, maintenance and refuelling is carried out at the main depot during the day.

However, the increasing complexity of modern buses means that it is more difficult to carry out running repairs at an outstation than for previous generations of buses. The risks that this poses to operational reliability and the possible implications for an operator's licence are generally now regarded as too great by larger operators, who have tended to reduce the number of outstations in consequence.

The physical size of the depot will ultimately limit the capacity of the number of buses, but other constraints may affect the height (barring all or some types of double deckers) or length (affecting large single deck buses and coaches).

Historically bus depots have been in locations that were often undeveloped at the time that they were built, but now find themselves in the midst of a residential district. They may no longer best meet current needs and can find themselves regarded as nuisance neighbours. As a result, relocation continues to take place across the country. New depots tend to consist of large amounts of open parking, with undercover facilities only for maintenance. These are typically located in industrial areas but are less likely to be directly on a bus route. Capital costs are minimized at the expense of greater operating costs.

Staff may have to travel further to work or have fewer alternatives to private transport. Staff car parking may therefore need to be greater than at existing locations, although some local planning authorities fail to recognize that a formal Travel Plan is difficult to implement for a shift-based workforce. A Travel Plan, a way to reduce car use and encourage more sustainable travel, is discussed fully in Chapter 13.

Scheduling

Having established the broad parameters for a bus route, detailed iterations of the scheduling process are likely to obtain an optimum timetable that meets the constraints of the service. This needs to take account of the resources available, as well as legal restrictions on drivers' hours, which may be supplemented by more restrictive local agreements.

At some depots, mainly those in large urban operations, drivers may be confined to operating on only one route, or just a very small number. More common is the splitting of drivers on to separate rotas, which may be arranged on a number of different principles, such as route groups, vehicle types, permanent early or late, part-time, or days worked per week (likely to be four long days against a standard of five normal days).

While these offer constraints to the scheduling process, they may offer other advantages, such as reducing the need for drivers to learn different routes, or for them to get to know customers better, or better retention of driving staff, by offering them a range of working practices to suit their individual circumstances.

Although computer-assisted scheduling is now widely used within the industry, smaller operators are less likely to use it, both for reasons of costs and complexity. Many local authority tenders for all-day operation are arranged on the 'one bus, one driver' principle, so there is limited need to draw up variable duties in such a circumstance.

However, for larger operators, a scheduling software package is likely to be the basis for drawing up detailed timetables, including vehicle workings and drivers' duties. To work to best advantage, it needs to be programmed to include all the constraints at a particular depot, such as maximum duty length, restrictions on driving one route after another, and all the appropriate points where a driver may take a rest break.

Despite computer assistance, experienced scheduling staff are a must for every large operator, as they will still be needed to make adjustments to timetables to ensure that it can operate with the minimum resource consistent with operating a reliable service. If a driver's duty needs to be shortened by 15 minutes at the end of the day to make it legal, a scheduler will be able to decide the most appropriate way to achieve this, which could include curtailing or retiming an individual journey. However, software enables the production of iterations and options for consultation with staff, which was generally a far too time-consuming process in the days of manual scheduling.

Conclusions

It is clear that bus services need to be well planned from the outset and then regularly reviewed. There are many issues to consider, whether it be the vehicles themselves, their staffing, the speed they can operate, where they go and how often, and the location of depots for their care and maintenance. Scheduling is an art in itself, especially if different parts of a route have different frequencies or buses operate on more than one route. Planning has to ensure efficient deployment of sufficient buses and drivers for the various times of the day and week. And in some cases buses may need to be specifically timed to connect with other buses or with trains.

The role of local authorities is crucial in obtaining, and then maintaining, efficient operation as buses need to operate at reasonable speeds, and then not be delayed by congestion, parking and roadworks. The challenge to try to address, and secure help from authorities on, is that delays can be different each day, both in location, timing and duration. Buses are more efficient than cars in terms of road space and fuel use, so should receive priority. That whole subject is discussed in detail in Chapter 11.

References

National Express West Midlands (2018) [accessed 6 February 2020] Transport Delivery Committee 11 June 2018, *West Midlands Combined Authority* [online] https://governance.wmca.org.uk/ieListDocuments.aspx?CId=134&MID=205#AI1333 (archived at https://perma.cc/P34N-ZRFF)

Traffic Management Act 2004 [accessed 6 February 2020] *legislation.gov* [online] www.legislation.gov.uk/ukpga/2004/18/section/16 (archived at https://perma.cc/S6FV-TNJD)

Transport Act 1985 [accessed 6 February 2020] *legislation.gov* [online] www.legislation.gov.uk/ukpga/1985/67/section/63 (archived at https://perma.cc/KBQ9-KA4B)

Vehicles and fuels

05

DAVID JENKINS AND JOHN BIRTWISTLE

Introduction

The first part of this chapter is a summary of the variety of passenger-carrying vehicles from minibuses to coaches, with explanations dealing with where they are best deployed. There is a wide range of vehicle types available to operators, including those of different dimensions, standards of finish and methods of propulsion. However, there are some common terms to describe the differences.

The second part describes the great advances now being made in fuel technology for all heavy vehicles. It explores the latest bus technology and examples of how this might develop in the next few years.

Section 1: Vehicles

Definitions

Buses and coaches are in law defined as vehicles which can carry more than eight passengers and are deployed on work for hire and reward. Buses are generally designed for shorter distance journeys, and any bus in regular use with more than 22 seats must meet the requirements of the Public Service Vehicle (PSV) Accessibility Regulations requiring provision for people with disabilities including wheelchair users.

Coaches are such vehicles generally finished to a more luxurious standard, and usually capable of maintaining a higher speed, though if used on scheduled services they must also comply with the PSV Accessibility Regulations. A coach is legally defined as a vehicle not permitted to carry standing passengers.

Minibuses

It is convenient to use the 22-seat cut-off to define a minibus, though in practice the style of vehicle, particularly in the case of coaches, may have a larger capacity. Minibuses are typically forward-engined with the entrance door behind the front wheels. In simplest form they are actually derived from van designs with internal steps and having only a manually-operated entrance door, especially where they are not used on local bus work.

This can include community uses. Where it is intended to allow travel for people with disabilities, it is common for entrance to be gained via a tail lift, giving access to the rear double doors. Some seats may be demountable to create a space for a wheelchair that is not permanently available. While such minibuses can perform local service work, principally community-based routes and low-demand services in very rural areas (for example in the Scottish Highlands and Islands), they are not ideal for busier routes. However, accessible minibuses have been available since 2001 – the Optare Alero – indeed even earlier in the case of the CVE Omni, albeit they are very much a niche product. Accessible minibuses are now deployed by a range of major operators, as well as with smaller undertakings, on a variety of work.

However, low floor minibuses still only have a very small accessible section, which may have as few as four seats, with the remainder reached by two or three steps. The economics of the operation of minibuses on local bus routes or on demand-responsive services is such that charging normal fare levels may not be commercially viable. Minibuses have a relatively very high rate of depreciation and although there are savings on fuel and other running costs, drivers also represent a higher proportion of costs than they do when driving larger vehicles.

The restricted capacity of a minibus means that they may not always be a commercial proposition for use on local bus services. The revenue from the fares cannot easily cover the costs of operation and ownership. They are, therefore, often likely to be found on a subsidized route with low demand, where the gap between costs and revenue is covered by the subsidy. This may be from a transport authority, or from another external funding source, such as an employer or developer.

Minibuses can be attractive to community bus operators, where the driver is an unpaid volunteer, thus removing the main cost of operation. There is anecdotal evidence to suggest that passengers do not like the cramped conditions in smaller buses, where these have been used to replace larger buses on urban routes. In rural areas, minibuses are more likely to be found on 'lifeline' routes where no other public transport is available. Minibuses potentially have a role to play where physical restrictions preclude the use of larger buses, but there is limited evidence that bus operators are choosing them for this reason.

Costs range between approximately £36,000 and £49,000, at 2020 prices, depending on specification and size (Ford, 2020). However, 30 Mercedes-Benz 'Sprinter' minibuses acquired by Stagecoach in Kent in 2017 cost £93,000 each (at 2017 prices). They are high specification, with low-floors, faux leather seats, and clean technology Euro 6 low-noise engines (Stagecoach Bus, 2017).

Buses

Choice of vehicle

Choosing a bus to operate a particular service represents a trade-off between an appropriate capacity for the expected number of passengers, physical dimensions of the vehicle taking account of the highways traversed, the benefits of standardization across the fleet and affordability.

In general, the greatest capacity will be needed in the peak hours. This is especially true in the mornings, when both adult commuters and schoolchildren will be travelling at the same time. As a result, buses are generally sourced to meet these peaks of demand, and, at other times of day, may have considerable unused capacity. It is often suggested that smaller buses should be used at off-peak times, but the main cost, the driver, will vary only marginally (if at all), while the capital and other operating costs are much higher for a small bus, on a per-seat basis, than for a large bus.

Examples of capital cost

These are mostly taken from operator and local authority press releases. They are based on 2019 prices:

- Small single decker: £150,000 (Salisbury Reds, 2019).
- Large single decker: £185,000–200,000 (BBC, 2019).
- Double decker: £240,000 (Stagecoach Bus, 2019).
- Hybrid vehicles may incur an additional £50,000–100,000 premium.
- Hydrogen fuel cell buses are much more expensive. A contract in 2019 by Transport for London (TfL) for 20 double deckers shows the cost as £542,509 per bus (TfL, 2019).

- All electric single deck vehicles are in the region of £350,000 whilst a double deck version may reach £450,000.
- A gas powered double decker can cost an initial £300,000 (Freeman, 2020).

These are just examples to highlight the initial capital outlay involved. As the new propulsion systems become more commonplace, it may be possible to see costs reduce.

Operators may choose to rent or lease vehicles, rather than make an outright purchase. This may reflect the cashflow implications for the business, differences in taxation treatment, and whether the vehicle is for general use, or acquired for a specific time-limited purpose. Businesses offering rent and lease options may be found advertising in the trade press.

Coaches

The cost of a high specification 53-seat coach which could be used for long distance services, charter or private hire work may cost in excess of £270,000 (Moseley, 2020); while a double deck version may be £390,000 (Scottish Citylink Coaches, 2020).

In all cases, both bus and coach, the alternative option is to arrange to lease such vehicles, eliminating any significant initial outlay. Cash flow, and in particular fares plus other income, would need to be disciplined to meet regular rental payments.

Specification

Buses and coaches are constrained by specifications and dimensions laid down in the Construction and Use Regulations. These govern width, length, height and weight, as well as numerous requirements for internal and external fittings.

Single deck buses

Almost all buses follow the same broad layout, of a low-floor section at the front of the bus, and a raised section at the rear, which also serves to accommodate the principal mechanical components. The engine is also at the rear but may be variously located transversely behind the rearmost seats, in a corner 'cupboard' or in line on one side.

Double deck buses

A double deck bus is typically 4.1–4.4 metres high, with a staircase located over the front offside wheel. Some buses for urban use have a centre door for passengers to use when alighting, in addition to the normal door at the front. Length can vary enormously, from around 9.8 metres to 12.0 metres on two axles, and up to 13.2 metres on three axles. This enables a wide range of passenger capacities to be accommodated, a two-door urban bus perhaps having as few as 65 seats, while a specialized three-axle bus may reach as high as 100 seated passengers. However, restrictions on axle loads sometimes mean that double deckers with large numbers of seats have a lower overall capacity than those with fewer seats but more space for standees.

Engines are universally located at the rear. To spread the load between axles, ancillary components such as fuel tanks are mainly located towards the front, often utilizing the space under the staircase.

Articulated buses

These vehicles are typically around 18 metres long, consisting of two portions joined by a flexible rubber bellows. The front section is on two axles, with the rear on a single axle, supported by a joint to the front section. The vehicle is permanently coupled and forms a single unit for passengers. Within the bellows, the floor is mounted on a turntable, which allows independent movement without affecting the fixed floor in either portion.

Articulated buses are ideal where large numbers of people need to get on and off simultaneously, or where there are large numbers of passengers making very short journeys (eg commuters arriving at London rail terminals, or car park to airport shuttles) who would be reluctant to go upstairs on a double decker. Seating capacity can be up to about 55 seats, though the layout is quite awkward, with more rear-facing seats than in a non-articulated bus, and also more located on sections raised above floor level. However, many buses have fewer seats to enable a greater number of standing passengers to be carried, giving an overall capacity of up to 120 passengers.

Articulated buses are capable of going anywhere a normal 12-metre bus can traverse, though they require more kerbside space at bus stops. This is especially so if a three-door layout is used: two in the front portion and a third in the rear portion, ahead of the rear axle. Street furniture needs careful positioning to ensure stops are free from any obstruction that could block the doorways.

The use of articulated buses has a chequered history in the UK, where a political decision to withdraw those operating in London helped to foster a public attitude of negativity towards them. However, they are frequently used to illustrate proposals for bus rapid transit schemes, especially if a more modern stylized design such as a Van Hool ExquiCity is used. Generally, their deployment seems to be easier where they operate on wider roads with few sharp turns.

The larger capacity comes at a price in fuel consumption, which at around four miles per gallon (mpg) is rather less than the c6–8 mpg of a 12m fixed bus, depending on the type of work on which it is used.

Fuels

Custom and practice has developed so that buses are most commonly fuelled at the end of the day when they return to the depot. Coaches used on scheduled services may function in the same way, but those used on irregular work will need to make ad hoc arrangements, especially if not operating from the main base (eg when on a holiday tour).

The size of diesel tanks is sufficient in almost all instances to allow operation of the bus until it returns to the depot up to 24 hours later. In so doing, an urban bus may have operated in excess of 250 miles, an interurban or rural service perhaps 300 miles.

Some alternative fuels are not yet capable of matching these mileages. Further details are available in the second part of this chapter.

Choice of vehicle

The type of vehicle employed on any particular journey will be determined by the size needed to cope with the busiest journey of the day. In many areas, this will be the morning peak when travel to school, college and work coincides. Schedulers will determine a pattern of work that places the appropriately sized vehicle in the appropriate place at the appropriate time (usually the peak period, as described above). The same vehicle is usually deployed during the rest of the day, unless there are physical restrictions, for example, a low bridge preventing use of a double deck bus; off-peak loads are smaller and unlikely to utilize the full capacity on any individual journey.

As the single biggest cost of operation is the driver, there is minimal cost difference in using double decker compared to single deck buses. Fuel consumption is marginally worse but outweighs the severe disadvantage of running large buses in the peaks and a separate fleet of smaller buses in the off peak.

On-board equipment

CCTV

Most new buses are fitted with multiple cameras, covering both the interior and exterior of the vehicle. As a minimum, exterior cameras provide a forward and rearward looking view, which is invaluable in helping to determine the circumstances of any accident, and potentially defending a claim against the operator. Newer systems may incorporate cameras providing additional coverage of the sides of the bus.

Interior cameras help to protect passengers and the fabric of the vehicle from vandalism and antisocial behaviour. Cameras in the cab area may also record audio, which again is invaluable in understanding any complaint against a driver – anecdotal evidence suggests that although drivers were resistant to such a feature, in most cases it is now welcomed as some aggrieved customers attempt to enhance their version of an incident to the detriment of the driver.

The images taken may be recorded and stored on the bus or transmitted to a central location. The DriveCam system permits drivers to press a button that will ensure the previous 30 seconds is stored. There are data protection requirements to be met in the use of the recorded images.

Cameras to replace mirrors

A number of operators are now using new technology, which replace conventional mirrors with cameras, relaying a view to two monitors one either side of the driver's cab. The benefits claimed are much clearer views in poor lighting and weather conditions, not hitting waiting passengers at bus stops, enabling the driver to get closer to the kerb, and, most importantly, the capital cost of the cameras is more than offset by the cost including labour of replacing mirrors and arms damaged in service.

Those deployed so far consist of a pair of cameras one each side, in the position usually occupied by a mirror mounting. This enables the driver's monitor to have both a conventional view mainly showing the vehicle, and a wider angle with more view of adjacent traffic.

Ticket machines

Almost all buses now have a computer-based ticket machine. This is not only for the purposes of issuing tickets to customers, and recording those without needing to make payment on the bus, but also to provide Automatic Vehicle Location, schedule adherence, and a (text) messaging service to drivers, though in a few cases this facility does exist in reverse. The extension of contactless payment means that ticket machines are effectively mini-payment terminals and subject to conditions imposed by the banking industry.

Ticket machines need to be mounted at a point in the cab where they are easily accessible by the driver, and if appropriate, also by passengers to touch in with either a smartcard, bankcard or other device. A touch pad can be mounted remotely from the ticket machine, where it is easier for passengers to use it, or as an additional facility to allow people to touch in remotely eg on the nearside, as used by Dublin Bus.

Ticket issuing equipment can also be mounted remotely. Some large city systems (National Express West Midlands, Lothian) site it on the staircase wall, which encourages passengers to move inside the bus after their transaction with the driver.

Fare collection box ('farebox')

In some locations, usually large urban areas such as the West Midlands, Nottingham, Edinburgh and Glasgow, buses are fitted with fareboxes. Passengers drop their fare into the box, which has a window on the driver's side so that they may check the amount paid. The driver then presses a lever or more commonly, foot pedal, to allow the coins and notes to drop through into a secure vault.

The driver has no access to the vault, and indeed takes no part in money-handling. They have no change to give to passengers who are required to pay the exact fare to drop into the farebox. If the passenger has insufficient change, some operators will issue an overpayment voucher from the ticket machine. This can typically be used as part-payment towards another fare or exchanged for cash at the operator's premises. The spread of contactless payments has reduced such an inconvenience for many customers.

Operators using the farebox system – usually described to the public as 'exact fare only' – have justified its use on the grounds of security and speed of operation. In most cases, it is used with only a limited range of fares. Further details on fares and revenue collection are contained in Chapter 7.

Next stop information

The Bus Services Act 2017 has provided for all buses to have audio-visual next stop announcements, though this requires to be enacted via a Statutory Instrument. Precise details are being determined, but commonly used facilities are a one- or two-line LED screen, or a larger TFT screen that can convey additional information eg indicating a fare zone boundary, departures by other routes and modes and general marketing information.

Stop information is generally controlled via the ticket machine. Each journey has an individual code, which the driver enters into the ticket machine. A pre-set list of stops matches each journey code, which are then displayed at the appropriate point, through the use of the ticket machine's GPS function. In some systems, the driver is able to initiate generic messages, such as asking passengers to move down the bus, make way for a wheelchair-using customer, or not stand on the top deck.

Automatic Vehicle Location (AVL)

AVL is now usually provided as part of the ticket machine system, though it can also be derived from other systems, such as driver performance monitoring. Vehicles fitted with AVL and used on eligible local bus services currently receive an uplift in the amount of Bus Service Operators Grant (BSOG).

Driving standards monitoring

Many operators now choose to fit a system that can record an individual driver's driving style, in part to encourage fuel-efficient driving, and to reduce behaviour likely to increase the risk of an accident or damage occurring to the vehicle. A gentler driving style will also normally increase passenger comfort.

Seat occupancy counting

Trials have been undertaken in London of a system that uses sensors to detect whether a seat is occupied or not. A screen on the lower deck displays to passengers the number and position of empty seats on the upper deck. The aim is to reduce overcrowding, and congestion around the exit, on the lower deck.

Depots or garages

Accommodating the fleet of vehicles has to take account of the space needed for the entire number of buses needed for the services being operated, plus spare buses enabling overnight maintenance and cleaning to take place. The exception is (and unusually) if a 24-hour service is offered when inevitably some buses will always be 'out on the road' and in use. To minimize dead running costs, the site should be adjacent to or nearby the routes being operated, and accessible (and with parking) for the drivers and other staff employed. Space is also required for engineering facilities to deal with regular maintenance and repairs, along with 'messing' facilities for staff.

While many older premises were designed as essentially covered structures with minimal or no outdoor parking, current practice favours outdoor parking areas with covered facilities only for buses undergoing maintenance or repair.

Ideally premises are laid out to allow the free flow of vehicles through them, taking especial account of the way buses arrive at the end of their duty. This is to ensure buses can queue for re-fuelling as they arrive, without causing congestion for other buses. Many premises are arranged so that buses can then proceed to a drive-through washing machine, but care needs to be taken with drainage and the subsequent route to reduce the amount of floorspace that becomes wet and could become a hazard to people working in the garage.

Maintenance regimes

Operators are required to have a system of regular inspection for their vehicles. Minimum standards are specified in the operator's licence. The basic premise is that the more frequently vehicles are used, the more frequently they are inspected. Major operators typically carry this out every 21 to 28 days. Smaller operators with less-intensively used vehicles may extend this to six to eight weeks, and the absolute limit accepted by the Driver and Vehicle Standards Agency (DVSA) is 13 weeks.

However, drivers are required to certify that a bus is fault-free, or to record defects that do not immediately prevent operation, on a daily basis before a bus leaves a depot. This procedure should be repeated when a bus is taken over from another driver during the course of the day.

The DVSA and Traffic Commissioners produce useful guidance to help operators (DVSA, 2015, 2018a, 2018b; Senior Traffic Commissioner, 2018).

Section 2: Fuels

This section, by John Birtwistle, is based on a paper to the Bus Policy Working Group of the Chartered Institute of Logistics and Transport, 2019, and reproduced with their permission.

Introduction

Great advances are now being made in fuel technology for all heavy vehicles. As the twin threats of global warming and poor air quality continue to grow and become more present in the public consciousness, the bus industry faces a tough battle in persuading politicians and the general population that buses are part of the solution, rather than the problem. The average double deck bus has the potential to remove up to 80 private cars from the road in peak hours, but is still commonly perceived as the source of air pollution and heavy fuel use.

Diesel and emissions

Diesel has been the principal power source for buses since the 1930s and for many years the perception was that a large, slow heavy engine was the most efficient and cost-effective means of propulsion. After experiments with lightweight vehicles with smaller engines in the 1950s, this trend continued and even at the beginning of the low floor bus era, heavyweight vehicles with 11 litre engines were commonplace.

The introduction of the first mandatory Euro emissions standards for new vehicles in 1992 indicated a realization that emissions were becoming an issue, with oxides of nitrogen, carbon monoxide, sulphur dioxide and particulates being subject to strict limits. However, one impact of ever more stringent Euro standards was to increase fuel use as engines were made less efficient by the exhaust treatments and operating cycles imposed to reduce these emissions. Only with the introduction of the Euro V limit in 2009 was there an opportunity to improve fuel consumption simultaneously.

The latest Euro VI limit, mandatory from 2013 apart from small series production exemptions, has also had a beneficial effect on reducing fuel use. But it has also seen a significant reduction in nitrogen oxide emissions compared with Euro V. Euro VI buses emit up to 99.5 per cent less NOx emissions and 98 per cent less particulates emissions compared to buses purchased in 2009 (DieselNet, 2019). Importantly, the achievement of the Euro standards for heavy vehicles has to be proven in the real world rather than under laboratory conditions as for the equivalent light vehicle standards, so there are no opportunities to 'cheat' the system.

Tests in 2017 comparing real-world heavy duty Euro VI bus emissions with real-world Euro 6 diesel car emissions found average NOx emissions from buses of 165 mg/km, nearly one-third or less of the average emissions from Euro 6 cars (480–560 mg/km) (International Council on Clean Transportation, 2017). Even given that, on average, a bus is only carrying 11.4 passengers and a car 1.5 persons, per capita bus emissions are at least 23 times lower compared with the cleanest diesel car.

Diesel electric

Diesel electric hybrid power was developed as a mainstream technology in the mid-2000s. The system uses a diesel engine to generate power which then drives the bus through electric motors and can deliver, manufacturers claim, up to a 35 per cent reduction in fuel use on a like-for-like basis. Two variants are produced:

- parallel hybrid, where the diesel and battery power are used together, with the battery providing initial starting torque and additional power up hills, being recharged under braking;
- series hybrid, where the engine always powers the generator which drives the electric motors.

Hybrid buses have a significant purchase cost premium over diesel and cost more to maintain, but use less fuel than diesel.

Hybrid propulsion has however fallen out of favour in many areas due to relatively poor performance, and the high cost of replacement batteries which have had a shorter life than anticipated. In London, where such costs can be recovered by operators under the contract costs, it remains popular, but elsewhere many hybrid vehicles are being converted to diesel power alone using Euro VI engines. A very few 'extended range' hybrids have been produced for Bristol and London which are able to operate for significant distances on electric power alone, taking additional charge from underground inductive charging plates – these vehicles have been very expensive to produce and the battery life is unknown, and this technology is considered unlikely to have much future application. Whilst outside London many diesel electric hybrid vehicles are now being converted to diesel-only power, within London development of hybrid retrofit continues, with Vantage Power having converted a range of older vehicles with experimental systems.

Addressing the battery life and replacement cost issue has caused manufacturers to look at supercapacitors. These are lighter-weight than the equivalent batteries and expected to have a longer life. Deployment has thus far been restricted to London on a small number of vehicles.

Hybrid flywheel power saw a brief interest around 2015, but only resulted in very small numbers of vehicles being built, and technical development appears to have stalled.

The micro hybrid concept has achieved considerable fuel efficiency savings by looking at the way ancillary components are powered, and using regenerated energy to achieve this. The concept is now commonplace on most UK-built buses.

Other fuels

Meanwhile, innovation continues with other fuels. Biogas is a sustainable fuel produced from waste, and at point of use produces emissions comparable to Euro VI diesel. It is carbon neutral and vehicle purchase costs have only a small premium over diesel, but specialist fuelling facilities and equipment are required. Deployment in significant numbers is ongoing in Reading, Nottingham and Bristol.

Electric buses are nothing new, with battery power being employed in the early 1900s, but today's batteries are far more efficient and relatively lightweight. The technology continues to improve rapidly and the concerns of limited range, battery longevity and capital cost are being addressed. Usually, battery powered buses are charged at the depot overnight for the next day's work. Battery powered buses are best suited to urban operation with shorter daily duty cycles of up to 150 miles, although this can be extended with 'opportunity' charging along the route. Overhead pantograph charging has been deployed in Harrogate, but the fleets in York, Manchester, Nottingham, Liverpool and London rely on overnight charging alone. There is a significant cost premium – up to 50 per cent – for electric buses compared with diesel, and whilst the technology is relatively new, apart from the costs of battery replacement the maintenance costs appear to be low.

Brighton & Hove Buses introduced 30 electric buses in October 2019 (Brighton & Hove Buses, 2019). They run in zero-emissions mode whenever they travel through Brighton city centre, a practice known as geofencing. The Enviro400ER buses, which are fully electric drive, run on batteries topped up via regenerative braking and a small Euro 6 generator if needed when outside the city's Ultra Low Emission Zone. Also in 2019 the company, and sister company Metrobus, secured government funding for 20 zero-emission fuel cell buses for Crawley and Gatwick Airport bus services (Alexander Dennis, 2019).

Hydrogen fuel cell vehicles are effectively electric vehicles that do not need charging. Hydrogen fuel reacts with oxygen to generate electricity and produce tail pipe emissions which are nothing more than water vapour, so the vehicles are as clean as electric at the point of operation. This is very new technology with vehicles currently operating only in London (Mayor of London, 2013); and, from 2015 to early 2020, Aberdeen (Aberdeen City Council, 2019).

The capital cost of the vehicles is thus far prohibitive for mainstream use (up to three times the cost of diesel buses), but increased usage requires production of additional vehicles which is expected to yield economies of scale and a significant price reduction. Specialized fuelling facilities are required and maintenance costs are high, but fuel costs relatively low and tailpipe emissions nil, and the need for charging – overnight or opportunistically – is obviated.

Returning to the theme of weight, buses are now substantially lighter this century – see Table 5.1. Manufacturers have worked hard to take unnecessary weight out of the structure whilst maintaining the necessary structural integrity. This has the benefit of reducing fuel use irrespective of the source of power. Table 5.1, by way of illustration uses data from a major UK operator.

Table 5.1   Bus weights, 1968 to now

DOUBLE DECK:				SINGLE DECK:			
Year	Type	Seats	ULW (tonnes)	Year	Type	Seats	ULW (tonnes)
1968	Routemaster	72	7.9				
1980	VRT	74	9	1981	Leopard	51	8.6
1990	Olympian	77	9.9	1990	Lynx	49	8.9
2000	B7TL	78	11.9	2001	B7	41	11
2012	ADL400	74	11.5	2011	B7RLE	44	11.7
2018	ADL400 MMC	74	10.6	2017	ADL200 MMC	41	8.5

ulw = unladen weight

Conclusions

A wide variety of vehicle types is available, though the choice for any particular use is influenced by appropriate size, cost and earning potential. Operators need to consider whether they intend to run the vehicle for the whole of its lifetime, or whether it may be needed only for a shorter period, for example to match the duration of a specific contract. This may influence whether a vehicle is leased or owned outright.

Increasingly technology is attempting to make the driver's job easier, as well as provide benefits for passengers. A number of features once regarded as optional, such as CCTV and Automatic Vehicle Location, are now largely accepted as standard features, while changes to legislation can mandate extra requirements, unforeseen at the time of purchase.

In summary, there appears to be a clear move towards vehicles capable of zero emissions at the point of operation, with battery power probably the cheapest and simplest option in the short term. But this remains a niche solution, and the cleanliness of Euro VI diesel is such that diesel power can deliver substantial benefits for air quality where the bus can be given optimum operating conditions to offer an attractive, efficient and timely service.

References

Aberdeen City Council (2019) [accessed 29 January 2020] Aberdeen's Hydrogen Buses 2019, *Aberdeen City Council* [online] https://consultation.aberdeencity.gov.uk/resources/copy-of-ahbp/consult_view/ (archived at https://perma.cc/TC5Y-X68H)

Alexander Dennis (2019) [accessed 28 January 2020] Thirty new Alexander Dennis Enviro400ER for Brighton & Hove in UK zero-emissions first, *Alexander Dennis* [online] www.alexander-dennis.com/media/news/2019/september/thirty-new-alexander-dennis-enviro400er-for-brighton-hove-in-uk-zero-emissions-first/ (archived at https://perma.cc/U8RT-ED62)

BBC (2019) [accessed 25 January 2020] McGill's invests £4.75m in 26 new buses, *BBC* [online] www.bbc.co.uk/news/uk-scotland-scotland-business-47733412 (archived at https://perma.cc/3MLJ-7BDR)

Brighton & Hove Buses (2019) [accessed 28 January 2020] First step towards zero-emission fuel cell electric buses for Metrobus Gatwick and Crawley, *Brighton & Hove Buses* [online] www.buses.co.uk/first-step-towards-zero-emission-fuel-cell-electric-buses-metrobus-gatwick-and-crawley (archived at https://perma.cc/62BX-MH66)

DieselNet (2019) [accessed 28 January 2020] Emissions Standards EU: Heavy-Duty Truck and Bus Engines, *DieselNet* [online] https://dieselnet.com/standards/eu/hd.php (archived at https://perma.cc/W9W9-VKZR)

Driver and Vehicle Standards Agency (2015) [accessed 25 January 2020] Commercial vehicle safety and maintenance guides, *GOV.UK* [online] www.gov.uk/government/collections/vehicle-safety-and-maintenance-guides (archived at https://perma.cc/X2R8-7W25)

Driver and Vehicle Standards Agency (2018a) [accessed 25 January 2020] Keeping commercial vehicles safe to drive (roadworthy), *GOV.UK* [online] www.gov.uk/government/publications/guide-to-maintaining-roadworthiness (archived at https://perma.cc/69VB-BKNM)

Driver and Vehicle Standards Agency (2018b) [accessed 25 January 2020] Public service vehicle (PSV): driver's daily walkaround check, *GOV.UK* [online] www.gov.uk/government/publications/public-service-vehicle-drivers-daily-walkaround-check (archived at https://perma.cc/L6G9-R9B7)

Ford [online] www.ford.co.uk (archived at https://perma.cc/UY2A-3XN3)

Freeman, J (2020) [accessed 25 January 2020] *First West of England* [online] www.firstgroup.com/bristol-bath-and-west/news-and-service-updates/news/open-letter-james-freeman-md-first-west-england (archived at https://perma.cc/A3U4-7ZQ5)

International Council on Clean Transportation (2017) [accessed 4 December 2019] NOx emissions from heavy-duty and light-duty diesel vehicles in the EU: Comparison of real-world performance and current type-approval requirements, *International Council on Clean Transportation* [online] https://theicct.org/publications/nox-emissions-heavy-duty-and-light-duty-diesel-vehicles-eu-comparison-real-world (archived at https://perma.cc/QH4G-4LY5)

Mayor of London (2013) [accessed 29 January 2020] Recent News from partners and industry, *Hydrogen London* [online] www.hydrogenlondon.org/projects/london-hydrogen-bus-project/ (archived at https://perma.cc/Q53Y-QYXD)

Moseley (2020) [accessed 20 July 2020] https://moseleycoachsales.co.uk/new-coaches/ (archived at https://perma.cc/UP6W-NE7B)

Salisbury Reds (2019) [accessed 25 January 2020] New buses coming this December..., *Salisbury Reds* [online] www.salisburyreds.co.uk/new-buses (archived at https://perma.cc/L6ZH-QNBK)

Scottish Citylink Coaches (2020) [accessed 25 January 2020] Largest fleet replacement investment in Scotland delivers new £7million fleet of luxury coaches linking Glasgow and Edinburgh, *Scottish Citylink Coaches* [online] www.citylink.co.uk/media090120.php (archived at https://perma.cc/8YED-L67C)

Senior Traffic Commissioner (2018) [accessed 25 January 2020] Senior Traffic Commissioner's statutory guidance and statutory directions, *GOV.UK* [online] www.gov.uk/government/collections/senior-traffic-commissioners-statutory-guidance-and-statutory-directions (archived at https://perma.cc/MGF4-5TN6)

Stagecoach Bus (2017) [accessed 28 January 2020] Big deal for Ashford as buses get 'little & often', *Stagecoach Bus* [online] www.stagecoachbus.com/news/south-east/2017/january/big-deal-for-ashford-as-buses-get-little-and-often (archived at https://perma.cc/VTU2-HJD6)

Stagecoach Bus (2019) [accessed 25 January 2020] Stagecoach in Oxfordshire announces roll out of new fleet worth £5 million, *Stagecoach Bus* [online] www.stagecoachbus.com/news/oxfordshire/2019/october/21-new-buses-for-services-s1-and-s2 (archived at https://perma.cc/J7VJ-N5XB)

TfL (2019) [accessed 3 February 2020] Supply and Purchase of Hydrogen Buses and Associated Services, *Contracts Finder* [online] www.contractsfinder.service.gov.uk/Notice/63f8fc28-0124-4552-9d2a-01e8a423cc7b?p=@QxUlRRPT0=NjJNT08=UF (archived at https://perma.cc/9HA5-WMEU)

Operations

06

TONY FRANCIS

Introduction

The operation of bus and coach services requires the successful coordination and management of the three elements that make up the business, namely the staff, the vehicles, and the services. This chapter summarizes the key priorities that need to be applied in not only delivering the services, but sustaining the undertaking through ever-changing and challenging social and business conditions.

Staff

'We must look after my men,' were words used to me in the 1970s by Geoffrey Fernyhough, Operating Manager of London Transport Country Buses and Coaches, which became part of the National Bus Company in 1970. He added: 'That is essential'.

Today we would refer to 'staff' or 'our people', but it underlines the fact that the business is all about people. Firstly, employees, who are entrusted with significant elements of the worth of the undertaking (the vehicles) to run services as accurately as possible and, importantly, legally and with absolute safety. They are often the only people interacting between the undertaking and its customers. Recruitment, training and retention of drivers, and giving them continual assistance, are priority issues.

Supporting the drivers are those overseeing the day-to-day operations at the garages. A manager of a major garage in the East Midlands with a large workforce was determined to know the given name of every driver and something about them as a person. Thus they could address them personally and be in a position to know if there were issues which might affect their professional duties. Traditionally, drivers signed on at a garage in the presence of a supervisor or inspector. Thus any issues or uncertainty as to their ability to undertake the tasks could be pursued. Increasingly, signing on can be done remotely, but systems are being applied which allow staff to communicate with the company and for their peers to report any issues of concern.

Vehicles

The prime output (or purpose) of an engineering department of a bus business is the provision of the required number of buses (or coaches) each day, according to the services advertised and available to the public. That requires a maintenance and cleaning (or presentation) regime which guarantees that requirement.

Most work in ensuring the vehicles are presented correctly is undertaken overnight at the garages. The essential prerequisite is to ensure each vehicle is cleaned, fuelled and free from defects. It must be correctly licensed, fitted out with information for the service(s) it will be working on and in all respects safe and legal. To help achieve this, there is a 'float' of vehicles to ensure there is the opportunity for maintenance and repairs to the entire stock of buses. This might mean a fleet of some 10 per cent or more above that needed to meet service requirements.

Unfortunately, accidents and other incidents such as breakdowns will occur whilst the buses are in service. Arrangements need to be made for the recovery of such vehicles (often this is subcontracted to specialists in this skill).

Services

These are quite often based on traditional routes linking small communities with larger towns providing opportunities for work, education, shopping, visiting friends and relations or just for leisure. Understanding the market for bus travel is essential; an example once arose where the local authority decided the weekly shopping service from a village should run in the morning, not, as it was, in the afternoon. This brought forward strong objections from the community, and the change was abandoned.

The lesson from this is to base services upon local intelligence. Today, with modern ticketing systems, there is significant data about current use, but there is a need to understand the potential for growth. An important part of operations is keeping in touch with passengers and ensuring one is offering the right type of service. 'Getting out on the road' or 'walking the shop floor' are expressions which encapsulate the need for those who take decisions to understand what is happening at the delivery side of the business. This is touched upon further in Chapter 15, *Working with the public.*

Buses, with a few exceptions where priorities are given to public transport, have to share their 'way' with a variety of other road users. Services are designed to reflect various factors; not only expected passenger numbers, but anticipated road speeds which vary according to traffic levels (for example, slower during the commute to and from work and school times and at busy shopping times).

However, this is no guarantee that these accurately reflect what happens on a day-to-day basis, as unexpected incidents can impact adversely on timekeeping. Accidents, roadworks including emergency repairs to utilities such as water and gas supplies, poor weather conditions, special events and sometimes reasons that are difficult to identify will delay buses. These can destroy timekeeping. Buses are delayed, which means, on a frequent service, they will catch up with each other and bunch together. This delays or even results in the cancellation of subsequent journeys that those buses were scheduled to run. In some extreme conditions, drivers may reach the limit of their legal driving time, adding to further disruption and cancellation of services.

It is thus essential that adequate supervision is given to the operation of services. Today, with the ability to communicate directly with the driver and know precisely where the vehicles are located, along with knowledge of the area and of previous incidents, it is possible to mitigate such situations. Nowadays, it is possible to apply Automatic Vehicle Location systems (AVL), ticket machine messaging and radio to support efficient management of the services. Use of computer technology means that the position of buses can be checked, for example, on hand-held devices to further aid quick decision making and transmission of instructions to staff.

But it is, nevertheless, a reality that road space is at a premium in many communities, and skills need to be developed to recover the scheduled timetable as quickly as practicable. This may mean introducing additional buses and drivers especially if the costs can be seen as maintaining the reputation of the business and retaining the goodwill of the 'customer base' (sorry – the passengers!).

A good lesson is to develop sound and mutually trustworthy working relationships with the highway authorities, especially to ensure that, at least, planned roadworks take proper account of bus services. Such a dialogue should provide evidence as to the adverse impact previous incursions have created, and perhaps agree measures that might mitigate delays and costs in future. Whilst a partnership is essential across the various disciplines within a bus undertaking, a significant coming together is similarly required with the authority that manages the 'track' or highway.

There are a few exceptions where the bus dominates. There are exclusive busways pioneered in such places as Runcorn, and one of the best in Cambridgeshire, but bus stations have been a feature of the business since its earliest times.

Bus stations

Location and size

These are a central point for the arrival and departure of buses and can be of considerable benefit to passengers, provided that they are located in the right place, have sufficient capacity and are otherwise fit for purpose.

Bus stations can fulfil that role, though a collection of closely related on-street stops may be sufficient provided they are near to the ultimate destination of passengers. There has been a long-term tendency to close bus stations in favour of on-street stops, while new-build bus stations replacing older facilities often have a reduced capacity compared to their predecessors. This is especially true of space provided for buses to layover between journeys. Where space in town centres may be in high demand, there has been a tendency for this to take place 'somewhere else'.

Examples of this include Northampton, where the capacity of the current Northgate bus station has to be supplemented by on-street stops in The Drapery. However, there are no specific layover spaces, unlike the previous Greyfriars bus station. As a result, buses cannot always use their intended stand, as a bus on layover is parked on it, resulting in potential confusion for passengers as the bus then has to use a different stand.

Layover space is important because it allows the stationing of spare buses to cover breakdowns and delays, and allows higher capacity at a stand compared to a layout without it.

Stand capacity

A bus station mainly serving routes that start and terminate at that location will need more stands than one where buses mostly pass through and pause only briefly en route to another destination. A common rule of thumb is to schedule no more than eight buses per hour in the former scenario. This gives sufficient leeway for early and late running while still maintaining an attractive throughput of buses.

Allowance may also need to be given to cover the time needed for a driver changeover, or where the bus has to reverse off the stand. In some bus stations, reversing manoeuvres may only take place when supervised by another member of staff, and it may take time to attract that person's attention.

Alternatively, reversing can be governed by signals that either forbid or permit a driver to reverse. At Hanley bus station, in the Potteries, the system operates on a time interval, which permits simultaneous reversing on a predetermined number of stands.

Buses to common destinations should be grouped as near as possible to each other to assist passengers waiting on the concourse.

Design

As far as possible, the movement of vehicles and pedestrians should be segregated and ideally separated entirely. This can often be achieved by a single concourse for passengers, with buses driving on and reversing off stands set at about 45 degrees to the concourse.

Alternatives include island designs with pedestrian access at clearly marked points – for example at either end of the island, or halfway along it, with an element of design to discourage people from walking in the roadway except at designated points.

Covered accommodation should be provided for waiting passengers, as a minimum in the form of shelters at each stand, and comfortable seating, ideally as a complete covered route from the moment of entering the bus station to boarding a bus. Each stand should also have a paper display of departures. This can be supplemented by electronic information, but should not be replaced by it, as it leaves no source of information if there is an IT failure or loss of power to the electronic equipment.

Automated systems do not allow for the possibility of a bus operating from a different stand, if it is unable to access that allocated. This can be overcome with manual intervention.

Interchange and detailed presentation

Bus stations are also interchange points, and making travel accessible for all is an essential prerequisite. Buses seldom offer a complete door-to-door service; there is a need to take account of the preceding and subsequent journeys, whether by foot or other wheeled transport.

Due account must be taken to ensure facilities are suitable for those people with disabilities, including, for example, provision for the setting down and picking up of people who may have to use private cars (Department for Transport, 2005). Good signing and information is necessary, but importantly kept up to date and well-presented. First impressions count, and bus stations may be regarded as a 'showcase' for the business, either attracting or discouraging users.

Staff welfare and control

Equally important, staff require toilet and possibly rest facilities at such locations. Such sites may also be ideal as a control or operational management centre for services.

These matters equally apply to all bus services regardless of their access to a bus station. In connection with staff welfare, it is important that toilet and refreshment facilities are provided at appropriately designated terminal points. Arrangements can be made with commercial premises, as well as provision of bespoke buildings although the latter can be expensive and sometimes controversial with local residents. It is also vital that matters such as fatigue and any potential loss of concentration can be identified, but preferably always avoided, by self-reporting and also monitoring schemes.

Summary and the future

Not only is there a need for those planning services to be watchful for today's (and tomorrow's) evolving social and work habits (for example the changing role of the high street), but those delivering the services day by day should take advantage of technology's advances. Moves towards the total elimination of the driver may not occur, but the technology that is arising towards this potential objective can ease the burden behind 'the wheel'.

Harnessing the ever-growing new opportunities to monitor and manage the resources of an operator will support the bus in increasing its contribution towards the population's mobility. However, teamwork across an undertaking is essential, recognizing the role each plays and supporting each other in service delivery.

Reference

Department for Transport (2005) [accessed 29 January 2020] Making transport accessible for passengers and pedestrians: A guide to best practice on improving access to public transport and creating a barrier-free pedestrian environment, *GOV.UK* [online] www.gov.uk/government/publications/inclusive-mobility (archived at https://perma.cc/DH3T-PHP4)

Further reading

Bus Archive [online] www.busarchive.org.uk/ (archived at https://perma.cc/9VM9-WELH)
Omnibus Society [online] www.omnibus-society.org/ (archived at https://perma.cc/582U-J9VC)

Fares, ticketing and other revenue – turning a social service into a business

07

JOHN BIRTWISTLE AND KEVIN HAWKINS

Introduction

In this chapter the various revenue streams that a bus or coach operator may exploit are examined. This concentrates on buses, although many of the concepts and opportunities apply equally to coaching in its various forms.

It must be remembered that whatever the political ideological or legislative regime, any form of business must cover its costs and make a profit. Profit is not a dirty word, it is the single pre-requisite for survival, whether it is just sufficient to keep the enterprise from insolvency, to facilitate renewal of assets and to ensure business continuity, or to provide shareholders with the confidence to invest and grow the operation. Not having a (sufficient) stream of income will guarantee that the operation cannot continue.

The chapter is specifically written with respect to legislation and prevailing policies in the United Kingdom at the time of writing (2019/20), but many of the principles are applicable to any operating regime. Where directly relevant, reference is made to the other potential regimes which might otherwise apply.

Costs

Running a bus service costs money. The cost elements can be allocated to various categories based on how they are incurred. It is simplest to start with operating, variable or direct costs – these terms are interchangeable. They relate to the wages drivers are paid and their on-costs (which will, as explored in other chapters, cover more than the hours spent driving) for the service; and the cost of fuel for the vehicles and tyre costs (which may be paid to a contractor on a pence per mile basis).

Semi-variable or indirect costs comprise the other elements of cost related to providing the service. These will include the depreciation and cost of capital, or financing costs of vehicles, vehicle maintenance and sundry overheads (tax, insurance etc) associated with the vehicles allocated to the route. Also included will be the costs associated with the need to keep spare vehicles to cover maintenance, breakdowns and operational interventions, and of spare drivers to cover for sickness, holidays and absence. Costs of cleaning vehicles and of maintaining appropriate licenses for operation also come under this category.

Overheads will include the other costs of providing any form of service and will generally include the upkeep costs for depot and maintenance facilities, management costs and those associated with any other office functions – administration, human resources, IT, etc, as well as promotion, information and customer services. For larger operators with multiple depots and/or operating companies, they may also include contributions to head office costs.

Semi variable and overhead costs will be allocated across routes on the basis of the hours operated by vehicles on that route, the miles (or km) operated on the route, or the Peak Vehicle Requirement (PVR) – the maximum number of vehicles needed at any one time to provide service on the route at any given time.

The margin – or profit margin – is generally calculated as the percentage of: the revenue less the costs, divided by the revenue. An operator's margin should be sufficient to allow for replacement of time expired assets in a timely manner, in addition to all costs and liabilities described above. Profit must not be considered to be a 'dirty word' or an undesirable concept – even a social enterprise with a growing business requires profit to be able to meet that growth with increased supply.

Fare setting

The actual values of fares will depend also on the expected mix of passengers – with historic and legislative impacts on this mix in terms of revenue generation. The bus industry is possibly unique in having elected – typically in the 1920s and 1930s – to offer younger passengers and sometimes other groups a cheaper level of fare than adults. Since when could a child pay half price for a bar of chocolate in a corner shop or supermarket?

As always, taking away such privileges causes massive ill-will and resentment and can have a detrimental effect on revenue – not just through elasticity, as explored later in the next section, but through the effect of these emotive impacts. So, they are probably here to stay.

The level of discount offered to children (and increasingly to students) is not fixed by any legislation and indeed is not mandatory. Typically, the discount level is between 25 per cent and 50 per cent, and is available until the child's 16th or 17th birthday – although some operators offer such commercial discounts up to ages as high as 25. And under-fives are traditionally carried without a fare being levied – provided that, in theory at least, they do not occupy a seat, and are accompanied.

Concessionary travel is something rather different and is explored in detail later in this chapter. But whilst the general rule is that an operator ought to be no worse off as a result of any concessionary travel, the position today is probably universal that there will be a lower yield per passenger than if the full fare was charged, even taking account of those same elasticity and emotive factors.

So, the fare charged to the 'average' passenger will be somewhat lower than the standard adult fare.

Competition

The standard fares regime may occasionally be suspended by an operator in an attempt to grow demand – either organically, or by attracting passengers from another mode or operator. This is explored in more detail later in this chapter, but it is worth touching briefly on the controls imposed through competition law.

In common with most businesses in the UK, the Competition Act 1998 sets out certain safeguards designed to protect the public and legitimate business interests. One of the latter is protection from predatory competition, which can be defined very simply as (inter alia) setting prices at a level that cannot cover costs.

A whole chapter, nay, a whole book, could be written on this subject but it is appropriate to record here that the Competition and Markets Authority (CMA) which administers and enforces competition law in the UK defines these costs as the sum of variable and semi-variable costs, and if overheads are not also covered there may be further factors taken into account. Failure to observe the Competition Act 1998's requirements is severely business- and career-limiting and may result in a spell behind bars, so is not recommended. If in doubt, consult a lawyer.

But of course, competition does occur 'on the road' from time to time and a new entrant to the market can sometimes appear, with lower costs and prices to match. This can result in the incumbent's inability to cover its costs with the reduced revenue resulting from attrition to the new entrant. Clearly an inability of an incumbent operator to react would be an unduly severe restriction on trade, and potentially would enable any new market entrant to deliberately destabilize an established operator, without fear of reaction.

So, there is a mechanism whereby an operator can introduce 'promotional fares' in response to another's cheaper prices and, provided these are set with an 'expiry date', if these promotional fares can be demonstrated to be increasing that operator's revenue such that they are reaching a position of renewed profitability, they will not be in breach of the Competition Act. However, it is of course much more complex than that and our advice remains: consult an expert!

Demand

Without demand, there is no need for supply. There is no room here for lessons in basic economics, suffice to say that bus travel is a derived demand subject to the usual principles of negative elasticity. That is to say that no-one (except bus enthusiasts and cold pensioners) makes a bus journey for its own sake, and, all other things being equal, as the price increases, demand for the service will fall. Of course, all other things are not equal and that complicates matters, but firstly we should consider that basic principle.

So, at the most basic level there has to be a price paid to travel which, taking account of the expected level of travel, will at least cover costs. The factors which a provider of bus services must consider when deciding how to calculate fares and charges comprise:

- Basic elasticity – the reducing propensity to purchase a product as its price increases. There are long- and short-term measures of elasticity pertaining to bus travel, but the general rule of thumb is that if you were to double the fare, you would lose sufficient passengers that your yield (the increase in total revenue accruing from those passengers who still travel) would be only 50 per cent. Now, that is not a hard and fast rule and **every local bus market is different,** but it does provide an indication that you don't simply get the full benefit of any increase.

- Cross-elasticity is the relationship between the price of X and demand for Y. So, in terms of bus travel if there is a competing mode of transport available, any change in its cost will affect demand for the bus service without that service changing – in price or indeed any other characteristic. For instance, a reduction in car parking charges in a city centre will result in reduced demand for bus travel, and vice versa. This always has to be remembered when amending fares.

- Boarding times have a massive impact on the costs of operation and will be affected by a great many different factors, not least the structure of fares. A simple fare structure that requires the minimum driver interaction will reduce boarding times – but may not maximize the overall fares yield.

- Trade-offs are often possible by passengers, hence the usual range of ticket products offered by operators, including singles, returns, day, week and month tickets and carnets. Whilst it might be expected that there would be a narrow range of multipliers between these products, that is very rarely the case, largely because **every local bus market is different.** There are some fairly obvious broad rules, however – returns should be cheaper than two singles, day tickets more expensive than two singles, week tickets cheaper than five days' travel and month tickets cheaper than four weeks – although this is often marginal, as once the passenger has bought a week's travel they are relatively committed. Finally, a carnet of 10 single tickets must offer a discount over 10 individually bought identical tickets.

- Loyalty is a major factor in setting fares – and not only as a result of competition. The principal competitor of the local bus is, no matter the local market structure, the private car. Competition with other bus operators and other public transport modes will always be secondary to that. But pricing to attract passengers to your service can be a valuable marketing tool – as long as it is accompanied by effective marketing!

- Fares experiments can be used to introduce a new service – and encourage customer loyalty – but remember these sit in the context of the various other external factors considered here. Consider it like this – half-price baked beans may encourage you to do your weekly shop at Tesco, but only if you eat a lot of baked beans. Aldi may still be much cheaper overall.

- Contra deals – the idea of offering discounts in retail and hospitality outlets for those who have travelled by bus – have been tried on many occasions although often with limited success. Where this has been successful is generally in association with attempts by retailers to encourage extra trade, such as evening shopping in the run-up to Christmas. Getting a half-price mince pie with your bus ticket can be sufficient incentive for some people to make an extra trip. Where it works better is when combined with marketing based on the convenience of leaving the car at home and avoiding the search for a parking space, but to succeed, the bus has to be able to access the attraction without sitting in the same traffic jam as the cars.

- Finally, the impact of latent and suppressed demand needs to be considered. Latent demand is where the introduction of a new service or a reduced fare encourages new travel as people consider it to provide a new opportunity to access a facility or attraction that was previously too difficult or too expensive to reach. Suppressed demand can be the case where the lack of a service to a particular area resulted in it being inaccessible without a car – and can be worth exploring with site owners and developers as a potential opportunity for contra deals (see above) and pump priming of services (as described later in the chapter).

Fare structures

Traditionally, fares charged to passengers depended on how far they travelled – on a crude 'pence per mile' basis in the early days of buses, but soon settling down to what is described as a tapered fare scale. That effectively charges the longer-distance passenger less per mile than the short-distance passenger, reflecting the fixed cost element of the journey and the variable mileage-based element.

Rather than having a separate fare for every possible combination of origin (boarding stop) and destination (alighting stop) – as with train travel – attempts were soon made to group stops together in 'fare stages' reflecting common groupings of land uses or geographical areas, or simply on a cruder distance-based scale. This made it easier for passengers and fare collection crew members to understand and remember the fares for journeys, but nevertheless some longer-distance services boasted impressive numbers of fare stages.

Whilst between 1930 and 1986 bus operators had to apply to the Traffic Commissioner for their area when they wanted to apply for a fares increase, and quite often had to attend a fiercely contested hearing in the Traffic Court only to see it refused (not infrequently on the basis of objections and 'evidence' from a train operator in common ownership!), today operators are free to set fares as they choose. But the tapered fare scale and associated 'fares triangle' (see Figure 7.1 later in this chapter), which sets out the fares applicable between each 'fare stage', remains the commonest fares structure for local bus operations in the UK.

In the 1960s, operators sought to reduce costs by eliminating the job of the separate conductor required to collect fares as the vehicle travelled the route, but to reduce the impact of this on boarding times as the driver collected fares from passengers, simplification became the order of the day. Many operators, largely those in urban areas, introduced flat fares on particular routes or across networks. The concept was that the passenger need not ask how much the fare was, or state their destination, and the driver would not be required to look up the appropriate fare.

Flat fare systems can have a significant impact – often negative – on yield, due to changes in individual fares, inevitably resulting in winners and losers amongst passengers, and the consequent effects of elasticity. Nevertheless, these were often introduced on new designs of buses with automatic fare collection. This proved unpopular and/or unreliable, bringing the concept into disrepute – and the baby was, often, thrown away with the bathwater. Replacement of flat fare collection systems usually also meant replacement of the flat fares structure itself – again in many cases putting individual fares up and reducing yield due to elasticity, as well as increasing boarding times once more with the need for additional fares interrogation by drivers.

More recently operators have begun to experiment with zonal fares – two models having been deployed, in broad terms – concentric rings, and distance-based zoning. Concentric or embedded rings are the simplest – consider a map of an urban area where the city centre is bounded by an inner ring road. Travel within that ring is charged at a set fare per single trip. Cross that ring to travel further out and you pay more. Travel entirely outside that boundary may be at a third price, or may match that of one of the other two prices. As many rings or zones can be included in the scheme as desired.

An unusual variation on zonal fares was employed in Bristol in 2012 where a solution was required to simplify a vast number of complex single fares – in some cases, for historical reasons, the same journey would differ in price dependent on the service boarded, even when the operator was the same.

The concept was that the new regime would charge a common value of £x for a trip of up to y miles, thereafter the cost increasing to £v for a trip of up to w miles, with three fares being used across the network. This was a necessary stepping stone to what became, several years later, a flat fare across the urban network (necessary to prevent any individual passenger's journey becoming immediately dramatically more expensive as a result of the change, but still maintaining a similar overall level of revenue to the operator). It is worth noting that whilst this was not the only contributory factor, bus use in the area increased by over 50 per cent between 2013 and 2019 (Department for Transport, 2019).

Some local transport authorities have funded free bus services in central areas in an attempt to improve public transport usage for more complex journeys. Routes such as Manchester's MetroShuttle provide links between public transport hubs and major trip attractors, but are largely unsustainable in an environment of reduced local authority funding (Transport for Greater Manchester, 2020).

Demand pricing – variable fares dependent on the number of people wishing to travel at certain times – is relatively uncommon in the bus industry. This is largely as a result of passenger research consistently revealing a desire for simplicity in fares, both in terms of the overall complexity of the regime, and in knowing what the fare is going to be for an individual journey at a given time. Demand pricing militates against this – particularly the latter – and goes against the increasing trend towards simplification. The only significant examples remaining are the legacy of 1970s attempts to boost off-peak bus patronage, at a time when peak period services required a far higher increase in vehicle and staff resources than the generally relatively flat peaks of today, by reducing fares to much lower levels between peak periods, often with local authority support to underwrite the revenue otherwise potentially lost. In a few cases such off-peak fares have been re-tained, by historical accident, by the current operators.

The increasing range of additional ticketing products might be expected to have gradually reduced reliance on single fares (and returns), and in many cases this is indeed the case. But in others, passengers remain wedded to the concept of paying for each journey at a time no matter what. Remember, every local bus market is different.

Payment

Cash was once the only way to pay your bus fare. Almost unbelievable in this day and age. Next, I'll reveal that there was an era before mobile phones when you had to use a fixed telephone in the street, and pay using coins...

Handling cash is a big issue for bus operators. It costs money – to count it, have it collected and paid into banks. It costs staff time to pay it in and process it. There is a risk of fraud from passengers with counterfeit and foreign coins and notes, drivers taking cash and not issuing tickets, and ad-ministrative fraud in cash processing. But it can also be inconvenient for passengers who, in an increasingly cashless society, still have to maintain a pocket of coins and notes to pay for their travel.

Cashless

In fact, for over 100 years we have had as an alternative to cash, the option to purchase paper or card-based season tickets – originally for a week's worth of specific journeys, more recently offering unlimited travel across a network for a day, week, month, term or even year. For operators, such tick-ets have the advantage of parting the passenger from their fare in advance, assisting cash flow, and in a competitive market can also encourage and engender brand loyalty.

The advantage for the passenger is a discounted cost of travel, more heav-ily discounted if a longer duration is chosen, along with obviating the need to carry cash. But these tickets have their risks – fraudulent reproduction for the operator, and loss or theft for the passenger. To ameliorate this, the long-est duration tickets – a month at least – have been accompanied for many years by photographic ID cards.

Smartcards have been around for a long time – the initial demonstrations of these for public transport use being planned in the late 1980s with an initial experimental application in Bolton, Greater Manchester. It has taken a lot of time and money to reach the situation where at the time of writing, public transport fares in London are handled by a proprietary smartcard system ('Oyster') and a separate open system with published protocols and schemes ('ITSO') delivers the concessionary travel schemes for England, Scotland and Wales, but very little else. Relatively few commercial smart-card applications have been developed, largely as a result of the high capital initial cost of developing systems.

A lower cost approach was adopted for some years by a few urban op-erators with magnetic stripe ticketing, as employed on the UK railways since the 1980s, for some bus systems – but with very limited success. These tech-nologies all are generally deployed as season tickets with a fixed duration – but can be used as stored value cards, with each journey made decrementing the remaining credit held on the card. This is explored further below.

Advance of technology

More recently, the advent of mobile phone technology has enabled pas-sengers to put such products onto their mobile devices with varying degrees of security, including 'QR' or 2D barcodes (often incorrectly re-ferred to as 3D barcodes!) and mobile or scrolling barcodes that are not reproduceable. Adopt an insufficiently secure approach, and the local pop-ulation will soon screenshot their passes and circulate them! The pass may be read by a relatively dumb or very sophisticated scanner on the bus; in some cases, a visual inspection by the driver has to suffice.

But this is largely missing the point of such ticketing, as the real value to the operator is being able to monitor the journeys made by an individual pas-senger – even if this passenger cannot be identified (or does not want to be). Sales of such tickets are largely through the internet or using a mobile ap-plication (app), where the purchaser may – or may not – consent to the shar-ing of their personalized journey data, depending on the payment system.

Whilst every local bus market is different, mobile ticketing has seen re-markable market penetration in some areas – over 40 per cent of transac-tions is not uncommon in a couple of years. This form of ticketing appears particularly appealing to the younger generation of traveller and particu-larly to the student population.

Only three years before this chapter was written in late 2019, it seemed inconceivable that you could use your bank card on the bus – but Europay, Mastercard and Visa (EMV – the three main card banking systems that have picked up the concept and run with it for retailing) allow contactless transactions to be made on-bus by presenting the card in proximity to a reader on the ticket machine. There are three forms of EMV:

- Model 1 is where the passenger uses the card instead of cash to pay for a product – which could be a single, return or season ticket of some form.

- Model 2 introduces the concept of post-pay, using a cap to guarantee that the passenger will pay no more than a set amount per day – or per week, based on the trips they have made. This can be deployed in a variety of environments either single or multi-operator and including multi-modal travel.

- Model 3 is otherwise known as Card as Authority to Travel – where the passenger has effectively pre-purchased a season ticket and uses their bank card as proof of that travel entitlement, rather than having a separate travel card.

Model 2 is emerging as a popular ticketing regime initially for operators' own products, but with aspirations for the rapid rollout of multi-operator products. The concept of paying for each individual journey and then settlement after the travel period is complete relies on the system knowing which journeys have been made – therefore, either a flat fare system or some means of recording alighting is required.

At the time of writing, both are in operation with the obvious simplicity and cost saving of flat fare being preferred where this can be a sensible commercial proposition, but for larger travel areas and routes beyond the urban core a continuing need for a graduated fare structure militates against this. Therefore, a separate 'exit reader' is required to record the passenger leaving the vehicle and a fare then being calculated. This lends itself best to dual-door vehicles with the exit reader sited adjacent to the centre exit.

Vehicles to this design are as noted earlier relatively uncommon, and therefore a compromise solution has been adopted with either a second card reader to the passengers' left as they leave through the front door, or even a requirement to 'touch off' on the same reader as they used on entry.

Such 'touch-on-touch-off' regimes are in their infancy, but the attempts to implement this with single-door vehicles appear to negate much of the intended benefit from reduced driver interaction seeking to reduce stop dwell time. Model 2 is likely to grow greatly in popularity at such time as technology enables reliable proximity sensing for passengers leaving or remaining on the vehicle. Technologies under investigation include face recognition, detection of the payment device passing through a 'virtual curtain' at the vehicle exit, and confirmation of the ongoing presence of the payment device remaining in the vehicle.

All the foregoing technological approaches are simply a means to an end, through the ever-growing application of IT, to increase the proportion of cashless transactions. As long as account is taken of those unable to travel using such technology, to ensure that there is a sufficient safety net to retain and encourage their use of buses, there are other advantages to operators besides the bus stop dwell time and cash handling benefits. Such use of technology facilitates the creation of a stronger relationship with the passenger, with access (where they give consent) to their travel habits and patterns, which should help improve service planning, and the ability to develop and market particular bespoke travel payment packages to encourage greater use (and as appropriate, brand loyalty).

All of which will be beneficial to operators, passengers and stakeholders alike – provided that the following fundamental principle is always remembered: Keep it simple for the passenger. And remember, if the system fails 'on the road', you still need to collect revenue and keep your passengers happy!

Ticketing equipment

History

Initially, bus and tram conductors carried a rack of tickets for specific journeys, together with a device to punch holes in, or remove a specific section of, the tickets. The punched or clipped sections were retained by the conductor, not to reduce litter, but to allow reconciliation of revenue by audit teams. Many of the clipping or punching devices emitted a ringing sound and a well-known version was made by the Bell Punch Company. A major disadvantage of this system was that the printed tickets had fare values printed on them and had to be reissued when fares changed – and even when the fare value was not shown, operators sought to replace the tickets with different colours when fares changed, to ensure old tickets were no longer being sold (at old prices). New routes required new sets of tickets, and conductors had to carry a heavy load.

In the 1930s, technology moved ahead with machines designed specifically to accommodate multiple fares on different routes. Systems such as Setright and TIM (the imaginatively named Ticket Issuing Machines) allowed the conductor to specify a fare, class of passenger (adult, child etc), single/return etc, route number, date, fare stage boarded etc. These were highly complex machines and worked remarkably well, also including registers that added up the total value of each type of fare sold to facilitate quick completion of waybill documentation to record the fares collected on each journey, and to provide useful audit data.

As one-person-operation (initially called one-man-operation or OMO) began to be adopted to save staff costs, devices were developed to allow these machines to be mounted on the driver's cab door – and, by the 1960s, to be powered electrically from the bus' own power supply, rather than relying on a handle being wound. Use of these continued at many operators into the 1980s and sometimes beyond. But there were new 'pretenders' introduced in the early postwar years, the most popular being the 'Ultimate' machine which used five or six sets of pre-printed tickets on a roll – back to the same problems as previously... These were used by drivers to issue a small range of fare values, unassociated with routes, to speed up boarding times – whilst, in most cases, continuing to offer change to passengers.

That too was soon to change in the 1960s with the advent of the Farebox. First used in the USA in the 1930s, this made its way to the UK at around the time that one-person-operation of double deck vehicles became legal in 1966. The Johnson Farebox, a type of hopper with a glass viewing pane for the driver to check, visually, that the correct fare had been paid, was often unpopular with passengers, as it frequently was accompanied by a 'no change given' policy.

It was followed by the rather more unusual 'Videmat' system where a large box was the repository of the passenger's coins, and which took a photographic image which was reproduced on the reverse of the passenger's ticket, showing the coins they had tendered. Woe betide the passenger relieving themselves of their post-holiday foreign coppers when the inspector boarded!

More extreme was the approach taken by London Transport and a few others (notably Sunderland Corporation) in the mid-1960s where passengers were required to insert a specific coin into a turnstile to be able to board. In the case of Sunderland, this was not even a coin – it was a token that had to be purchased in advance!

But most operations continued using the driver – or increasingly rarely, conductor operated Setright or TIM into the early 1980s when the bus ticket machine industry entered the modern era with the advent of the Wayfarer machine. The TGX150 was revolutionary when introduced in the 1990s. Whilst there had been ticket machines that provided flows of data to bus companies before, this was a bespoke machine designed with the operator in mind which provided detailed transactional data to facilitate greater-than-ever route and network analysis. Soon competitors emerged, and by the 2010s Wayfarer and ERG had a high proportion of the UK market.

Since then a component-based approach has been adopted to ticket machine supply as a degree of resistance has emerged against the power which equipment providers can wield. Modern systems such as current market leader Ticketer are using relatively low-cost pieces of equipment tailored to the specific needs of bus operators. Operators also use competitive systems including INIT, Flowbird and VIX, but concerns are again emerging about the risks associated with a small number of suppliers able to control the market.

Who knows where we might go next – the abandonment of ticketing with all passengers recorded using mobile phone or bank card detection, facial or iris recognition or even 'wearable' technology is no longer as far-fetched as it seemed in the white heat of the 1980s technological revolution. Tomorrow's world, tomorrow, perhaps.

Passenger flow

Not every operator has always issued tickets and in efforts to speed up boarding and reduce stop dwell time, there have been many experiments with passenger flow. As mentioned above, in the mid-1960s turnstiles were deployed by some operators including London Transport and Sunderland Corporation. The use of such devices necessitates a separate exit from the bus entrance. The concept is to separate boarding and alighting passengers to allow speedier boarding and alighting simultaneously, and to encourage passengers to 'flow' through the vehicle in a single direction.

Whilst several experiments took place in previous decades with sometimes seated conductors collecting fares as passengers boarded at the rear of the bus, on the open platform, alighting at the front (Cardiff and Bournemouth were keen proponents of this method), the age of the one-person-operated bus required a different solution. Thus, from the early 1960s the use of two-door buses with a front entrance and centre exit became more prevalent, and with double deckers becoming so designed once their one-person-operation became legal in 1966. This also often led to staircases moving rearwards, the theory being that passengers could move into the lower saloon whilst others were still boarding.

So why are so few buses two-door (other than in London) today? Apart from the increased capital (purchase) cost and maintenance costs, the main reasons are a concern in some locations that the driver has insufficient control of and supervision of a central exit, and the design and layout of bus stops and bus stations being unable to accommodate central exits. Nevertheless, there remain some areas – Bristol, Reading, Edinburgh – which remain supportive of the concept.

The ultimate passenger flow must be to have the entry and exit points at the extreme opposite ends of the vehicle, but this is a concept which has been rarely employed. One of the first was the Leyland low-loading trolleybus of 1935, a design at least 50 years ahead of its time. Having to be conductor-operated by law, this double decker maintained the then almost universal concept of passengers boarding at the rear, but with two staircases and an exit at the extreme front, under driver supervision to improve safety, it potentially achieved the perfect passenger flow. Furthermore it was a low-floor, step-free vehicle, anticipating the 1990s designs that are now universal.

Unfortunately, it never entered production – too much, too soon – and probably too expensive. Despite Walsall Corporation emulating this vehicle, but with front entrance and rear exit, with its Daimler CRC6-36 in 1968, the concept failed to take off – probably in the latter case due to reliability and cost issues with a unique design.

In 2003, Dennis SPV – precursors of today's ADL – introduced the original Enviro 200 prototypes. Five were built, as single deckers somewhat short of the full 12m length to which many operators bought, and with innovations such as a full step free low floor from front to rear, 'super single' rear tyres to reduce wheelarch intrusion, an engine in the rear offside corner and a rear door that when open extended beyond the rear of the bodywork.

It was, however, never put into production, despite trials with some operators including operators in London. Why? Again, probably cost and unfamiliarity – the UK bus industry can be very conservative, and super single rear tyres were a novelty considered beyond the realm of reasonable experiment. A great pity, as practical experience of this vehicle confirmed its ability to speed up passenger flow.

There are important lessons to be learned from these experiments, especially as operators are increasingly challenged to reduce stop dwell time in order to maintain service operational efficiency in the face of ever-increasing traffic congestion. The main one is the need to reduce conflict between boarders and alighters. This puts the concept of 'touch-on-touch-off' ticketing, considered later in the chapter, into context. Whilst some operators contend that this is possible using one card reader per bus, and employing strict rules of 'No boarding until everyone has alighted', this simply does not work in the busiest urban environments.

Having a separate exit reader is therefore almost essential, but the need to maintain gangway width to enable passage of passengers in wheelchairs militates against the use of barriers to separate the flows, as was done in the age of the turnstile to prevent those paying the exact fare from interacting with the driver. So, we are back to two-door buses again – and I idly wonder whether the front entrance, rear (rather than centre) exit concept may yet have its day.

Many readers will be wondering how London fits into this story. There are very few one-door London buses – only the smallest – and almost all have front entrance and centre exit. The 'New Routemaster' is the exception with its three doors – front, centre and rear – but the use of these has changed since the concept was first seen on the streets late in 2012. At that time the rule was 'board or alight at any door' and the doors at the rear were kept open at times to allow alighting between stops in traffic congestion. That practice soon ceased due to fears over passenger safety, but open boarding and alighting continued until early 2020.

Their introduction was accompanied by the cessation of cash collection on-bus, as all passengers were required to pay using the Oyster smartcard or with a period pass (and later with an EMV card). However, revenue was being lost by passengers not 'touching on' at the centre and rear doors, and by early 2020 the rule was that you must board at the front and interact with the driver. An interesting repeat of London's previous experience of three-door buses with open boarding in the 2000s, with articulated single deckers that provided a free ride for many passengers until a revenue inspector was spotted.

The COVID-19 pandemic in 2020 led to buses running 'free' in London for several weeks, with operators elsewhere not issuing change and in some cases not accepting cash in order to minimize driver/passenger contact. What next? Well, we are unlikely to adopt the mainland European concept of general open boarding and self validation of tickets – only London has gone down this route, and is now itself abandoning the practice. If we see an epidemic of franchising with local authorities taking control of local bus networks and taking the revenue risk, we may yet see this – but not where commercial operators are accountable for their own finances. But as explored in the ticketing equipment section above, new technologies will emerge and may enable greater strides to be made in the achievement of passenger flow.

Travelcards

Developing the concept from the multi-journey tickets introduced in the early years of the 20th century, operators began to realize that there would be demand for tickets that allowed the user to make 'unlimited' journeys. London Transport were early pioneers with these, Red and Green Bus Rovers giving users the freedom of the London network from 1962.

Having been trialled in many of the larger metropolitan areas in the 1970s, such tickets are now commonplace and typically offer an adult, child or student, or a defined group travelling together, travel across a defined area for a day, week, month, term or even a year. Single operator tickets are easy to introduce – the principal consideration being the price at which they are pitched.

Unlike the rail industry's standardized multiplier system, operators are free to choose the price points for these products, the general intent being to encourage the passenger to 'trade up' to something more than they might otherwise consider, whilst giving them a discount on what they would pay in cash for each trip. So, for instance, a day ticket will cost more than two single fares, a week ticket will cost less than ten single fares – and less than five-day tickets (by definition).

For the operator the advantages are various:

- cash upfront;
- reduced cash handling on bus, reducing bus stop dwell time and fraud;
- brand loyalty in a competitive situation;
- overall reduced cash processing, therefore reduced costs.

As discussed above, new purchase options have rendered these tickets ever more popular – but there still remains considerable demand for 'singles and returns' – and every bus market is different.

More recent initiatives to try to fill empty off peak capacity include evening tickets designed to appeal to those seeking a car free night out, and hour tickets allowing multiple connecting journeys within an hour of the first boarding.

A criticism often levelled by politicians at bus operators is the lack of tickets valid on any bus. This is generally an unfounded criticism – a better one would be the lack of publicity about such tickets. For passengers, such tickets have the advantage that the single operator restriction does not apply, and therefore come at a higher price. For the operator the benefits can be reduced as there is an inevitable administration cost, and a revenue risk, as explored below.

The logical extension of the multi-operator ticket is the multi-modal one, additionally valid on trams, trains or ferries. These are generally available in metropolitan and other major urban areas where there are meaningful local light or heavy rail systems – but the relatively high ticket costs of the latter compared with bus generally make these considerably more expensive products with niche usage.

It is interesting to reflect that given the caveat that every local bus market is different, demand for multi-operator tickets rarely exceeds 5 per cent of the overall market, and that for multi-modal is often tiny. Surprisingly, most people continue to make the same outward and return trip, on the same bus provided by the same operator, every day they travel, and rarely use anything else. So, whatever we can do to persuade them to be more adventurous must be a benefit – to them and to operators alike.

The Competition Act 1998 Ticketing Schemes Block Exemption Order 2001 (as amended) is the enabler of these multi-operator and multi-modal tickets. Its very title indicates the nature of the legislation – it is founded in competition law and technically complex. An entire book could be written about competition law and the bus industry, with several chapters on ticketing – but this is not its rightful place. So what follows is by necessity a brief introduction and the reader is strongly advised to take expert (or even legal) advice before making use of the powers in what is commonly referred to in the industry as the 'Block Exemption'. That said, it is mainly common sense and should certainly not be considered as a blocker or inhibitor of implementing such tickets.

From first principles, competition law is intended to achieve two broad aims – to ensure that there is a level playing field on which rival organizations can compete fairly and without external influence imparting an unfair advantage or disadvantage, and to protect the consumer from collusive or orchestrated behaviour that reduces their choice or inflates prices. These two broad principles are the basis of the two Chapters of the principal piece of UK competition legislation – the Competition Act 1998.

Under Chapter 1 of the Competition Act, providers of goods and services (which includes bus operators) are prevented from (inter alia) colluding over prices and agreeing how the market is to be served. So, this would effectively prevent operators agreeing to accept each other's tickets or establishing multi-operator (or multi-modal) ticketing. But as described above, such tickets have been in operation for many years across much of the UK – so a mechanism was required to enable their continuation. A 'Block Exemption' is a piece of legislation which exempts certain types of agreement from being illegal under (in this case) the Competition Act, provided they meet pre-specified criteria.

The Block Exemption was originally introduced in 2001 by the then-Office of Fair Trading (OFT) for a five-year period, and has been renewed (with very minor changes) since then, in more recent years by the Competition and Markets Authority (CMA) which superseded the OFT. It defines four types of ticket – the multi-operator travelcard, the multi-operator individual ticket, the through ticket and the add-on. For the Block Exemption to apply to the ticket in question, its requirements applying to that type of ticket must be met, and there must be a written ticketing agreement.

The multi-operator travelcard (MTC) is a ticket valid on services operated by multiple operators (and may cover multiple modes) for unlimited travel within a period of time and a defined geographic zone. So it could for example be a one-day unlimited bus ticket for Birmingham. For such a ticket, the definition of validity, price and method for redistributing revenue collected from ticket sales, to reflect the value realized by the passenger from use on each operator's services, can be agreed between the participating operators.

These types of ticket are sold as a single transaction, but used on a variety of different journeys on services provided by different operators. Therefore, there is a need to have some means of ensuring that the participating operators receive some payment for the passengers they carry using the tickets. Otherwise they will not be participating operators any longer. There are various means available to achieve this, but one which might appear obvious to the casual observer is not permitted by the competition authorities.

The OFT and CMA consider that 'revenue foregone', where the operator accumulates the value of the journeys made using the MTC on its services, each operator then aggregating these values into a central pot and the total MTC sales revenue being redistributed on the basis of each operator's proportion of that value, is not compatible with competition law principles.

Their belief is that each operator would, therefore, be incentivized to seek a higher percentage share of that pot, and could achieve that aim by increasing the price of all its tickets – thereby making its 'revenue foregone' higher. Such an action would not be in the interests of the customer (the bus passenger).

That is absolutely correct, but omits one vital point – that demand, as we have explored, is elastic, and therefore such increased fares would reduce demand from the operator's purchasers of all other tickets. Since multi-operator tickets typically account for less than 5 per cent of total revenue, this would be a very perverse course of action for the operator. Nevertheless, reimbursement on the basis of 'revenue foregone' is prohibited under the Block Exemption, and only one specific exception has been made to this rule in the 18 years since its introduction.

The alternatives are many and various. Some MTC schemes allow all revenue to lie where it falls – the operator selling the ticket keeps all the revenue. This works where all participants consider that they are as likely to sell MTCs as they are to see use of them on their local networks. Reimbursement on the basis of journey boardings is acceptable, but will only work for participants if each has a similar journey length and/or fare scale. Overall market share, based on registered service mileage, is also acceptable and will work where each operator is equally proportionately likely to see the use of the MTC on its services. Periodic surveys of usage and travel diaries can be used to apportion revenue, provided that a proxy fare scale is used rather than operators' own fares, to avoid the problems with 'revenue foregone'.

These methods can be and often are used in combination, for instance 25 per cent of revenue lies where it falls, and the remaining 75 per cent is distributed on the basis of registered mileage share, thereby incentivizing participating operators to sell the MTC. The CMA's preference is for passenger miles to be used, but these can only be calculated where passenger pass usage can be attributed to individual passengers – recorded from smartcard or mobile phone use – and some measure of journey length deployed, such as using exit readers or asking the passenger to identify their alighting stop on boarding (thereby deleting much of the benefit of reduced stop dwell times that such products yield to operators). So, in practice this is rarely if ever used.

To ensure that whichever mechanism adopted is not unduly biased to particular operators, all are required to sell the tickets at the same price and any discounts for whatever reason must be applied consistently by all participating operators.

The multi-operator individual ticket is valid for a return trip (and exceptionally a single) on a service provided by two or more operators. Typically issued as a return ticket, it will allow the holder to return on the issuing operator's service, or on the equivalent (generally competitive, or coordinated under a qualifying agreement) service provided by another operator. Each operator sets its own price for the ticket and retains all the revenue. These tickets are not common and are now exclusively bus-only. In the 1960s and 1970s the then-nationalized transport providers issued 'bus/rail inter-available returns' which accepted return bus tickets on trains and vice versa across parts of urban England and Scotland – but these are very much a thing of the past.

Through tickets are generally also bus-only, but there are examples of bus–rail ticketing under this definition. The providers of these tickets tell the other operators participating in the ticket how much they will charge them to carry each passenger bearing the ticket. This is called the 'posted price' and cannot be discriminatory between other participating operators.

What does that mean? Consider three bus operators: A, B and C. Operator A runs buses from Bigtown to Metroville. Operators B and C each run services from Metroville to Hamlet. There are through tickets from Bigtown to Hamlet. Operator A tells operators B and C that it will charge them £3 for each passenger bearing such a through ticket that it carries from Metroville to Bigtown. It cannot charge operator B £3 and operator C £4 – that would be discriminatory. But of course, operator B's price for carrying a through ticket holder from Metroville to Hamlet may not be the same as operator C's price for the same trip. Which would be confusing for the passenger were it not that the posted price need not be reflected in the fare. It is just the transaction behind the scenes that makes the through ticket work for the operators.

Each operator will need to record the trips made with the through ticket and make appropriate payments on a regular basis to the other participating operators. And the scheme has to be documented.

Most bus–rail through tickets were swept away when the PlusBus ticketing concept was developed in the early 2000s as described below, but a few examples remain.

Finally, we have the add-on. Whilst there are technically two types of add-on defined in the legislation, we can avoid this additional complexity and consider the generality of how add-ons work. The most prevalent example is the 'PlusBus' ticket, which provides unlimited travel on local bus services of participating operators in a specified zone centred on one (or several) rail stations. The tickets are sold as bus add-ons to the train journey, and have standard terms and conditions with only the price, zone, and participating operators, plus a choice as to whether to offer just daily, or daily plus season tickets, to be decided locally. They are effectively bus MTCs acting as add-ons to rail travel. Of course, these are not the only add-ons available… but I struggle to think of any others which have been established.

All these tickets require some form of governance to be set out in their written agreement. For those other than the MTC this can be very light-touch, just requiring a mechanism for price and validity review and admittance of new operators, as well as cessation of the scheme. MTCs can be done on a similarly light-touch basis – for instance tickets aimed at occasional tourist purchasers covering large rural areas with few sales and little impact on operators' revenue, but the larger MTC schemes – despite their relatively small market penetration – can still account for considerable revenue and require more complex and formal governance.

This can be done by appointing a management committee and chair to meet and review on a regular basis, or even setting up a limited company with shares held by the participating operators, as has been the case in many major metropolitan areas. These bodies, often called 'Ticcos' (ticketing companies) have a measurable cost of operation and therefore generally require a small levy top sliced as a percentage of the overall sales revenue from the MTC.

Remember – if your multi-operator or multi-modal ticket is not compliant with the Block Exemption, it is most likely illegal. The penalties for not complying with competition law in the UK are severe on both a personal level and corporately.

The Transport Act 2000 (as modified) established the principle of ticketing Schemes. A local transport authority has the power to require all bus operators within a prescribed area to sell and accept tickets valid for use on all operators' services within that area. The powers available to the authority are limited to specifying the area of the scheme, the type of tickets and the type of passenger entitled to use them (adult, child, etc) and the medium on which they must be issued. There is no locus for the authority to set the price of the ticket which should be determined in the usual manner for that ticket type – which to date, has always been a multi-operator travelcard – although there are very few such Schemes in existence. Starting the process for new tickets, or changing the scope of the ticket as specified above, requires a prescriptive statutory process including consultation.

The ticketing Scheme will still require a ticketing agreement between the participating operators in order to be Block Exemption compliant, and will require the establishment of an appropriate management regime as specified above, to include the local authority making the Scheme for good order.

There was a vision promoted in the early 2000s, largely by politicians and local authority officers, that integrated ticketing ought to offer people the choice to book a journey from their home in suburban Warrington to their sister's boyfriend's house in a village outside Gdansk... and to buy the ticket online. One small problem with this was the cost of integrating the various ticketing systems not being justified by the tiny demand for such journeys. However, the buzzword of recent years, and one which is likely to have greater traction in future is Account Based Ticketing, or ABT.

As noted earlier in this chapter, the use of contactless EMV bank cards to pay for travel is now widespread and the emerging popularity of 'Model 2' transactions allows the user to travel without limit on various operators' buses, or even various public transport modes, and to pay at the end of the day or week, capped at a level which would equate to the cheapest price at which that travel could have been bought in advance – for instance a multi-operator or multi-modal day travelcard. This is also known as ABT. Whilst not yet rolled out in its ultimate form, there are at the time of writing (late 2019) examples of single or multiple operator ABT being trialled, but there remain technological and commercial challenges to be overcome before the full-service model is available.

The logical extension of MTCs that has been pursued already is that of offering these for pre-purchase at discounted prices, by major potential users – typically local authorities, National Health Service (NHS) Trusts and other major employers. A sliding scale of discounts may be offered dependent on the number of tickets bought, as this not only encourages take-up of public transport, it also brings the revenue to the operators earlier than it otherwise would. Such purchasing employers are also often encouraged to sell the tickets to their employees at a further reduced cost, or even free of charge. This type of encouragement features along with other 'ingredients' in Chapter 13. However, despite considerable lobbying over many years to HM Treasury, these tickets are treated as a taxable benefit for the employee.

An alternative approach adopted in 2019 by Transdev is the concept of the employer's travel club, whereby joining employees can benefit from discounted purchase of advance travel passes from operators.

Revenue protection and standard fares

When operators were not forced to take such stringent cost cutting measures as they are today, the revenue inspector was a common traveller on the bus and struck fear into passengers and bus crews alike! Now, however, they are far less common – which makes revenue protection an area where operators are seeking greater automation. Pre-paid tickets fulfilled on smart or electronic media are easier to validate by the driver, as they will either 'pass' or 'fail' when presented to the ticketing machine, and are a major improvement on paper pre-paid passes, the home production of which became a major cottage industry in some parts of the UK. Nevertheless, the only way to ensure that a cash paying passenger does not over-ride beyond the point to which they have paid can still only be detected by physically checking their ticket.

Bus operators' conditions of travel will set out the consequences of failing to have the correct ticket or pay the required fare. These are generally referred to as Standard Fares. It is, strangely enough, not permitted to call them Penalty Fares – the concept of a Penalty is enshrined in law and only the railway operators, and Transport for London (as successor to London Transport) are able to call them by that title. Nevertheless, the ability to specify a Standard Fare at a level which ought to deter fare dodging is within the right of any operator of local bus services, provided that the level of that Standard Fare and any associated conditions (such as leniency for prompt payment through a reduction in the value) are clearly specified in those conditions of travel.

Concessionary travel

The National Concessionary Fare Schemes – background

Starting with Northern Ireland in 2001, then Wales and Scotland followed by England, introduction of nationwide free travel for older and eligible people with disabilities has clearly substantially grown the use of buses by these users. Before 2006, there were a number of local schemes ranging from flat fare, half fare or, in certain cities, free travel but with travel limited to just local residents.

There is no doubt that where bus routes still operate, the national schemes provide benefits of social inclusion and mobility and promote active lifestyles, although there have been stories of free users riding on the buses to keep warm in the winter. However, in line with the national pension age and to save money in an age of tight public expenditure, the initial qualification age of 60 for women and 65 for men has since risen in England and is now heading for age 67 in line with national pension age limits.

England has the most complicated schemes to administer, compounded by being devolved to Travel Concession Authorities (TCAs) which are generally County, Combined Authority or Unitary Authorities. Scotland, Wales and Northern Ireland have simpler arrangements which are outlined later in this section.

The English scheme

In England, there is a legal requirement to offer free travel to pass-holders during the core times of 09.30–23.00 on Mondays to Fridays and all day at weekends on registered local bus services. There are some services which may be excluded, including Park and Ride routes, limited stop coach operations and specialized tourist services. One of the changes made early in the 2020 COVID-19 emergency was the Government telling authorities to remove the 09.30 restriction, and this became a condition of receipt of the COVID-19 Bus Services Support Grant financial support.

The legal core offering can be extended by TCAs adding non-statutory elements. These could include free travel for companions, wider time bands on Mondays to Fridays or additional modes such as trams. Unlike the core scheme, the extensions can be, for example, for all pass-holders, solely for disabled users or just for users of those passes issued by the local scheme TCA.

Concession authorities are obliged to reimburse operators for pass-holders boarding at stops within their own area. Some TCAs have therefore seen variations to what would have been expected from local pass-holders. For example, seaside resorts can see an influx of visitors with passes issued by other authorities, whilst a major shopping centre will result in return journeys to other areas being the responsibility of the local TCA. The funding allocations to TCAs have become blurred within the overall Revenue Support Grant since the initial amounts in 2011, and authorities are generally arguing that they now face shortfalls in meeting the core requirements of the scheme.

Operator reimbursement

The process for operator reimbursement is the most contentious part of a scheme. Put simply, it is calculated as follows:

journeys made × the average fare foregone × the local reimbursement rates

In England, Department for Transport (DfT) guidance includes a comprehensive Calculator devised in 2011, with assistance from Leeds University, and which is updated annually. This goes into much detail, but the included default values can be replaced in many areas by locally experienced values. Hence there is scope for debate although, with the inclusion of long-term fare inflation compared to 2005, the resulting reimbursement rates have tended to reduce year-on-year despite rising bus operating costs.

The recording of journeys has improved in accuracy with the use of smartcards, particularly with ticket machines that can record boardings by individual bus stops. However, this medium is not 100 per cent reliable, resulting in the use of manual recording on ticket machines as a back-up when a failure occurs.

The average fare foregone in England is usually calculated by considering the normal adult single, return, day and weekly tickets used on each route to reflect discounts offered for more than single trips. However, as the minimum qualifying age now rises, it could be argued that, usually retired, 67 year olds would have been very unlikely to have purchased weekly tickets if there had not been a scheme!

Setting reimbursement rates is the most complicated part of the process. Furthermore, TCAs and bus operators, who otherwise may work in positive partnership, often face disagreement or conflict in this area due to the ability to use local factors instead of the DfT default values. Operators naturally see reimbursement as a key revenue stream whilst the TCAs see the costs of the scheme as a substantial commitment on their often-declining budgets.

Generation

The main principle of the schemes is that operators should be left no better and no worse off than they would have been without the scheme. If reimbursement is made greater than this, it could be seen as State Aid, contrary to EU law.

An operator needs to receive full reimbursement for those passengers who would have travelled anyway without a scheme. For additional journeys generated by the scheme, they should not receive reimbursement for the fares but instead receive the marginal additional costs of carrying them. If buses overload as a result of the scheme, the operator is entitled to be paid the net cost of putting on an additional bus or a bus with larger capacity.

The principles of generation are explained further in Figure 7.1.

Figure 7.1   Explanation of generation

⊕ Without free travel, a number of people will use the bus.

⊕ With free travel, some of these will still travel but no longer pay.

⊕ And a number of extra passengers will travel because it is free – known as GENERATED passengers.

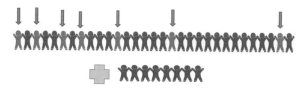

⊕ The operator needs to be paid for those that would have travelled before free travel was introduced – at the fare they would have paid.

⊕ But he does NOT get paid the fare for the generated passengers, only the extra cost to him of carrying them – called marginal additional costs.

⊕ How do we calculate that in reality?
EXAMPLE
   o   Add the seven passengers who paid before but now travel free to the eight new passengers.
   o   The total number of concessionary passengers is 15.
   o   But we are only paying for seven of those.
   o   So we pay the fare for 7/15 or 47% of the total (the Reimbursement Factor).
   o   And we pay marginal additional costs only for 8/15 or 53% of the total.

⊕ But what if the bus is now overloaded because of the extra passengers?
   o   The operator is entitled to be paid for the net cost of putting on a larger bus or an extra bus.

   o   This is an Additional Capacity Cost Claim

Marginal costs

Marginal operating costs and administration costs are those that are incurred by an operator to carry generated passengers. Examples are the use of ticketing equipment, publicity and other administration costs but also the impact of increased boarding times at bus stops. The DfT recommend a fixed rate for much of this element, but this is also particularly dependent on passenger journey lengths.

Marginal capacity costs are again calculated for each generated passenger and cover such costs as fuel usage, wear on vehicles, and third party insurance. A standard rate is normally set for each TCA based on government guidance. However, these are often challenged, resulting in local figures unique to some operators. The calculation uses factors including costs per vehicle hour and mile, the percentage of concessionary journeys, bus speeds, vehicle occupancy, average commercial fare and service elasticity.

By their nature, as schemes are already in existence, the process of determining reimbursement rates is necessarily theoretical and employs detailed spreadsheets and databases. There is therefore often a role for internal experts or specialist consultancies on both sides to try to achieve a fair level of reimbursement within the recommended DfT rules, usually involving a degree of compromise. One option can be a fixed deal with an individual operator which includes an element to cover for additional costs that could be claimed but which provides stability for both parties over the duration of the arrangement. The deals will need to be supported with evidence to avoid breaching state aid rules.

If no agreement can be reached on reimbursement, there can be an appeal to the Secretary of State for a determination.

Scotland

The Scottish scheme covers both local bus and scheduled long distance routes for travel at any time of day. Travel is within Scotland or to directly served destinations across the boundary with England. Elderly pass eligibility is from age 60, although this is under review.

The scheme is administered nationally by Transport Scotland to improve effectiveness of administration, made simpler by use of a standard reimbursement rate. However, operator payments are subject to a scheme cap which kicks in if the annual budget limit is reached. This has happened in some recent years. There are some local discretions that include rail, ferry and tram services.

Wales

The Welsh scheme also has a current eligibility limit of age 60 for bus travel within Wales and for direct trips across the English boundary but, as in Scotland, is currently under review. Some rail services within the country are also included and travel can again be made all day.

Reimbursement rates are administered by local councils. There is a single reimbursement rate set by the Welsh Government. This was formerly set against the average single fare on each route. However, this has now been replaced by an average fare calculation for each operator's depot following concerns that some routes had seen disproportionate increases in single fares compared to other categories of fare. Interestingly, the proportion of concessionary journeys against all bus trips is significantly higher in Wales than in either Scotland or England.

Northern Ireland

Free travel at any time of day on buses, trains and on two ferries within Northern Ireland is available from age 60. However, from age 65, a Senior Smart Pass is available which gives travel into and throughout the Republic of Ireland as well on State transport plus some independent operators. Similar travel for Irish Republic pass holders is not available until age 66.

The scheme is administered by Translink and covers seniors plus blind and war disabled pass holders.

Children and young people

Whilst not a statutory requirement, a number of local authorities operate concessionary fare schemes aimed at other categories of people, notably for children and young people.

Most operators have their own commercial arrangements for young person fares and discounts. However, two examples of county-wide schemes across all operators are as follows.

In Greater Manchester, the Combined Authority's Travel Concession Scheme includes, as well as the core elderly and disabled travel, discretional products for children and young persons (up to age 16) and older students (up to age 19). Travel for these groups on bus is either for free travel or for travel at discounted concessionary fare levels. Reimbursement procedures are at tailored calculation rates.

In Kent, the county council operates child and young person schemes that are run outside of the statutory concessionary fare scheme, but with similar mechanisms. The Kent Freedom Concessionary Travel Scheme was introduced in 2007 as a pilot scheme under the terms of the 1985 Transport Act, expanding to become county-wide in 2009. In 2012, a further scheme, the Kent 16+ Travel Card was introduced. Both schemes operated with a fee for the pass, which then gave free travel for that school year. Budget restrictions by 2014 caused a limiting of the available times of use to weekdays between 6am and 7pm, although the larger operators have since allowed wider free travel to pass-holders on a voluntary basis. However, during the 2020 COVID-19 emergency this offer was suspended to deter unnecessary bus travel on those buses that remained operating in the evenings. It will be interesting to see if this concession is reintroduced after the emergency is over.

The pass price has risen substantially from the initial £100 in 2009 to £350 in 2019, with much higher prices for the 16+ version. The pass is now known as the Kent Travel Saver and still offers substantial discounts over any commercial fares. In its initial years, the scheme had been shown to reduce traffic congestion at some key locations at school start and finish times, including between Tonbridge and Tunbridge Wells.

Other income – service support

The 1985 Transport Act changed everything in respect of how operators planned and licensed routes. Moving from a system where an operator sought permission from the Traffic Commissioner to run a new service or amend an existing one, with objections possible from (inter alia) local authorities, other operators, train operators, the police or the local farmer (no, not really – but it seemed like that), operators were obliged to identify which services they would run at their own risk, without any financial support, from 26 October 1986.

The 1985 Transport Act requires local authorities to identify what services within their area of jurisdiction are not being provided commercially by bus operators, but which are considered to be 'socially necessary' – maybe a service in the evening or on Sunday where there is a commercial daytime service, or a route which is no longer served. The original intent was that when operators in 1985–86 had identified their commercial networks, the local authorities would 'fill the gaps' by funding the provision of 'supported services' following competitive tendering exercises against services specified by the authorities.

However, local authority spending has been cut back significantly by central governments since then, and it is notable that the 1985 Act does not require the authority to do anything about this perceived lack of services. Since public transport expenditure of this nature is deemed to be discretionary, unlike some of the statutory duties of those same authorities (for instance elements of education and social services spending) then it is an easy budget line to cut. If the choice is between a new roof for the infants' school and an hourly Sunday bus between the village green and the shopping centre, it's easy to see which will be funded. Some local authorities have now cut their 'supported services' budget to nil.

For those that retain a supported services (also called tendered services) budget, there are three broad types of tender that are awarded. These are gross cost, minimum subsidy and resource contract.

A gross cost tender is where the local authority specifies the fares to be charged and takes all the revenue. The operator is simply paid to run the route – at the total cost which they have bid. Minimum subsidy tenders allow the operator to set the fares (usually) and to keep all the revenue they collect, so the overall level of payment by authority to operator is lower. The risk transfers substantially to the operator since, as part of their tender bid, they have to estimate their income from fares and net that against their total operating costs. Resource contracts are now very uncommon – the local authority pays the operator a 'daily rate' for a fixed number of hours of operation, all driver and vehicle costs being included, usually with a cap on the maximum mileage that will be operated at that cost during that fixed time period. The authority then decides how that resource is best deployed.

The foregoing assumes a clear split between what can and what cannot be operated commercially. In practice there is rarely such a clear distinction, and an operator could be prevailed upon to extend a commercial service geographically, or temporally, or to instigate a minor diversion, to meet an otherwise unmet need. Local authorities have the ability to make money available to operators, without having to go through a competitive tender exercise, through their use of 'de minimis' powers. In any given year an authority with a budget for supported services exceeding £600,000 may spend up to 25 per cent of that budget securing services under 'de minimis' powers; an authority with supported service spending below this threshold is restricted to a total 'de-minimis' spend of £29,999.

There are no restrictions on the number of service enhancements – or indeed operators – that can be funded under these powers; indeed, one operator or even one service may be the sole beneficiary. Whilst most local transport authorities make extensive use of these powers and are able to enhance the 'commercial' bus network considerably as a result, a few refuse to spend money in this way, citing 'risk of legal challenge' as the reason.

Third party funding can form a useful source of income to keep otherwise non-commercial services afloat. Some NHS Trusts and private employers see the provision of no, or off-site, parking, as being preferable to the stagnation of high development value land adjacent to their main sites by this land use. Such policies require shuttle services to take employees (and site users) to and from these sites and commercial contracts are formed with local bus or coach operators to this end. Such contracts can be closed – only available to pre-registered users – or open, where the public can board, usually having to pay a fare for the privilege. Similar arrangements can be made with schools, either directly or through the local authority who may 'sell' surplus capacity on services they are obliged to provide for free home to school transport.

Finally, the local planning process can be used to underwrite local bus services particularly where new housing developments are planned, but also with applications for commercial, employment and health developments. Rather than requiring the developer to pay for additional road infrastructure to enable access to their new facilities, some local authorities seek to reduce the amount of on-site parking provided at the development and instead extract a fee from the developer equivalent to the cost of such improvement measures.

Such a fee, known as a 'section 106 payment' after the corresponding section of the Town & Country Planning Act 1990, is used to guarantee the provision of a defined route and frequency of local bus service, in a tripartite agreement between developer, local authority and operator. Some of these have proved highly successful and at the end of their (up to five year) funded beginning, become commercial services. The more successful schemes offer new residents or employees at the development site a free travel pass for at least a month at the start of their operation, and provide comprehensive and updated public transport information throughout the development area.

Kick-start campaigns

A similar principle was adopted by national government in the early 2000s seeking to stimulate new service initiatives with the promise of match funding – a 'kick-start' campaign. Various 'urban bus challenge' and 'rural bus challenge' competitions were initiated but had a common failing – with a few honourable exceptions, when the funding ran out, the service ceased.

These well-meaning initiatives attracted service proposals which would not otherwise have seen the light of day, and in many cases were so woefully un-commercial that their growth opportunities in the early, funded years were minimal, condemning them to abandonment when the funding streams, which were always promoted as being of fixed duration, expired. This took resources and management time away from the more deserving cases on the margins. Not a mistake to be repeated, hopefully – for a few years at least.

The green bus fund

Increasing governmental concern about air pollution and climate change has led to attempts to incentivize the early adoption of new technology, as explored in other chapters. Typically, one of the biggest challenges to over-come is the capital cost premium of the new technology. Incentive schemes have therefore sought to bridge the funding gap between a conventionally fuelled vehicle and one powered by a 'greener' source of energy.

This topic is only present in this chapter to consider the funding mechanism. Application for grant funding was conditional on a bidding process which ranked the contribution sought per vehicle and paid the 'least demanding' first. Contributions were calculated on the basis of the capital cost difference adjusted with respect to any operating cost savings over the first five years of vehicle use.

Adopted by both the Department of Transport and the Scottish Government, these schemes led to the early, and not always successful, adoption of diesel-electric hybrid and pure electric buses, starting in 2009. Whilst this did to some extent pave the way for bus electrification, there was an unintended side effect of the grant funding – the expected reduction in manufacturers' prices with product maturity and (relative) volume increase did not materialize, and these vehicle types now have to be made affordable by other means.

Major projects and government initiatives

There is a growing trend towards central government initiating competitions for local authorities to bid for additional funding streams, designed to stimulate specific outcomes. With the increasing awareness of the need to address the environmental concerns of poor air quality and climate change, increasing economic stagnation of our major urban areas through the effects of congestion, and the health and societal problems caused by social isolation, efforts have been made in the late 2010s to stimulate a shift to public transport.

Starting with the Transforming Cities Fund and Future Mobility Zones, authorities in partnership with their local bus operators are providers of 'green' travel solutions such as cycle hire and car share clubs. They have been challenged to embrace the latest digital technology, and adopt innovative yet sustainable transport and land use planning initiatives to generate bids for substantial infrastructure and supporting investment from central government. At the time of writing (late 2019), there were no decisions on the successful bidders or the projects to which the funding was to be applied, but this does provide a potentially useful marker towards future funding opportunities for public–private sector co-operative working. Early 2020 has seen major new funding competitions announced in England covering bus fleet electrification, support for rural networks and experiments with low-fare, high-frequency urban networks supported by substantial bus priority measures.

Advertising

A bus is a large and highly visible object – from all angles, inside and out. The people it carries become a captive audience for external messaging during the course of their journey. And they often get a souvenir of their trip – a ticket – which has important information on one side. So, there are lots of opportunities for messages to appear on and in buses that have a high intrinsic value to those who want to promote their own goods, services and offers. Advertising is big business.

Until the 1970s, many bus operators negotiated with their local shops and businesses and promoted a variety of local products on the outside of the vehicle, and on the 'cove' panels running along the insides where the roof joins the side of the bus. These advertisers paid the operators directly for the privilege. But there were also national advertisers – frequently producers of cigarettes and alcohol, who sought to achieve national coverage and dealt with the major national operators with local subsidiaries, to negotiate more extensive advertising deals. A few very large advertising agencies now control the majority of the UK bus market, but operators will sometimes reserve parts of the bus for their own advertising.

This trend has continued, with the 'local' advert now being the exception rather than the rule, for larger operators, and on the vehicle outside, at least. Technology has also changed, with a move from hand-painted adverts through paper rolls applied with adhesive to vinyl adverts and lightweight boards carried in 'frames' on bus sides.

Advertising 'downtime' – space which cannot be sold commercially – is often made available to local charities or used by the bus operator to promote its own services and offers, or to promote other messages about bus travel.

In the early 1970s the bus advertising concept gained a new element – the all-over advertising bus. These were sold at a considerable premium in the major urban areas, giving their purchaser the opportunity to have a full-size mobile advert on view in a different area every day, and have proved popular ever since. Some operators will insist that the front of the vehicle remains in their livery, to ensure that waiting passengers can recognize their bus more readily, especially in competitive environments.

Bus tickets are another operator medium which has become a popular advertising site in recent years, with operators offering passengers contra deals through commercial agreements with third parties – such as 50p off a cup of coffee in a high street coffee shop if you show them a bus ticket bearing today's date.

Operators communicate increasingly with their passengers through websites and mobile phone 'apps' both of which are attractive media for third parties to advertise their goods and services – another small, but growing, source of commercial income for operators.

The Bus Service Operators Grant

In the late 1960s there was considerable concern that the provision of bus services in rural areas was becoming increasingly expensive, as fuel costs and wages increased steadily. The advent of one-person operation described earlier helped to offset these costs, and the principle of cross-subsidy – then perfectly legal – allowed these services to be maintained by the profits derived from operation in more urban areas, where these were provided by the larger (and often state-owned) operators.

Nevertheless, there was a perceived need to address the trend towards ever-increasing fares and the risk of rural isolation. This introduced the concept of Fuel Duty Rebate, usually abbreviated to FDR. Unlike rail and air services, bus operators have always paid duty, or been taxed, on the fuel they use – just like private motorists – ever since fuel was taxed. Buses tended to use more fuel (in absolute terms, not per mile) in rural areas where routes were longer, as distances were greater between trip attractors and generators.

So, FDR was the simple solution, with the original desired intention of keeping bus fares low, by reducing costs where they were highest, in rural areas. At first introduced in the Finance Act 1965, the rebate was 100 per cent and was linked directly to the fuel tax – which still had to be paid, but was rebated.

This situation obtained for many years, although there was periodic Government disquiet, as environmental awareness grew, of there being a payment to operators linked directly to fuel use. This led to a misconception that operators were not concerned with fuel economy. That would hardly be the case unless the tax element of the fuel cost vastly outweighed the net price of fuel, which was not the case – so why would an operator waste money on fuel they need not consume?

Nevertheless, it was time for a major change, and in 2012 FDR was replaced by the Bus Service Operators Grant (BSOG). At least in name the connection with fuel use was severed. But the debate continued as to how this could be severed in practice, and a number of alternative methods of replacing the payment, which was universally acknowledged to still bring advantages to passengers, were investigated. The two mechanisms can be categorized as PPK – pence per km – or IPP, incentive per passenger. Assuming that the total quantum of payment remains the same, the former can be demonstrated to favour longer distance, rural or suburban services with higher running speeds and lower patronage; the latter to favour urban services with high usage and passenger churn and lower operating speeds. So, the former can be used to support rural services which are hard to justify commercially, but will have a deleterious effect on urban buses which are the ones having the greatest impact achieving modal shift from car use, and vice versa.

In 2014 a further amendment took all supported services out of scope of BSOG in England, and payments instead were made to the local authorities directly, in lieu of the payments that operators had previously received. These payments were guaranteed for three years and the intent was that through contract price negotiations operators would be unaffected by the change in payment regime.

So, what to do? Leave well alone, for now at least – unlike in Scotland where, in 2012, a move to pay BSOG purely on pence per km, with the same total national budget, led to a resurgence of rural services, but at the expense of some marginal urban ones.

Wales took a different approach again, replacing BSOG with the Bus Service Support Grant, or BSSG – paid on the basis that all operators were entitled to a certain rate, but with an additional payment based on 'quality' and determined on a regional basis.

Reductions to FDR took place during the 1990s and again in 2012 when the rate was cut by a further 25 per cent.

Incentive payments were introduced in England in 2010 to encourage operators to equip their vehicles with the capability to provide 'real-time' feeds – essentially a periodic confirmation of the geographic location of the bus, with a time stamp, and to read ITSO smartcards. These incentives were paid as uplifts to the basic FDR payment of 2 per cent and 8 per cent respectively, and have continued since that date.

A further uplift to BSOG for 'green' buses was engineered to prevent any perverse incentive for bus operators to not invest in vehicles which use less fuel! At a fixed rate of 6 pence per km operated, the incentive was payable in England for a vehicle which could be demonstrated and certified by its manufacturer to achieve a 30 per cent reduction in fuel usage compared with its Euro IV standard diesel equivalent. This was intended to encourage the purchase of diesel-electric hybrid vehicles – in conjunction with the Green Bus Fund mentioned above. Scotland went a stage further, offering a 100 per cent BSOG uplift for vehicles meeting the same criterion.

Vehicle eligibility criteria have since been modified on each side of the border to match the latest 'Low Carbon Vehicle' standard, which pits the 30 per cent fuel efficiency saving against the latest Euro VI diesel comparator, and the topic of BSOG reform is unlikely to remain quiet for long.

Private hire

A supplement to operator income can be the hiring of vehicles for use by private parties – not coaching work per se, but 'private hire'. As explained in other chapters, the requirement to operate such work under 'EU hours' can add considerably to the cost base of the operation unless dedicated driving staff are available for secondment from non-driving duties. But vehicles out of use inter-peak, in the evenings or on Sundays can be used – if they are fitted with tachographs.

Why is this relevant? It is another income stream – and one which local bus service operators tend to forget, largely, these days. But a modern double deck bus is a very cost effective, not to mention green, way of transporting 80–90 people in comfort and safety, bringing in much needed additional revenue at marginal cost to the operator.

Conclusions

Income is derived principally from customers, but, in particular circumstances, also from public authorities in return for carrying, for example, young persons, along with older people and people with disabilities.

Payment is made by way of fares which generally vary according to distance travelled. Such payments are traditionally made when boarding the bus by way of cash, but increasingly in advance or by way of a credit/debit card or mobile phone.

It is quite simple really – understand your cost base, set your fares to cover your cost base, bid for tenders and contracts at a sustainable level, and anything else is a bonus!

References

Department for Transport (2019) [accessed 12 February 2020] Annual bus statistics: year ending, March 2019, *GOV.UK* [online] www.gov.uk/government/statistics/annual-bus-statistics-year-ending-march-2019 (archived at https://perma.cc/Z9KU-2XJQ)

Transport for Greater Manchester, 2020 [accessed 25 February 2020] Free bus – free travel around Manchester city centre, *Transport for Greater Manchester* [online] https://tfgm.com/public-transport/bus/free-bus (archived at https://perma.cc/4KDV-DWJN)

Further reading

Passenger Transport (nd) [accessed 21 February 2020] The Magazine, *Passenger Transport* [online] www.passengertransport.co.uk/the-magazine/ (archived at https://perma.cc/U2T5-L359)

Confederation of Passenger Transport UK [online] www.cpt-uk.org/ (archived at https://perma.cc/V7Z5-WT4A)

Human resources case study: Metroline

08

STEVE HARRIS

Introduction

Metroline is a London bus operating company. As the Managing Director, I am uniquely positioned to discuss the human resource challenges for road passenger transport companies. Metroline depends on maintaining an effective workforce of around 4,700 bus drivers. It is the bus drivers who go out and provide the services to the people of London, which brings in almost all of the company's revenue, and it is the bus drivers whose conduct 'on the road' will form people's opinion of the company. There need to be enough bus drivers to carry out all of our bus services, and they need to be good enough at every aspect of their job to make Metroline the obvious choice to win and retain contracts to operate routes.

Average driver turnover for Metroline and typically other London bus operators would be between 8 and 12 per cent; this translates into around 400–600 drivers for Metroline. It is a huge task simply to 'stand still' on driver numbers (Metroline, 2019). So, it is vitally important that companies overcome this average by coming up with strategies and solutions to retain staff. Nevertheless, drivers do leave and new route contracts do require additional resources, as contracts are won and lost at route level and it is difficult to predict gains and losses, although we have the flexibility to loan staff between the 15 garages. In 2018, to accommodate for this, Metroline successfully recruited and trained 600 drivers to help the business continue to deliver services and generate revenues.

This chapter aims to highlight that recruiting and training bus drivers is a complex challenge, and requires much resource and a dedicated team to deliver. The approach adopted by Metroline is to combine the recruitment and training functions under one department, which ensures that all members understand the challenges and direction. Information can be shared more effectively, processes changed more easily, and staff who are on leave can be covered more flexibly.

To begin, this chapter usefully outlines the bus operating context in London within which we operate.

The London scene

Background

The Greater London area is currently the only part of Great Britain where local bus services are regulated, although this could potentially change if, for example, Greater Manchester secures a franchising scheme, as provided for in the Bus Services Act 2017. Thus, explaining the London scene of franchising may be helpful.

The management of public transport in London culminated, in 1933, with the formation of the London Passenger Transport Board (trading as London Transport). This had an almost total monopoly in the provision of road passenger transport, plus the Underground rail network, over a large area within and surrounding the capital. Although changes were made subsequently, including, in 1970, transferring services outside of the then-newly formed Greater London Council to the National Bus Company, the overall system remained unchanged until the mid-1980s when deregulation of road passenger transport was being applied.

London was initially exempt from this application of the free market, although it prepared for such an eventuality. Bus operations were divided into 13 separate commercial based companies and sold to the private sector. However, deregulation did not occur. In 1997, a newly elected Labour government determined that there should be a new governing body for the capital – the Greater London Authority (GLA) – including public transport. To enable the GLA to deliver its responsibilities, a new organization, Transport for London (TfL), was formed in 2000.

The overall framework

TfL and its subsidiary, London Bus Services Limited, are responsible for the planning and provision of local bus services in Greater London. The elected Mayor of London and the GLA have a duty to formulate and implement policies that promote and encourage safe, integrated, efficient and economic transport services. Thus, almost the entire local bus network in Greater London is determined by TfL, including the precise detail of individual local bus services.

TfL is also responsible for the Underground rail network, the Docklands Light Railway, some local services on the National Rail network (the 'Overground'), Croydon Tramlink and London River Services. Additionally, it is responsible for taxi and hire car licensing, the strategic highway network and Victoria Coach Station, terminus of many long-distance coach services.

Bus operators can, with the consent of TfL, provide services within the GLA area, which are not part of the TfL network. These are largely tourist-based services.

The contracted system

Contracts for each service are awarded to operators, normally for five years, following a period of competitive tendering. Contracts are focused on delivering best value for money, whilst accounting for safety and overall quality, but incentivized to improve standards and performance.

They have an option to be extended by up to two years, based on meeting a heightened performance target gauged over a two-year performance period. There is a pre-qualification system to ensure the financial stability of the undertakings is satisfactory, along with an understanding of their capabilities to provide public transport services. Approved operators are issued with a Bus Services Framework Agreement, which sets out the business arrangements between operators and TfL.

Experience in providing services for TfL

Each operator is contributing towards a single network, a single fares and marketing system, so far a unique environment for Great Britain. Tendering for such services depends upon an ability to have operating premises within easy reach of the route, plus the capacity to accommodate vehicles and recruit and retain staff. Contracts are monitored analytically by TfL to ensure there is full understanding as to the reasons behind variations in performance and where, for example, any shortcomings are beyond the control of the operator.

Unlike bus operation outside London, operators are not primarily concerned with revenue generation, as that is for TfL. However, the financial and budgetary position of TfL affects operators both in what is expected from them and the quality with which it is presented. Operators have to primarily concentrate on ensuring contractual terms are met through safe provision and in providing the full scheduled service. But there is an awareness to take account of, for example, the priorities and objectives of the elected Mayor. These may well change from time to time.

This has previously resulted, for example, in the very quick design and provision of the New Routemaster bus. More recently, a greater involvement of trade unions in policy making has emerged. There are now tripartite meetings with these bodies, alongside TfL and operators. An objective of the current (late 2019) Mayor has been to launch 'Vision Zero' to eradicate deaths and serious injury on London's transport network by 2041 (Mayor of London and TfL, 2018). This involves operators working with not only TfL but also for example bus manufacturers and other innovators designing and implementing practices that achieve this outcome.

Currently (late 2019), high priority is being given to improving air quality through the Low Emission Zone, encouraging hydrogen, all electric and hybrid propulsion systems (TfL, 2019). This has accelerated fleet replacement, although the current fares freeze (2017 to 2020) has created an expectation of further productive improvements, albeit challenged by increasing traffic volumes and resulting congestion (Mayor of London, 2017).

Forums exist for operators to deal with common operating issues, without infringing competition rules. One issue being reviewed is that of driver fatigue, to ensure steps are taken to eliminate such possibilities, balancing for example the desire of staff to undertake overtime while still being able to cope safely with all that is required of them. A report in 2019 commissioned by TfL found that: 'bus drivers are an understudied group within research relating to fatigue'; and that solutions are a shared responsibility among drivers, managers, operators at all levels, TfL, borough councils, unions and the Department for Transport (Loughborough University, 2019).

The fares freeze has increased pressure to not only ensure expenditure is within budget, but greater efficiency is enviably sought in every activity.

Overall, the arrangements represent the need for sound and trustworthy partnership in challenging conditions. The results show this is achieved.

Metroline's workforce planning

Metroline will budget for the attrition highlighted in the above introduction; however, it is somewhat predictable as this has been a constant for many years. The percentage of people leaving due to new career opportunities (Uber or Amazon delivery roles, for example), or illness, or family reasons, will be relatively static one year to the next, and will be spread across all locations. Similarly, the number of applicants across Metroline's area of operations will normally be somewhat predictable and evenly spread as well.

Where workforce planning becomes more challenging, is when Metroline succeeds in 'winning' the bid to operate an additional bus route. While Metroline will normally be given around nine months' notice of the change, the realities of suddenly having to find up to 120 additional drivers for a single location – over and above recruitment of replacements for natural turnover – can present a major challenge. While in theory Metroline could demand that a recruit in East London undertakes work based from a garage in West London, the reality is that that person will have little trouble finding similar employment much closer to home, and the company would run the risk of losing the investment in recruiting and training.

In order to facilitate effective workforce planning it is necessary to keep up-to-date data on the current staffing position of each of the 15 garages (target staff level versus actual staff level) and make this into a forecast showing natural staff turnover plus adjustments for any planned changes in workload. This last information comes mainly from Metroline's Head of Planning and Tendering, who will be the first to know of any relevant changes: incoming routes, outgoing routes, routes being lengthened or shortened, made more frequent or less frequent or even, at times, being transferred internally from one Metroline garage to another due to capacity issues.

The staff position forecast, then, is a document requiring constant updating and care. But what practical difference does it make? Well, on the most basic level, any applicant who lives close to several Metroline garages can be allocated to whichever is going to be in most need at the time they are expected to complete their training. The company can also be proactive in timing and targeting advertising for a particular location. Where a major route is being lost to a competitor, and there is no other work coming in locally, the company may also make a decision not to allow drivers allocated to that route contract to remain at Metroline, and effectively force the drivers to join the new operator under Transfer of Undertakings regulations (TUPE) (GOV.UK, 2019).

Recruitment

The first stage with any recruitment begins with attracting candidates, and in this respect Metroline has a number of advantages.

Metroline has been a large and highly visible local employer since its formation in 1989; our buses carry over a million people every day and are seen by far more. For that reason, more than half of our applicants are attracted in some way by our reputation in the community: 26 per cent are referred by a family member or friend who works for or has worked for the company (though we offer no specific incentive for this); 21 per cent research us specifically for our brand reputation, while 8 per cent are returning former employees.

In terms of advertising, ads on buses are efficient (12 per cent of applicants), as are banners outside our garages (almost 7 per cent) while internet advertising counts for 13 per cent. The remaining 13 per cent come from a mixture of job centres, job fairs, or agencies referring experienced bus drivers from elsewhere in Europe.

In order to gain and train 600 recruits in a year, it is necessary to interview around 3,000, which itself requires us to attract and filter over 8,000 applications. To help us with this mammoth administrative task, we use an online software application. There are many such applications on the market, all designed to help companies manage vacancies, applications, and interview schedules while enabling efficient communication with applicants through the recruitment process.

From the applicant's point of view they see an online application form, and once their application is vetted they have access to book their own interview date. From the recruiter's point of view they see all information related to a vacancy or applications in one place, with easy access to template emails and letters. Meanwhile, managers can quickly access useful statistics to gauge the effectiveness of the recruitment process.

With employment levels at record levels, and competition for skilled drivers particularly fierce as the cab and home delivery markets surge, one of the key factors for recruitment is speed. With this in mind, the application form is kept simple. A recruiter checks for newly completed applications throughout the day, filters out any with clear disqualifying features (such as driving bans) and immediately sends an invitation to book their own interview date which, depending on our existing bookings, is often as early as the next day.

Metroline runs assessment centres every other day, with up to 15 slots available for candidates. Things commence with a presentation outlining what life is like as a Metroline bus driver, and what is involved in training to become one. This ensures that every single candidate receives clear, consistent and, importantly, realistic messages about the role they are hopefully going to sign up for. The life of a bus driver can be challenging in many respects and is not for everyone; if we are going to make an investment of significant time and money in training a candidate, it is vital that candidates thoroughly understand what to expect on this journey.

While candidates are given this presentation and complete a short literacy test, their legal entitlements documents are vetted. This particular phase of recruitment is heavily regulated; candidates must give informed written consent to process their personal data, or we cannot legally conduct the vital checks.

Like any UK employer, Metroline is bound by legislation which states every recruit must provide satisfactory proof of their right to work in the UK. While the majority of these are relatively straightforward – an in-date UK or EU passport, for example – more complex cases also occur on an almost daily basis. In the most difficult cases applicants present documents which they think are acceptable, and may even have been accepted by a previous employer, but which do not meet government guidelines. This can be very frustrating for them and lead to lengthy delays in the process, as they await new passports and visas.

Recruiters must be knowledgeable, rigorous, professional, patient, and assertive because these rules cannot be broken. The penalty for employing someone without the proper documents is currently (2019) £20,000 per person, and, once an employer is known to have done so, they are likely to attract far more checks from the authorities in future, which would be disruptive to the business.

The other very important document to be checked is the candidate's driving licence. The candidate must obtain an access code for the Driver and Vehicle Licensing Agency (DVLA) online checking tool, which the recruiter can then use to check for bans, penalty points, categories and expiry dates as well as any codes restricting the use of the licence; the most common being a restriction that corrective eye-glasses should be worn.

If checking documents in a legally compliant way is the science of recruitment, then the art of recruitment is the interview. It is an art because each one is unique; the style of the interviewer meets the style of the interviewee to discuss the specific life and work experiences that they can bring to the role, in a way that is different every time. Still, even art is based on fundamental techniques and structures, and the art of interviewing is no different. The interviewer must be able to build a quick rapport with candidates of different backgrounds, in order to gain real insight into them and develop a view on what sort of employee they might be and how they will fit into the life of a bus driver.

There are times when even the best interviewer has real difficulty building or maintaining rapport with a candidate. Often this occurs when aspects of a person's work history do not quite add up and have to be challenged. This, together with disappointment over rejection for the role, can lead to complaints, and it is important that these are always considered carefully. Ideally, even unsuccessful candidates should feel that they were treated so well that they would recommend us to their friends and family.

A successful literacy test and interview is not quite the end of the recruitment journey. Depending on driving experience, we may require candidates to undergo a preliminary assessment of their skills in a Metroline car. In every case, there will be a drug and alcohol test for safety reasons, a company medical with a qualified occupational therapist, a criminal records check and reference checks. For someone who does not hold a bus driving licence already, they must have the medical before a provisional licence can be requested from the DVLA, and thus there are often four weeks between interview and eventual start date.

Staff passes

As with the majority of workplaces, the job perks are sometimes what entice new employees the most and the bus industry does not fall short of this standard. Whilst the average Londoner will spend between £2,000 to £3,000 each year for train and bus travel, bus drivers, and all those that work within the establishment, receive a free travel card and nominee card to get around the network, courtesy of Transport for London. This discretionary benefit not only supports employees travelling to and from work, but gives value for the job we do.

Metroline has a current (late 2019) workforce of 4,700 bus drivers, and an additional 1,000 working behind the scenes in our 15 depots. That is a lot of employees with travel cards! Each employee must follow a simple application system when applying for their own/their nominee's pass, and this also applies to any loss, damage or cancellations made throughout their bus driving career. It is very important that the administration of this benefit is performed well. It requires a great deal of coordination from all depot administrators because cards must be recovered, or cancelled, whenever an employee leaves.

Induction

Driver induction takes place once a week and introduces the new trainees to the company, its values and the training department in particular. As this date is agreed with each trainee when they sign the employment contract, we find that the majority of trainees do attend on the date and time agreed.

The main challenges are that the trainees sometimes do not bring the information they need to complete some of the Human Resources (HR) forms and for us to order their uniform. Additional time is given for them to complete the HR forms and a tape measure usually resolves the uniform ordering challenge. At the end of this full day, the trainees will be introduced to their training instructor.

Computerized tests

Trainees who do not already hold a bus licence will need to pass three computer-based tests, a theory (module 1) test, a hazard perception test (module 1a) and a bus-related case study (module 2) – see Table 8.1. By having our own computer testing facility and approved invigilators, we have reduced the likelihood of trainees missing Driver and Vehicle Standards Agency (DVSA) appointments.

The challenge of ensuring trainees have the knowledge to pass these tests has been met by supplying trainees with books and tablets that contain test questions and information, plus the chance to take mock tests.

Table 8.1 The three tests

Test	Marks available	Pass mark	Time allowed
Module 1	100	85	2 hours
Module 1a	100	67	45 minutes
Module 2	50	40	1 hour 15 mins

Some of the language used in the test questions is unusual to the trainees, so we provide them with a dictionary to assist them. Trainees who have English as a second language are also encouraged to obtain a mother tongue to English dictionary which they are permitted to use during these tests.

The in-house theory test centre is audited by the DVSA on average three times a year, and the standard we maintain has not attracted anything more than a few minor continuous improvement notices.

Basic training

Basic training is given to all trainees. For those without a bus licence the process takes about five weeks; for bus licence holders the process is more of a refresher course and is not normally expected to take more than a week. There is a structured training programme that the driving instructors work to, ensuring that even if a change of instructor is required, a candidate can still achieve progress.

At the end of the basic training programme, trainees wanting to acquire the bus licence will take an 'on-road' (module 3) test and a 'show me–tell me' test (module 4) which is related to bus safety. These tests are carried out with one of our two delegated driving examiners. The examiners are authorized to test anyone who is an employee of Metroline, but not people from outside of the company, and are audited regularly by DVSA. In addition we also have two module 4 examiners, who are authorized to assess Metroline trainees taking the module 4 test only.

For trainees who already hold a bus licence, their driving standard and bus safety checking is assessed too. These assessments are in fact much the same as the tests taken by trainees trying to acquire the bus licence, but they do not need to be audited by the DVSA and are carried out by specially trained instructors.

One of the challenges is to maintain the availability of training buses to use during times when the fleet is required to receive its periodic maintenance, and to overcome this several instructors (and their trainees) will work shifts. The scheduling of trainees to instructors, instructors to buses, basic training assessments and the booking of DVSA tests is carried out by a dedicated senior trainer.

Pre-service training

Pre-service training takes place after trainees have passed their tests or assessments. It is classroom based training that covers all subjects related to driving a bus in London, including contractual requirements from TfL, communication skills, equality, wellbeing and interactive learning for ticket machines and radio systems. This five-day programme is run on a rotation system, with each day's course being standalone (not relating to the previous day's subjects). Using this system gives us the flexibility to add trainees into a pre-service programme on any day of the week.

The main disadvantage of the rotary system in pre-service is that if a trainee misses one day in the middle of the programme, they will need to wait for a week for that training day to come round again before they can move on. From induction day onwards, we tell all trainees that missing days in pre-service is not acceptable and although a few miss days due to illness, most arrange their lives so that no time is taken off during this week.

The day following a trainee's pre-service training, they will sit an exam to confirm learning. The exam also forms part of the City & Guilds qualification trainees are required to attain.

City & Guilds driver qualification

Part of Metroline's contractual agreement with TfL is to ensure each driver holds a level 2 City & Guilds (C&G) qualification related to London bus driving or is working towards it if in the first year of employment. Formerly, this was achieved by drivers completing a Business and Technology Education Council (Btec) qualification – however, this changed to a C&G qualification in January 2016. Drivers holding the correct Btec qualification are not required to take the C&G one; therefore trainees who join our company already holding one of these qualifications will pass to garage directly after finishing their pre-service training.

The C&G Level 2: Certificate in Professional Bus Driving for London requires the trainees to complete 16 written tasks, have two observations and pass a confirmation of learning exam. The written tasks have been divided into sections that are completed during basic training, pre-service training and at garage with assistance from garage mentors. The exam, which takes place on the day after trainees finish pre-service, consists of 10 multiple-choice questions plus 15 short written answer questions to be completed within 90 minutes. A maximum of 60 marks are available, of which 48 marks or above is a pass.

On average, 88 per cent of trainees pass the exam first time; however, our largest challenge comes with organizing re-sit exams for the ones that do not achieve a pass. As re-sits dates need to be arranged to fit with the trainee's garage shifts, dates are made available on a spreadsheet and garage allocation staff book places for the re-sits.

Once a trainee's portfolio is completed, the work is checked by one of our Internal Quality Verifier (IQV) specially trained team members.

There is a considerable cost implication to delivering this training. Apart from training staff time and producing the training materials, a dedicated administrator is needed and C&G charge a fee of £57.20 per trainee registered with them. In 2018 alone, 551 trainees were registered for the C&G qualification, totalling £31,517.20. This fee is not recoverable if the trainee leaves after 30 days from registration date.

Sampling of candidate portfolios, the work done by the IQVs and the administration systems used to track trainees' progress is audited by a C&G External Quality Verifier (EQV). With most companies this will be done for all trainees' portfolios before a certificate can be claimed. However, at Metroline, due to the robust systems used to collect, check and track trainees' work, we have been granted the highly sought after 'Direct Claims Status' which allows us to claim certificates without the EQV seeing all portfolios. Metroline has held direct claims stature since our first EQV visit in June 2016, and is one of only two London bus companies who can boast this accolade.

A requirement of C&G is that all staff involved in this training must have standardization meetings. For our on-road instructors standardization takes place during some of their regular team meetings. The IQV team meet at least three times per year and a full day of standardization is given to our 58 garage mentors once a year.

To date, over 1,000 trainees have completed this qualification, and a further 400 are working towards it.

Apprenticeship scheme

Metroline strive and take pride in employing the best possible bus drivers, and we are the first London bus operator to embrace the new bus driving apprenticeship. There are a few challenges we face on a daily basis, such as liaising and chasing down our allocations team, complying with strict government rules, keeping the apprentices enthused and booking them in for workshops.

We work in partnership with a training company, and have monthly progress meetings with them. Industry-related training is given by our instructors/trainers; however, functional skills and workshops are solely delivered by the training provider. We resolve our challenges by stressing the importance, to the relevant people, of what needs to be done, as well as involving line managers when they are unresponsive. In order for us to keep the apprentices positive, we ask them for feedback to help further their experience with their apprenticeship.

Ongoing driver training

The law requires that each bus driver maintains their knowledge by completing 35 hours of periodic training every five years. The regulations on delivering this training are overseen and audited by a government agency called the Joint Approvals Unit for Periodic Training (JAUPT). This training is also known as CPC training, as the drivers are working towards a Certificate of Professional Competence.

So that we can undertake this training, we have qualified as a recognized centre with JAUPT. There are many aspects to having centre approval, including having robust schemes of work, ensuring we have trainers with sufficient knowledge and keeping accurate records. Centre audits can happen at any time with or without notice, but it is usual for notice of a visit to be given in order that any achieved records can be retrieved.

Individual courses must also be submitted to JAUPT for approval – this ensures that all courses cover subjects related to the driver's job role. A detailed description of the course, its timings, paperwork and a list of trainers qualified to deliver the course will accompany the application form and £252 registration fee. Course approval will be valid for one year, and JAUPT will send in their own quality control staff, without notice, to audit the course delivery and timings.

When the course is completed, the hours earned are registered against the driver's licence number and a fee of £8.75 per driver is paid. Once the 35 training hours have been reached the DVSA will issue a driver qualification card as proof of competency.

Drivers who do not accumulate enough hours before their card expires are not legally allowed to drive a bus with passengers; therefore, the importance of organizing periodic training and delivering it in-house is crucial to the operation of the company.

Vigil vanguard training

This in-house training course deals with corrective training for drivers who have been involved in minor collisions. The course has additional company rules attached to it so that drivers cannot repeat the learning within three years, and although the drivers can obtain periodic training hours when completing this course, its primary function is to give advice and guidance to the drivers.

Conclusions

The challenges around delivering bus services in London are immense. Whilst the tendering process and quality of service is world-leading, the nature of this causes HR planning issues, against a background of greater challenges required to employ customer-focused employees. The world of work is changing, with many choosing to work from home or requiring flexible working arrangements that do not necessarily sit well with a bus service operating 24/7.

Additional challenges around maintaining vehicles required to sit for long periods in the London congestion can consume additional resources and result in penalties. TfL continue to innovate along with the operators, and London will soon see the launch of the gas bus alongside an already established fully electric bus network.

References

GOV.UK (2019) [accessed 9 October 2019] Business transfers, takeovers and TUPE, *GOV.UK* [online] www.gov.uk/transfers-takeovers (archived at https://perma.cc/XEG2-37AT)

Loughborough University (2019) [accessed 4 October 2019] Bus Driver Fatigue, Final Report, *TfL* [online] http://content.tfl.gov.uk/bus-driver-fatigue-report.pdf (archived at https://perma.cc/7WND-BYUB)

Mayor of London (2017) [accessed 9 October 2019] Freezing Transport for London fares in 2017, *Mayor of London* [online] www.london.gov.uk/what-we-do/transport/freezing-transport-london-fares-2017 (archived at https://perma.cc/PD3Z-JMND)

Mayor of London and Transport for London (2018) [accessed 9 October 2019] Vision Zero action plan, Taking forward the Mayor's Transport Strategy, *TfL* [online] http://content.tfl.gov.uk/vision-zero-action-plan.pdf (archived at https://perma.cc/7JN8-8C5M)

Metroline (2019) Internal statistics

TfL (2019) [accessed 9 October 2019] Low Emission Zone, *TfL* [online] https://tfl.gov.uk/modes/driving/low-emission-zone (archived at https://perma.cc/7C8M-Q3VQ)

PART TWO
Wider engagement

The present and potential market for public transport

09

PETER WHITE

Introduction

The market for public transport may be viewed in three ways:

1 The existing patterns of demand, defined by trips made, shares by different modes, purposes of journeys, etc.

2 The potential market – for example, from the viewpoint of particular modes such as bus – examining scope for growth, by diversion of trips from other modes, or stimulating new travel.

3 The 'market mechanism' in the sense used by economists, ie a mechanism for allocating resources within an economy, mainly by use of pricing, to reflect costs of production and user preferences. This will, for example, be evident in price elasticity of demand.

In this chapter, the first definition is the main one used, but reference will also be made to the other two.

The current market for public transport in Britain

The definition of a passenger 'trip' may seem obvious: however some care is needed when comparing different sources of data. From the individual traveller's point of view, a trip or journey is usually undertaken from one activity to another, for example home to work. Typically, this involves a journey in one vehicle (such as a car or a bus), with a walk stage at each end although in the case of car this may be very short. 'Stage' is used here to cover a part of a journey by a particular mode, not the 'stages' on a distance-based fare scale.

This approach of defining trips by the journey purpose at each end promotes the idea we are considering transport largely as a 'derived demand', ie not undertaken for its own sake. This applies to the great majority of trips, although some will be undertaken for their own sake, notably in rural or tourist areas.

The convenience of a service will also depend on its ability to fit in with the traveller's time constraints, for example start and end times of work, or a medical appointment. Higher frequency of service will thus stimulate greater demand, by increasing the probability of matching these constraints.

Considering a different perspective, when data received from bus operators are used, a 'trip' is usually equated with a passenger boarding a vehicle, traditionally when paying in cash, but now usually validating a pass, smartcard, contactless bank card or using mobile payment. Each time another bus route is used as part of the same journey, a second 'trip' is thus recorded. The term 'boarding' is more precise, as used in the National Travel Survey (NTS). Whilst most bus journeys involve the use of only one bus, up to one in five journeys involves a second route (ie the ratio of 'boardings' to trips is about 1.15 to 1.20).

The shift from cash payment to smartcards and similar technology enables bus operators to analyse their passenger markets in much more depth than before, especially by route, and time of day. Where the number of cards on issue is known, an average trip rate per card may also be calculated. However, in most cases, cards are only validated on entry to the bus (with exceptions such as the 'Mango' card of Trentbarton, where validation on exit is also required, like existing rail stations fitted with ticket barriers), hence trip timing is defined by entry to the bus.

If we wish to examine origins and destinations of trips (at least at the level of bus stops) some inferences may be drawn. For example, if passengers make a simple 'trip chain' (as defined below), such as home–work–home, then it may be reasonable to assume that the alighting point of the home-to-work trip is also the boarding point of the later work to home trip, and likewise the alighting point of the latter close to the starting point of the former. However, this assumption does not apply in all cases, for example where only one bus boarding is recorded on a specific day (eg walking or using a taxi in the other direction), or where more complex trip chains are found.

Where systems such as smartcards are used, it is also possible to infer bus-to-bus interchange by examining an anonymized sample of card records for trips throughout a day. When two successive boardings occur on different routes within a short interval, it is reasonable to assume that they form part of the same linked trip. This approach can also be applied to inter-modal transfer when the same ticketing system is used (for example, between bus and Underground on the Oyster card in London). Where passengers complete a travel diary, then such interchange can be described directly.

The PLUSBUS ticketing offer outside the London area enables a simple 'add on' ticket to be purchased for bus feeder or distributor trips at each end of a rail journey (usually by pre-purchase when booking the rail journey, providing a day ticket for the bus travel), although it is not generally possible to link data directly for specific trips. Examples of inter-modal linking can also be found in the long-distance market, notably the growth of express coach services to airports such as London's Heathrow.

Operator-based data can be used to estimate annual trip rates, by dividing total trips recorded by the population served. Care must be taken to ensure that areas covered by operators match, as far as practicable, those for which population data is available. For example, in England the Department for Transport (DfT) requires bus operators to submit annual data on journeys (ie boardings) by named administrative area, enabling averages to be shown. This indicator can also be used to make international comparisons between cities, and for other public transport modes where boarding data are available (usually for rail, and sometimes for taxi).

However, operator data are limited in some respects. For example, they give no information on trip purpose, or user characteristics (such as age, gender or car availability). They do not record the whole journey (eg the walk stages at each end of a bus ride, or use of a car to join the bus at a park and ride site). For these purposes, a household-based survey is generally preferable. In this, data are collected on individual respondents, and they each complete a travel diary for all trips made. Usually this is only for one or two days, but the NTS in England is one of the most comprehensive in the world, collecting data for a seven-day consecutive period, and carried out continuously for over thirty years.

Such data give a very useful understanding of the public transport market, but the sample is not sufficient to describe origins and destinations for at a local level (unless a specific local study is carried out). There are also some limitations on reliability of self-reported data, for example in estimating length and duration in time of the walk stage to and from bus stops. To an increasing extent, mobile phone data are now being used in travel surveys, to give much larger samples in specific areas than possible in household studies. This can be particularly useful to give very detailed information on trip timing and length.

The characteristics of movement can also be analysed to infer the mode being used (eg a low average speed for walking, a 'stop-start' pattern for bus compared with car). Subject to ensuring anonymity of respondents' data, it therefore greatly enlarges our understanding of the spatial and temporal distribution of trips. However, it does not give data such as trip purpose or user characteristics.

The concept of the 'trip chain' is also useful at this point. By this, we do not refer to successive links in a one-way trip (eg home to work by walk, bus and train), but to 'chaining' of activities outside the household through the day. For example, if there is only one activity outside the home before returning (such as work, or shopping), a 'simple' trip chain is observed: the great majority of public transport chains are of this type. However, 'complex' chains may also be made, in which successive activities are connected by trips before the traveller returns home: for example, home to work, then to evening shopping, then home.

These complex chains tend to be associated more with car than public transport use (except in large cities) and with travel associated with childcare and/or part-time work. They may produce particularly complex patterns at peak periods – for example, an adult car driver dropping a child at school then continuing to work. Understanding these chains is useful for the public transport operator, since the convenience to the user will depend on being able to complete trip chains by public transport.

For example, if someone goes into work at 12.00 and returns home at 20.00, then the level of service frequency in the evening will affect their modal choice. When an operator is considering withdrawal of a poorly-used evening service, this needs to be borne in mind. Traditional ticketing systems, based on boardings for one-way trips, do not give these data, but they may be derived from household surveys such as the NTS, or – where all successive trips are made by public transport – from smartcard data.

Table 9.1 shows the composition of the public transport market in England for bus and rail services, showing both the shares within each mode for different trip purposes, and the share of all trips by purpose taken by each of these modes.

The following conclusions can be drawn from Table 9.1. The rail system is far more utilized for commuting, comprising around 48 per cent of all trips on that mode, compared to 19 per cent for buses. Transport for education, the other main component of weekday peak demand, shows the reverse pattern, comprising of only about 6 per cent of all trips for rail, but 19 per cent for buses.

Overall, peak demand for buses is less marked than for rail, but much of it derives from education travel, which may be more sharply focused on school start and finish times. Rail's overall demand trends are thus strongly influenced by those for work travel, which due to growth in employment in the centres of large cities since about 2000 has helped rail in this respect. The coincidence of adult journeys to work and school trips between 08.00

Table 9.1 Composition of bus and rail journeys by purpose, England, 2018

Trip purpose	Percentage of all bus trips	Bus market share of all modes' trips	Percentage of all rail trips	Rail market share of all modes' trips
Commuting	18.75	6.3	47.06	11.1
Business	2.08	2.0	8.82	10.0
Education*	18.75	7.1	5.88	1.6
Shopping	25.00	6.4	5.88	1.1
Personal business	10.42	5.4	5.88	2.2
Leisure	20.83	3.9	26.43	3.5
Other purposes**	4.17	1.3	0	0
All purposes	n/a	4.9	n/a	3.3

SOURCE National Travel Survey Table 0409 Average number of trips (trip rates) by purpose and mode (DfT, 2018).

NOTE that data in that table are shown with trips per person rounded to a whole number, from which above percentages are derived. In the case of rail, the published grand total is 33, but adding separate purposes together gives 34, which is used as the base for percentages within the rail market, from which the above percentages are derived. 'Bus' comprises 'Bus in London' plus 'Other local bus' (and thus excludes school services not open to the public). 'Rail' comprises 'London Underground' plus 'Surface rail'. Note that recent NTS data for bus use show substantial fluctuations on a year-to-year basis (giving a greater rate of decline than in operator-reported data), so that the bus share of the overall market appears considerably lower than in the previous year, for example.
*including 'escort' trips.
**including 'other escort'.

to 09.00 tends to produce a higher peak in demand in the mornings than afternoons, when a better spread is found. In rural areas, adult use of buses for the work journey is very limited, peak demand being determined overwhelmingly by education travel.

The largest single trip purpose by bus is shopping at 25 per cent, compared with only 6 per cent for rail. Together with personal business and leisure travel, this gives bus a better spread of demand during the working and shopping day, but the shopping market is clearly vulnerable to the shift to online retailing (shopping trips by all modes are declining).

The overall market shares by public transport are relatively small – about 5 per cent of all trips for bus, 3 per cent for rail – but bear in mind these are UK national averages. Higher shares are found for flows into the centre of larger cities, especially at peaks – in London, over 80 per cent of trips into the central area between 07.00 and 10.00 are by public transport, largely rail.

Use of a 'trips' measure is a useful starting point, but does not take account of trip length, which tends to be greater for rail than other modes. Again, using the NTS for England, we can show that in 2017, about 90 per cent of all bus trips were under 10 miles, a similar distribution to that for taxi/private hire sector, but for the London Underground this share was only 57 per cent, and for surface rail 27 per cent (DfT, 2018).

The aggregate totals for distance travelled by mode can be used in giving a national picture, and making international comparisons. In this respect, the UK as a whole is fairly typical of western Europe. Bus represented 5.2 per cent of all motorized passenger-km in 2015, rail 8.5 per cent, and trams and metro 1.7 per cent, compared with car at 84.5 per cent. For all 28 EU member countries at that time, the overall bus and coach share was somewhat higher at 9.4 per cent and rail lower at 7.6 per cent, but bear in mind this also included countries in Eastern Europe with lower car ownership levels (EU, 2018).

NTS England data also show that the distribution of public transport use by age and gender displays substantial differences between bus and rail in England. By age, the highest trip rates per year are shown for those aged 16-20, followed by those of 60 and over. Bus in particular tends to have a lower rate of use among those of working age, whereas rail does better in this respect, reflecting its higher component of commuting (see above). Age-based use of public transport is also influenced by fares charged, especially the free travel on local buses for the retired, and railcard discounts.

By gender, females make more use of buses than males in all age categories. For rail, males' trip rates are higher, but the differences are less marked. This partly reflects car availability, but also some differences in travel patterns, for example the role of shopping. A comprehensive analysis of demographic variations in bus use is given in a recent Independent Transport Commission report (Le Vine and White, 2020).

Trends over time

From a very high trip rate per capita, bus use declined sharply from a peak in the early 1950s. To a large extent, this is attributable to the rise in car ownership over that period. This not only diverted trips directly from bus to car but – as a secondary consequence – resulted in operators cutting services and raising real fares to offset the loss of revenue. This in turn had further impacts on demand, discussed further below. In recent years, some decline has also been attributable to factors such as the general reduction in shopping trips. However, it must be emphasized that a wide range of outcomes is seen at the local level, associated with policy differences, quality of service and factors such as parking policy. Park and ride services have proved successful in shifting car use back to bus, at least for part of the journeys made.

For rail, the pattern has been very different. Growth in car use had an impact in the 1950s and 1960s, with network cuts also having effects on demand, but growth in intercity travel offset this in terms of passenger-km travelled. Since 1994/95 a marked growth – of over 100 per cent – has occurred in both passenger trips and passenger-km, despite some further rise in car ownership.

Table 9.2 shows overall trends in bus use within England in 2002/03 in terms of absolute totals (millions of trips) and the trip rate per head, the latter being influenced by population change during that period (notably in London).

Table 9.2   Trends in bus use in England, 2002/03 to 2017/18

Area	Total trips (millions)	Trips per head
English metropolitan	1,182 to 907 (−23.3 per cent)	108 to 76 (−29.6 per cent)
English non-metropolitan	1,255 to 1,223 (−2.5 per cent)	40 to 35 (−12.5 per cent)
England outside London (sum)	2,437 to 2,131 (−12.6 per cent)	58 to 46 (−24.1 per cent)
London	1,527 to 2,225 (+45.7 per cent)	207 to 252 (+21.7 per cent)

SOURCE DfT, 2020

In London, the trips per head figure peaked at 285 in 2008/09, but then declined. The much greater fall in the metropolitan areas than the rest of England is noteworthy, as is the very marked differences in trips per head between the metropolitan areas and London, despite the 'Mets' being areas of up to around 2.5 million people (West Midlands and Greater Manchester).

Table 9.3 shows the current cross-section relationship between car ownership, driving status, and use of bus and rail services.

It can be seen that bus use is very much lower for persons in car-owning households, especially 'main drivers', whether expressed in trips or person-miles. Conversely, rail use (the great majority of the 'other public transport' category) varies much less and is, indeed, particularly high for the 'other driver' category. The relationships in this table could be used as a crude forecasting device for the effects on bus use of any further growth in car ownership, but note that changes at the margin may not be the same as averages derived from the population as a whole. For example, car ownership and driving licence holding among younger adults has declined substantially

Table 9.3 Public transport use by car access, England, 2017

Trips per person per year	Average for all persons with vehicle	Main driver	Other driver	Non-driver	Average for all persons in non-car households
As car driver	475	793	231	4*	9
As car passenger	232	96	257	461	76
Buses	31	14	41	58	161
Taxi/PHV	6	5	7	8	24
Other p.t. (a)	29	24	70	23	62
Distance per person per year (miles)					
As car driver	3,982	6,681	1,726	33*	114
As car passenger	2,076	1,299	2,528	3,274	702
Buses	186	75	197	312	669
Taxi/PHV	49	47	54	50	182
Other p.t. (a)	686	745	1,394	368	806

SOURCE Table NTS0702 Travel by personal car access, gender and main mode: England, 2017 (DfT, 2019)
'Buses' corresponds to 'Bus in London' and 'other local bus', and 'car' to 'car/van' within NTS0702
'Other p.t. (a)' corresponds to 'Other public transport', comprising surface rail, London Underground, air, ferries, and light rail. Data in NTS0702 for walk and 'other private' is not shown.
*in some cases, a person who does not drive a household car may drive a company vehicle

since about 2000, while it is growing among those moving into the retired age bracket, but their patterns of travel may not match the average car usage (for example, a lower level for travel to work by all modes).

It is also noticeable from Table 9.3 that those using buses also tend to be the main users of taxis and private hire vehicles, with 24 trips per head per year, compared with six for those in car-owning households.

A very marked difference can be seen in car ownership levels and trends between London and the rest of England. London has for many years displayed a strikingly lower car ownership rate, now only 305 per 1,000 population, which has declined slightly since the mid-1990s, compared with an average of 494 in other regions, the lowest (outside London) being the North East at 428. It is noticeable that some of the strongest car ownership growth has taken place in regions in which it was previously at a low level. For example, between 2002/03 and 2016/17, the percentage of households with no car or van in England outside London fell from 24 per cent to 20 per cent, but this was particularly marked in the North East (from 37 per cent to 29 per cent) and Yorkshire and The Humber (30 per cent to 24 per cent), which may help to explain the greater decline in bus use in the metropolitan areas noted above.

The lower car ownership in London may reflect external constraints, such as the cost of housing and parking restrictions, but also the very comprehensive public transport alternatives available. The percentage of households with two or more cars is particularly low. A similar pattern may be seen in other cities (often capitals) elsewhere in Europe, where despite high per capita gross income, lower car ownership and higher public transport use than the national average is shown (for example, Paris in relation to the rest of France, Stockholm within Sweden, etc).

A recent study for the Urban Transport Group (Sloman and Cairns, 2019) indicates that the bus share of the journey to work market (from census data) may be very largely explained by external factors such as population composition, but cases of greater than expected market share can also be identified, associated with factors such as service frequency.

Other factors affecting use of buses and coaches in Britain

Figure 9.1 shows variations in bus trips per head of population (on the vertical axis) with car ownership (expressed as the percentage of zero-car households) on the horizontal scale – hence one would expect bus use to rise

Figure 9.1   Bus journeys per head in relation to car ownership

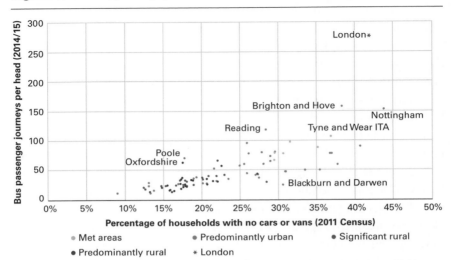

Bus trips per head in England in 2014–15, in relation to household car ownership from the 2011 census, using DfT data for trips per head reported by bus operators. Note an exceptionally low outlier (Rutland) has been omitted – year-by-year data for this small area shows marked fluctuations.

This diagram first appeared in the author's book *Public Transport: its Planning, Management and Operation* (6th ed, 2017) and is reproduced with consent of the publisher.

toward the right, as is indeed the case. At low levels of zero-car households the observations are mainly closely grouped along a trend, with the notable exceptions of higher bus use in Oxfordshire and Poole.

There is a much wider scatter to the right, some areas having much lower bus use levels than might be expected from the general trend (such as Blackburn and Darwen), but others (notably Brighton and Hove, and Nottingham) much higher (note that the data here are subject to the definition of the trips per head indicator, as discussed earlier).

Comprehensive reviews of factors affecting bus use may be found in two reports: *The Demand for Public Transport* (Transport Research Laboratory, 2003), and the *Soft Measures* report (DfT, 2009). An update to some aspects of the 2003 report was produced for the DfT in 2018 (Dunkerley *et al*, 2018). All may be downloaded free of charge from the TRL and DfT websites.

The first deals mainly with the 'hard' indicators that are readily quantified from existing aggregate data, such as fares or service levels. The latter deals with those not readily quantified, such as quality of passenger information and vehicle accessibility. In practice the distinction may be less relevant from the passenger's viewpoint – they perceive changes in price and quality of service offered (which may be mediated through subjective perceptions) and then change behaviour accordingly. The text below summarizes some of the main findings, but much fuller details can be obtained in the original reports.

A concept used for measuring the effects of readily-quantified factors is 'demand elasticity', expressed in simple form as:

elasticity = % change in demand / % change in a factor affecting demand

For example, if a 10 per cent increase in average fare causes a 4 per cent decline in trips, the elasticity is –4/10, or –0.4

Note that price (fare) elasticity is usually negative, since an increase in fare will normally cause a decline. The –0.4. value shown here is typical for the 'short run' elasticity, ie within about one year of the fare change, ensuring that over a shorter period care has to be taken to allow for usual seasonal variation, by reference to an equivalent period in the previous year. It will be clear that revenue in this case would rise, since we have 96 trips for every 100 trips previously, but each produces 10 per cent more revenue.

This value varies by trip characteristics, especially length. Very short trips, for which walking and cycling are alternatives, are most sensitive to price; those around 3–7km show the lowest sensitivity, but it rises again with longer trips (where alternative destinations may exist, eg a suburban shopping centre versus the city centre). There is little evidence for differing elasticities for reductions or increases in fares of the same magnitude, so the elasticity concept may be used to forecast the effects of fare reduction, including completely free travel.

Over a longer period (5–10 years), the elasticity for a given fare change is greater, as more substitutes exist (eg buying a car, relocation), and given the underlying turnover in the market, new users may be more sensitive to price. These are typically about twice the short-run value. Hence, whilst it is tempting for an operator to increase fares in the short run to increase revenue, in the longer run this could be self-defeating.

The same elasticity concept can be applied to changes in service level, usually expressed as bus-km run. In most cases this reflects a change in service frequency (for example, if a service were increased from two to three buses per hour, bus-km would rise by 50 per cent), although in some cases it may reflect a change in network size, and/or length of time a service operates during the day or week. In this case the elasticity value is positive, ie an improved service will attract more passengers. Coincidentally, its magnitude is about the same as the fare elasticity, ie +0.4 (a 10 per cent increase in bus-km will produce a demand growth of 4 per cent), and higher in the medium to long term.

A simple 'across the board' service increase will thus generate revenue, but not sufficient to cover extra costs if the additional bus-km incur the same unit costs as those previously run. However, where service expansion is at off-peak times, the marginal cost may be much lower. Alternatively, if smaller vehicles are used, cost per bus-km is lower (although cost per seat-km is higher). The extensive high-frequency minibus conversions in the 1980s confirmed an elasticity figure of about +0.4, and were made commercially viable due to lower wages paid to their drivers. However, this did not prove feasible in the longer run, and such services reverted to larger vehicles. An attempt to recreate the concept in Ashford, Kent in 2018 was only partly successful due to the need to offer the same wage rates to minibus drivers as those for full-sized buses. A fuller discussion is provided elsewhere by the author (White, 2019).

In addition to the private car, modal competition also arises from rail and taxis/private hire vehicles (PHVs). For example, as congestion has grown, some demand in major cities has moved to existing 'heavy rail' services (more people now commute into central Birmingham by rail than bus, despite the very limited rail network in the region). This can also be seen in new or extended light rail systems (such as Nottingham Express Tram, or Manchester Metrolink). As discussed in Chapter 1, there has been a sharp growth in the supply of taxis and PHVs in recent years, especially since 2013. At the aggregate level, this has not been matched by growth in use, but some cases may have occurred of trips diverting from bus to this mode.

Attitudinal data

In addition to observing behaviour, survey data can also be collected on attitudes to transport modes. This gives an understanding of user perceptions, and may point to areas needing managerial attention.

A limited amount of attitudinal data is collected by the NTS, but the main example is that collected by Transport Focus, twice-yearly passenger surveys on all train operating companies in Britain, and a large sample of bus users annually – see Chapter 15. A five-point scale is used to assess many aspects of service provision, including an overall measure of satisfaction, whose determinants can be derived from other ratings. Comparisons are made by area, and also named operator groups.

The NTS data is broadly similar, but also includes London (not covered by Transport Focus) and non-users, who tend to rate buses less favourably than users (but nonetheless is a useful indicator of perceptions).

Factors affecting overall levels of local travel

For many decades, a general growth in travel by all modes has been observed, but much more marked in terms of distance travelling than person trips. Much of the expansion has been in the form of longer-distance trips. A broadly stable amount of time in travel per person per day (about one hour) has also been seen, both in Britain and other countries. The underlying growth was associated with a shift to faster modes, so that greater distance could be covered in a given time, and also increases in real income.

However, a striking shift has occurred this century. For example, between 2002 and 2015, trip rate per person (by all modes) in the NTS fell from 1,074 to 943, albeit recovering to 986 in 2018 (a net drop over the whole period of 8.2 per cent). In particular, younger people are travelling less than equivalent age groups previously, and have much lower levels of car ownership and driving licence holding – again, a pattern not unique to Britain.

This change in behaviour has two effects. Firstly, simply extrapolating past trends is not an appropriate method of forecasting, given uncertainty about the future. Secondly, if demand per head is stable or falling, then total demand will only rise where population growth offsets this decline (there may of course be growth in specific modes, eg if car ownership rises then more road space may be required). The lower level of travel in general may be associated with factors such as teleworking, and online shopping, together with some changes in social behaviour.

In terms of forecasting, one method is to use 'scenario forecasting'. Rather than extrapolating a single trend (perhaps with upper and lower bounds), alternative futures may be considered, eg in terms of overall mobility levels, patterns of employment, social behaviour, impacts of new technology, and energy availability. A good example is the studies conducted in New Zealand examining alternative outcomes for 2045 (Ministry of Transport New Zealand, 2018).

Future opportunities for the bus industry

A rather negative impression might be gained from the preceding text, given the impacts of car ownership on bus use, and more recent trends in travel in general. However, given the industry's modest market share (Table 9.1), even a fairly small shift in market share could represent a large absolute growth in bus use. It could also represent a wider role in society at large by the bus, for example in reducing social isolation, widening employment opportunities and reducing energy use and pollution by stimulating modal shift from cars.

As indicated in Figure 9.1, there is a wide scatter of bus trip rates, even allowing for variations in car ownership, with some areas producing noticeably higher usage than others. In many cases this reflects a much more positive approach to improved service quality and associated marketing, for example by 'More' (part of Go South Coast) in the Poole area, or the main operator in Brighton and Hove. Supportive local authority policies, such as parking control and provision of bus priority (see Chapter 11) clearly assist. A number of specific opportunities include:

- Bus rapid transit (BRT). The use of sections of road or track solely for bus use (either guided or unguided), usually linked with the rest of the road network, on which conventional bus priorities are provided. The marked gains in speed and reliability enable substantial ridership growth, including diversion from car (about 20 per cent of all BRT use comes from previous car trips). This has been particularly marked in the Cambridge busway case. Using conventional economic assessment such as that in 'WebTAG' (the standard assessment framework specified by the DfT), very good benefit/cost ratios can be derived from existing experience. A fuller account is provided by Whelan and White (2019).

- Scope for using driverless vehicles. Extensive testing is under way in many countries, ranging from small cars to larger vehicles. In the context of bus travel, much attention is being given to using small vehicles for the 'last mile' link to places not currently served, or low-density sections of existing routes. However, if driverless vehicles are shown to be safe and acceptable, this concept can equally well be applied to existing bus services. Removing driver costs would make smaller vehicles commercially viable, enabling large increases in frequency, with consequent stimulus to demand.

Conclusions

Extensive data are available to show the trends in demand for bus services in Britain, and the composition of the market. Bus use is associated (negatively) with car availability levels, but also strongly influenced by fares, service frequency and other service quality factors.

In contrast to rail, bus has a slightly greater share of the market by all modes (measured in passenger trips), but is much less focused on the journey to work, with a better balance between peak and off-peak demand, notably the importance of shopping. Variations by age and gender indicate that bus use is concentrated in younger and oldest age groups.

Acknowledgement

Helpful comments were provided on an earlier version of this chapter by Roland Clausen-Thue.

References

DfT (2009) *The Role of Soft Measures in Influencing Patronage Growth and Modal Split in the Bus Market in England*, London

DfT (2018) [accessed 14 February 2020] National Travel Survey: England 2018, *GOV.UK* [online] https://assets.publishing.service.gov.uk/government/uploads/system/uploads/attachment_data/file/823068/national-travel-survey-2018.pdf (archived at https://perma.cc/6GQB-MTBT)

DfT (2019) [accessed 14 February 2020] Travel by personal car access, gender and main mode or mode: England, *GOV.UK* [online] https://assets.publishing.service.gov.uk/government/uploads/system/uploads/attachment_data/file/821434/nts0702.ods (archived at https://perma.cc/B7KV-CTQZ)

DfT (2020) [accessed 14 February 2020] Passenger journeys on local bus services by metropolitan area status and country: Great Britain, *GOV.UK* [online] https://assets.publishing.service.gov.uk/government/uploads/system/uploads/attachment_data/file/852282/bus0103.ods (archived at https://perma.cc/CL75-AC6R)

Dunkerley, F et al (2018) *(RAND Europe and SYSTRA) Bus fare and journey time elasticities and diversion factors for all modes: A rapid evidence assessment*, for UK Department for Transport

EU (2018) *EU Transport in Figures 2017 Statistical Pocketbook*

Le Vine, S and White, P (2020) [accessed 14 February 2020] The shape of changing bus demand in England, *Independent Transport Commission* [online] www.theitc.org.uk/wp-content/uploads/2015/03/ITC-Bus-market-in-England-Jan-2020.pdf (archived at https://perma.cc/6E32-M8LN)

Ministry of Transport, New Zealand (2018) *Public Transport 2045*

Sloman, L and Cairns, S (2019) *What scope for boosting bus use? An Analysis of Intrinsic Bus Potential of local authority areas in England*, Transport for Quality of Life for the Urban Transport Group

Transport Research Laboratory (2003) *The Demand for Public Transport: A Practical Guide*, Report TRL593

Whelan, G and White, P (2019) Chapter 9: Assessing Bus Rapid Transit Outcomes in Great Britain, *in* F Ferbrache (ed) *Developing Bus Rapid Transit*, Edward Elgar

White, P (2019) [accessed 20 February 2020] The influence of regulatory environments on public transport service provision: A British case study, *Research in Transportation Business & Management*, 32 [online] www.sciencedirect.com/science/article/abs/pii/S2210539519300859 (archived at https://perma.cc/8Y7J-4EUG)

Bus provision and land use planning

10

TIM PHAROAH

Introduction

This chapter emphasizes that bus services do not exist in a vacuum; they are linked to the spatial distribution of people and activities. It argues that land use and public transport should be planned together to maximize the benefits, ie integrated planning to meet sustainable transport aims.

The chapter outlines how urban activities can be arranged to maximize the use of bus services, and support the provision of an integrated public transport network. Equally, it argues that new developments can be the catalyst for improved bus services that will benefit the wider community.

Benchmarking, targets and aspirations

Urban planning at whatever level, whether through neighbourhood plans, local plans, local transport plans, or wider regional or strategic plans, should include aspirations for the role that buses (and other public transport) will play, together with the means of meeting that aspiration. The location and form of urban developments will determine to a large degree the role that the bus is able to play in the transport mix. Whether that role is fulfilled in practice will depend on a range of other policy and practical interventions. These are discussed later on in this chapter.

A useful tool is to set targets for the proportion of travel by bus (bus mode share), to be reached by a specified date. Targets need to be clearly defined in terms of what is being measured, and the area covered, and data need to be collected over the plan period to monitor progress in relation to the targets. A robust system for measuring mode split is the KONTIV survey design developed by Socialdata in Germany (Socialdata, 2019), which has also been applied in more than 30 British towns and cities. This uses interview surveys to establish the mode of travel for all trip stages, rather than just 'main mode' as used in the national census (of England and Wales) for the journey to work (Office for National Statistics, 2011).

To be supportive of a 'sustainable transport' outcome, the required target bus mode share is likely to be in excess of 25 per cent of all trips. The other 75 per cent will need to be heavily in favour of walking and cycling if car use is to be kept small (eg under 25 per cent). The London Mayor's Transport Strategy 2018 includes a target for 80 per cent of journeys to be made by walking, cycling or public transport by 2041. This may seem ambitious, but can be seen in the context of a large increase in public transport use in the previous 20 years. Bus and rail accounted for 26 per cent in 1997, but had climbed to 37 per cent by 2017 (Transport for London, 2018). Smaller cities and towns will struggle to reach that level, principally because they lack the intensity of employment and other activity in their central areas, and have a much smaller presence of rail services.

A target of 25 per cent of trips by public transport is not unreasonable, certainly for larger towns and cities, as levels of around 20 per cent for the journey to work are already achieved in some places, for example Dundee, Liverpool, Newcastle upon Tyne, Nottingham, Norwich, Oxford and Thurrock (Office for National Statistics, 2011). The challenge will be much greater in those cities where the bus mode share is around 10 per cent of all trips or even less, such as Exeter, Gloucester, Ipswich, Peterborough, Preston, Watford and Worcester (Socialdata, nd).

An alternative to measuring the bus mode share in town or city (which can involve considerable survey resources) is to specify the bus passenger numbers to be achieved, as a proxy for the intended mode share. In rough terms, people make just under 1,000 trips each year, so a bus mode share of 25 per cent should produce at least 250 bus rides in the area (per person, per year). Account needs to be taken, however, of trips involving more than one bus ride, and also of bus rides taken by non-residents. The latter can be very significant in popular tourist destinations.

It is important that the target chosen is clearly specified, together with the data source that will be used. For example, alternatives might include:

- mode split of trips (by main mode or trip stages) generated by residents or occupiers of a development or a particular area, based on periodic interview surveys;

- mode split of all trips to and from a development, or area (including visitors), based on periodic cordon surveys;

- bus (or other public transport) passenger journeys per year (of both residents and non-residents) based on operator statistics;

- any of the above related to a single journey purpose (for example, the journey to work, or to school) based on, for example, workplace or school travel surveys.

Having established a target, it will subsequently be necessary to carry out surveys at intervals to monitor progress towards that target over time. If progress is not being made, or progress is too slow, then various interventions will need to be modified or introduced to speed the pace of change. The land use planning mechanism can be used for this purpose, such as the granting of permission for higher density developments that will increase trip demand, or clamping down on the amount of parking provided as part of new developments in order to shift travel demand in favour of public transport.

Even without new developments, mode shift towards the bus can be achieved with various non-planning interventions, such as bus priority on the streets, reduced fares, stricter parking controls and higher parking charges.

The planning mechanism

Buildings and the activities within them are dependent on transport and access provision, whatever the balance of modes. Equally, transport activity only arises because of the trips generated by different land uses. Land use and transport are thus inextricably linked. While this is indisputable, understanding how to intervene in order to achieve better developments or better transport is not straightforward. In the UK, land use and transport tend to be planned separately, which can create difficulties when trying to achieve more sustainable solutions, including the higher take-up of bus services.

This section takes a broad look at the planning system, and highlights aspects that work against the improvement of bus services.

That urban developments and the transport that serves them need to be planned together sounds obvious. If people were unable to get access into or out of a building, that building or development would be worthless and pointless. Nevertheless, in Britain at least, the importance of this joined-up approach has not always been recognized, and it is not encouraged by land use and transport planning systems that are to a large degree independent of each other. A report from 2011 said: 'the extent to which an understanding of the transport infrastructure has been the starting point for land use planning is strikingly limited' (Transport for Quality of Life, 2011). Not much has changed in the years since 2011.

Even with general acceptance of the need to integrate land use and transport, it is considerably more difficult to say how land use and transport should be planned together. It immediately involves ideologies and policy priorities, whether these are stated explicitly or not. The default position too often is the laying out of development to suit access by car. To shift from this position so that travel by bus is not only enabled, but also positively encouraged, requires very different planning parameters. These can be strongly resisted when it is realized that they involve less convenient, less generous or more costly provision for car parking and car use. Thus although both spatial plans and transport plans almost without exception contain policies for increasing the use of sustainable modes, such plans rarely contain any specific mechanism or policy for reducing the use of cars. Yet increasing the use of sustainable modes inevitably requires mode shift away from the car, since people cannot ride in cars while at the same time walk or cycle or ride the bus.

The big question is, does the current planning system work to deliver integrated solutions to achieve sustainable transport outcomes? The short answer for England is that it does not.

Firstly, authorities responsible for land use planning in many cases are not responsible for highways or public transport, and vice versa, especially in areas with two-tier local government, ie with county and district councils. Local planning authorities are required to produce Local Plans for controlling land use development and change, which may or may not include or be coordinated with transport plans. Local highway and transport authorities prepare Local Transport Plans, which may or may not be focused on development issues.

Immediately, therefore, integrated planning requires cooperation and agreement between two different authorities, each with their own interests and priorities, and often with different politics as well. Local transport authorities in England outside of London are required to produce a Local Transport Plan

(LTP) under the Transport Act 2000, as amended by the Local Transport Act 2008. Guidance has been produced on how LTPs should be produced (Department for Transport, 2009). Local Planning authorities are required to produce a Local Plan, which sets out their policies for the use of land in their area (Planning and Compulsory Purchase Act 2004). The transport implications of this plan have to be assessed, using as guidance a Government web page entitled 'Transport evidence bases in plan making and decision taking' (Ministry of Housing, Communities and Local Government, 2015).

Secondly, the system of planning inquiries into major development plans and schemes is not necessarily obliged to scrutinize transport policies and proposals, even though they will affect land use outcomes. As a Planning Inspectorate spokesperson stated (in response to a question about why the spatial and transport plans for the West of England Plan differed): 'It isn't uncommon for there to be a difference between a spatial plan and a Local Transport Plan, given that they have different purposes and are subject to different legislation' (Local Transport Today, 2019). LTPs themselves are not subjected to inquiries in the way that Local Plans are.

Integrated planning is needed at both the strategic and local level. At the strategic level, sites for development, and redevelopment, need to be identified simultaneously with the public transport that will link them with centres of activity. A broad indication of density and land use mix also needs to be specified. At the strategic level, this will often require adjacent local authorities to collaborate for cross-boundary solutions. Plans for new or improved public transport need to be accompanied by mechanisms for funding and implementing them, with timescales coordinated with those of major new development.

Unfortunately, statutory mechanisms for regional or strategic planning have largely been abolished, with the exception of the big cities, including London and Greater Manchester, and areas that have 'Combined Authority' arrangements. There is no consistency, however, with some having an elected mayor, some having devolved powers, and others not. In addition, to muddy the water further, there are various mechanisms that operate almost independently of the local government system, bringing democratic accountability into question. Such mechanisms include, for example, Local Enterprise Partnerships, which produce 'strategic economic plans', and so-called Enterprise Zones, within which planning controls are reduced.

Also, since 2015 in some areas Local Transport Bodies (LTBs) have been set up, basically to oversee the spending of Department for Transport (DfT) funds. The areas covered by these LTBs are larger than local authority areas, and their membership may not necessarily include representatives from the local planning authorities (Campaign for Better Transport and Campaign to Protect Rural England, 2013).

Government guidance has also been drastically reduced, including that for planning and transport. Planning Policy Guidance Transport (PPG13) was abolished, along with other guidance, in 2012. Reliance is now placed on the National Planning Policy Framework (NPPF), which is too general to be of much practical help for local authorities attempting to coordinate transport and planning. In any case, it does not focus on transport, which is overseen by a different ministry, the DfT.

The NPPF does indicate in general terms that local plans, and local planning should aim to promote sustainable transport. It states that, for example: '…opportunities to promote walking, cycling and public transport use [should be] identified and pursued'. The emphasis, however, is on identifying the impacts of development on transport, rather than on the integration of spatial and transport planning. In practice, the main issue dealt with is whether the road network can accommodate additional (mostly car) traffic generated by new developments, and whether additional road capacity needs to be provided.

National Planning Policy Guidance is provided on many aspects of planning and plan making, but there is only one dealing specifically with transport, focusing on the transport evidence that should be taken into account (Ministry of Housing, Communities and Local Government, 2015).

One of the key aspects of policy affecting the design and layout of development, and the transport outcomes, is the amount of parking provision. Parking, and access to it, easily can account for half of a development site. High levels of provision for parking offer no disincentive to car ownership, and hence can limit the demand for public transport. Former policy guidance (PPG13) argued for maximum parking standards for non-residential development, to: '…be designed to be used as part of a package of measures to promote sustainable transport choices and the efficient use of land'.

The 2019 NPPF, by contrast, states (para. 106) that:

> Maximum parking standards for residential and non-residential development should only be set where there is a clear and compelling justification that they are necessary for managing the local road network, or for optimizing the density of development in city and town centres and other locations that are well served by public transport (Ministry of Housing, Communities and Local Government, 2019)

The difference in approach is that NPPF regards areas well served by public transport as fixed, whereas PPG13 called for an integrated approach whereby development could itself be used to generate better public transport.

Parking provision is not a neutral aspect of development. The more parking that is provided, the more car use is enabled or encouraged. The less parking provided, the more encouragement and scope there will be for higher levels of public transport provision. Nor is excessive parking provision easily remedied, at least in residential developments. Once habits of car ownership and use have been established, there is little chance of retrospectively increasing public transport provision or mode share.

At the local level, the planned outcomes should fit within the broader strategic context, and specifically should give priority to the 'sustainable' modes: walking, cycling and public transport, as prescribed by the NPPF (2012 and as subsequently amended). At this level the specific sites for development will be identified, along with requirements for density and the mix of uses, along with the facilities that will be provided (such as employment and schools). Public transport will be (or at least should be) a key consideration in determining these aspects at the local level. Given the reliance on the private sector for public transport provision, and the separate arrangements for bus and rail provision, it is difficult for local authorities to guarantee services in relation to new developments.

To achieve real progress towards sustainable transport, the extra travel demand that new developments generate should be used to enhance the public transport offer, which would benefit existing as well as new areas of development. Instead, the present mechanisms often result in proposals for new housing being used to justify the provision of new road capacity. Rarely will it be used to justify the provision of significant new public transport routes or services.

A practical problem arises from the fact that most local planning authorities have no statutory duty to plan for or operate buses or other public transport. As a consequence of this, they do not employ officers with public transport experience or expertise, unless the authority has taken on some particular initiative in this area. Even in local transport authorities, the absence of responsibility for mainstream bus operations since de-regulation has meant that knowledge and expertise can be hard to find in-house.

The result of this is that the integration of land use development with bus service planning and operation either does not happen, or it relies on external consultancy expertise being brought in on a case-by-case basis, which obviously precludes it from being the mainstream activity that it needs to be.

The crucial point here is that planning for sustainable transport outcomes has become very difficult in the face of divided responsibilities, and a private sector development industry that seeks primarily to maximize profits and opportunities, rather than to create sustainable development for the public good.

The mechanism in Britain for planning land use and transport is so varied, complex and fragmented that it is difficult to set down on paper what it is, let alone how it works. In summary, as at 2019, the system is not fit for purpose.

Urban form needed to deliver a significant role for the bus

Spatial planning influences, or even determines, the transport that can be provided for. At the same time, the transport facilities provided will influence the character and spatial arrangement of urban activities.

The planning of land uses and urban form therefore should reflect the expected or desired role of the bus in meeting the travel needs of inhabitants and visitors to an area. The density of population, and the intensity of activities, will have a direct bearing on the density of the network of services that can be provided.

This concept was succinctly presented in Government guidance issued in 2001 (subsequently withdrawn):

> By shaping the pattern of development and by influencing the location, scale, density, design and mix of land uses, planning can help to reduce the need to travel, reduce the length of journeys and make it safer and easier for people to access jobs, shopping, leisure facilities and services by public transport, walking and cycling. Consistent application of these planning policies will help to reduce some of the need for car journeys (by reducing the physical separation of key land uses) and enable people to make sustainable transport choices. (Office of the Deputy Prime Minister, 2001)

As a general rule of thumb, developments will be successful in this regard if bus (or other public transport) services can be provided that are financially self-supporting, without any need for ongoing subsidies. Equally, if a bus route needs financial support, this probably indicates either that the population density is insufficient to support a good level of service (in which case steps should be taken to increase it), or that car provision is excessive, or both.

An exception to this may be in areas that are being newly developed, where short-term subsidies can ensure that services are running when the first new residents move in and before the threshold of passenger numbers needed for viability has been achieved. Bus services that are financially viable overall nevertheless involve some internal cross-subsidy, for example to maintain frequency in the early morning and late evening, and on Sundays.

Urban form that is oriented to bus (and other public transport) is not just about the overall density and level of activities within the catchment areas of stops. The access routes to those stops are also a key consideration. Although not generally in the sphere of responsibility of bus operators, the success of their services will depend in part on how easily accessible they are. This involves careful planning for pedestrian movement.

In most of Europe it is assumed that all urban developments will need to be accessible by pedestrians, and so in most developments footways are provided as a matter of course, even though their quality may not always be ideal. It stands to reason that if footways are to be used, places have to be located within walking distance of other places. Given that not all activities can be found within walking distance, the footway and footpath network needs to give direct and high-quality access to bus stops (and tram and rail stations). Provision for walking as the main 'access mode' is crucial to the effectiveness of the bus network. This is a prime requirement for the layout and design of urban developments.

If public transport is to play a key role in serving movement generated to and from developments, then this will (or rather should) determine more generally the form, layout and density of development, and the spatial distribution of various activities. Two guidance documents provide further details on this point (Chartered Institute of Highways and Transportation, 2018; Stagecoach, 2017).

The main requirements are to:

- build in a compact form to sufficient density;
- arrange developments within easy walking distance of bus stops;
- provide high density around rail stations (including light rail);
- ensure that trip attracting uses (such as schools, retail, leisure and employment) are grouped together around public transport stops or interchanges;
- design direct and attractive walking routes to bus stops.

Urban layouts that do not support the frequent use of public transport are instead likely to be arranged to make driving and parking easier. Such car-oriented places will be the opposite of those planned around public transport; that is, with low density, dispersed activities and lots of parking.

The requirements of car-based travel and bus-based travel are in so many ways incompatible. Therefore, every aspect of the arrangement of paths, streets, roads and parking, and access ways to public transport services, expresses a particular idea of what should have priority, and what is considered important for the users of a development. Of course, a compromise will usually be sought, but there is no getting away from the fact that the more the car is provided for, the less suitable will be the design for attracting bus users. Urban planners and designers would do well to make the trade-offs explicit at the time plans are being made and planning permissions are being sought.

There are contrasting practices when it comes to the making of plans. The conventional but now widely discredited way is so-called 'predict and provide'. In essence this involves using models based on comparator developments elsewhere to predict the vehicle trips likely to be generated by the proposed development. The plan is then drawn up to provide enough road capacity to accommodate the predicted traffic levels. There is little to recommend such practice, because it is derived from and constrained by an engineering paradigm. Predict and provide may be adequate for deciding on the capacity of a sewer to meet the demand from a building, but it is completely inappropriate for dealing with the very much wider ramifications of urban transport. In planning future transport provision, predict and provide simply reinforces and perpetuates car-based travel.

The alternative practice, now becoming more widespread, involves setting out from the start what kind of transport outcome is desired. This may be called the normative approach, often described as being 'objectives-led' or 'vision led'. In this approach, discussions and consultations lead to an agreed set of aims and objectives, including for example to achieve a particular mode share by sustainable modes. The process of setting targets already described fits into this process. Models are then used to test whether a particular plan, or set of measures, will achieve the desired objectives.

A variant that is suited to strategic or long-term plans is the 'scenario-based' approach, whereby a number of future scenarios are put forward for consideration. The most favoured scenario then becomes the basis for the more detailed objectives of the plan. A number of cities have adopted a normative approach for their overall plans, for example the Greater Manchester Transport Strategy 2040.

Within the agreed vision or scenario, a planning strategy for the development of a town or city will need to identify more specifically what sort of public transport network will be provided. Smaller towns and cities will generate shorter travel distances that in all likelihood can be served by a network of bus routes. Cycling may also be a more significant mode, as in cities like Oxford and Cambridge, thus moderating the demand for public transport. In larger towns and cities, however, it is more effective to provide rail-based public transport in order to meet higher capacity requirements, and higher speeds for longer journey distances.

In this case the network of bus services will play more of a supporting role, catering for shorter local journeys, providing access to rail stations, and serving lower density districts that generate insufficient demand to support rail services. Integration and coordination of the bus and rail services is, however, essential to maximize their use. Interchange between bus and rail involves not just the physical linking up of services, but also integrated fares, tickets, marketing and timetables.

The success of the bus network will depend not only on its role vis-a-vis other public transport, but also the configuration of the routes. For example, bus ridership in the small town of Lemgo, Germany, increased sixtyfold when the bus services were arranged to provide half-hourly interchange between the three town bus routes at a central rendezvous point.

Another crucial aspect of urban development for the success of bus services is the need for development to be arranged in corridors of limited width, thus ensuring that everyone is within easy walking distance of bus stops. The corridor arrangement can be seen, for example, in some seaside towns such as Brighton and Hove, and Southend. Bus services operate on parallel roads around 600–800 metres apart, coming together in the town centre. This enables most areas to be within a 300–400 metre walk of a bus stop.

More difficulty arises when the network of main streets is further apart, as is often found in outer suburban areas, and in places laid out primarily for car use such as Milton Keynes. There the main roads are spaced one kilometre apart, which means that many places are more than half a kilometre from the nearest bus stop. Runcorn was designed to incorporate a segregated busway system, but again, insufficient attention was paid to the means of accessing bus stops on foot.

In conventional towns with a predominantly radial road pattern, bus routes come together in the town centre, but as they fan out towards the suburbs, the distances between the main routes increase, thus increasing the walk necessary to access them, or requiring the insertion of additional routes. This is not a problem if development densities are high enough to support these additional routes.

The arrangement of bus stops along bus routes is often referred to as resembling 'beads on a string'. However, this description is generally more relevant to railways, where stations are more widely spaced. In continuously built-up areas, bus routes may be more appropriately viewed as development 'corridors', since the walking catchments of stops usually overlap.

The spacing of bus stops is another key consideration. For ease of access, keeping walking distance short, closely-spaced stops are favoured, but this must be balanced against the extra journey times associated with frequent stops. Where buses share the streets with other traffic, the provision of bus priority measures can speed the bus, thus compensating for extra time at stops; see Chapter 11.

A further requirement in the planning of development and the bus routes that serve them is that activities, or destinations, should be grouped together at bus stops, and should be visible from them. High inter-visibility between buses and the activities they serve helps to maintain a high profile in people's minds, and also helps navigation for people unfamiliar with an area. Segregated bus routes can be a problem in this respect, an example being the Runcorn segregated busway, which often is not visible from the development it serves.

Bus routes in general are focused on major destinations such as town and city centres. Other destinations are distributed more widely through the urban area, such as secondary schools. There is still a need, however, to group these activities as far as possible around bus stop locations. There is synergy, for example between a school and a corner shop, or between a health centre and a chemist. Play areas likewise should be close to other facilities that people use either before or after using the bus.

The communities themselves need to have connected street and path networks, and not be separated by distributor roads that have neither frontage development nor footpaths. Connected layouts are more bus-friendly because they are also more people-friendly.

Other attributes needed in support of high bus mode share

Integrated transport and land use planning is not confined to the physical and spatial arrangement of land uses and transport infrastructure as discussed above, but includes a range of policy measures that either encourage or limit, or otherwise influence people's choice of mode. The key measures (at least potentially) are to do with the pricing of public transport vis-a-vis the pricing of roads, parking and car use, and the regulation of road and parking space.

Perhaps the most important of these are policies and provisions for car parking, especially in town centres and other destinations for which the bus competes. A good example is the Workplace Parking Levy in Nottingham, which has had a direct influence on encouraging the use of trams and buses in the city, both by making car commuting more expensive, and through public transport improvements funded in part by revenues from the Levy itself. It has also led to the re-purposing of some city centre parking sites, thus strengthening the city centre demand for access by public transport (Nottingham City Council, nd).

Other examples of measures to limit competition from the car include road user charging, management of road capacity giving priority for buses over other traffic, and provisions for cycling.

In addition, there are many measures that can help to make buses more attractive to users. In this respect it is important to recognize that the quality needed should not be measured by reference to existing users, important though they are. Almost by definition the quality of services is adequate for existing users, and equally the quality is inadequate for those who currently choose not to use the bus. For example, the often-quoted acceptable walking distance to bus stops of 400 metres is probably too great to attract people who have a car sitting outside their house. The city of Zürich, Switzerland, applies a maximum of 300 metres to the nearest bus or tram stop, and it has one of the highest levels of public transport use in Europe.

Fare levels, the ease of ticketing, and the ready availability of information on routes, interchanges and service times, especially in real time, have a major impact on whether people choose to use the bus.

The presence or otherwise of rail services unsurprisingly has a huge impact on the demand for buses, but distribution of demand between bus and rail is less important than achieving high levels of public transport use overall. This requires the different services to be coordinated and integrated. Munich, Germany, provides a good example, with bus, tram and suburban rail networks integrated and marketed to provide 'One Network – One Timetable – One Tariff'.

One of the most striking features of cities in continental Europe is the prevalence of trams. They have the advantage not only of supplying higher capacity on the street than buses, but also higher passenger appeal. There is a benefit of having readily visible infrastructure in the street, ie the tramlines, because this conveys permanence and certainty. By contrast, people do not so easily trust buses because their routes can easily be varied, or even discontinued, even though this rarely happens in practice.

There is benefit too in finding your way around. Ask directions and people can say 'just follow the tramlines'; that would be difficult for bus routes to match.

Generally, trams are considered suitable only in cities above a certain size, say 250,000 population, where the density of passengers justifies the infrastructure investment and maintenance costs. However, there are also small cities with trams in countries where public operation and subsidy go hand in hand, and where public transport is regarded as an essential public service rather than a commercial entity. For example, Gmunden in Austria has a tramline, but a population of only 13,000!

The mix of bus and rail in a city can, if properly integrated with development, serve a very high proportion of total trips, as indicated by the fact that, in 2017, 76 per cent of car trips were under 10 miles in length, suitable for rail travel, and 55 per cent were under five miles, suitable for bus and cycling (DfT, 2015; 2016; 2017).

Conclusions

The key message explored in this chapter is that land use development and transport are inextricably linked, and consequently that the planning of both needs to be integrated. The type and form of urban development has a strong influence on the ability of buses to serve it. At the same time, the type and scale of public transport provision determines what sort of development is required to support it.

Unfortunately, in Britain land use planning tends to be undertaken separately from transport planning. This makes it very difficult to shape transport outcomes, in particular to achieve high levels of sustainability. The result is much new development being built around the car, rather than people using buses and active travel modes. Urban form that suits car use is to a large degree the opposite of what is required to generate high levels of public transport use.

Also, given the generally agreed aspirations for more sustainable transport choices, it is difficult to avoid the conclusion that the current planning system is not fit for purpose. Strategic planning mechanisms are notable for their absence, while at the local level, planning authorities lack both responsibility and expertise in transport matters.

The chapter has set out the various design requirements for what might be termed 'bus-friendly' developments, and these need to be included in the remit of planning authorities with the power and resources to implement them. It has discussed the role of spatial planning in securing a high level of bus use, together with the importance of other transport factors in supporting bus demand.

It is important to recognize, however, that the actual level of bus use in any particular town or city will depend just as much on the socio-demographic make up of the population. Lower income areas will have lower car ownership, and thus a greater degree of dependence on public transport. Even so, it is important to ensure bus services are of a high quality, so that public transport mode share is maintained as and when people's economic position improves.

Finally, it is worth summarizing the essential features of a high-quality bus service:

- Frequency should be as high as is reasonably justifiable relative to the density and intensity of the area served.

- Departures should be at regular intervals (eg every six, 10 or 12 minutes) to provide a 'turn up and go' service without need for timetables. Less frequent routes should operate on a 'clockface' basis, ie at easily remembered numbers of minutes past each hour.

- Services should run throughout a long day, albeit thinned out in the late evening.

- Services should be broadly similar on every day of the week, albeit Saturday and Sunday timetables will omit the extra runs required in peak hours during the working week.

- In order to maximize memorability and to simplify presentational design, timetables should be identical hour-by-hour and should avoid variation.

- Timetables should ensure easy interchange between services.

- Timings should be symmetrical in the two directions in terms of journey times and interchange arrangements.

- Bus services should be coordinated with rail services.

- Fares should be reasonable and tickets and permits should be easy to find, to understand and to obtain.

- Town and city networks should be marketed under a single brand, albeit with sub-brands to recognize local identities or special services.

References

Campaign for Better Transport and Campaign to Protect Rural England (2013) *Where the Money's Going: Are the new local transport bodies heading in the right direction?*, London

Chartered Institute of Highways and Transportation (2018) *Buses in Urban Developments*, London

DfT (2009) *Guidance on Local Transport Plans*, London

DfT (2015) [accessed 25 February 2020] National Travel Survey: England 2015, *GOV.UK* [online] https://assets.publishing.service.gov.uk/government/uploads/system/uploads/attachment_data/file/551437/national-travel-survey-2015.pdf (archived at https://perma.cc/88ZM-JXTM)

DfT (2017) [accessed 25 February 2020] National Travel Survey: England 2016, *GOV.UK* [online] https://assets.publishing.service.gov.uk/government/uploads/system/uploads/attachment_data/file/633077/national-travel-survey-2016.pdf (archived at https://perma.cc/W9KB-7EP4)

DfT (2017) [accessed 25 February 2020] National Travel Survey: England 2017, *GOV.UK* [online] https://assets.publishing.service.gov.uk/government/uploads/system/uploads/attachment_data/file/729521/national-travel-survey-2017.pdf (archived at https://perma.cc/4WV4-S4K7)

Local Transport Today (2019) Different visions in WoE's LTP & spatial plan, *TransportXtra* [online] www.transportxtra.com/publications/local-transport-today/news/59905/different-visions-in-woe-s-ltp–spatial-plan (archived at https://perma.cc/4KAZ-FY6B)

Ministry of Housing, Communities and Local Government (2015) Transport evidence bases in plan making and decision making, *GOV.UK* [online] www.gov.uk/guidance/transport-evidence-bases-in-plan-making-and-decision-taking (archived at https://perma.cc/286Y-MSJG)

Ministry of Housing, Communities and Local Government (2019) *National Planning Policy Framework*, London

Nottingham City Council (nd) Workplace Parking Levy, *Nottingham City Council* [online] www.nottinghamcity.gov.uk/wpl (archived at https://perma.cc/LM8T-FF6T)

Office for National Statistics (2011) [accessed March 2019] National Census of England and Wales, *Office for National Statistics* [online] www.ons.gov.uk/census/2011census (archived at https://perma.cc/72LF-Q2W7)

Office of the Deputy Prime Minister (2001) *Planning Policy Guidance 13: Transport*, London

Socialdata (2019) [accessed March 2019] The New KONTIV® Design, *Socialdata* [online] http://www.socialdata.de/info/publikationen.php?lang=en (archived at https://perma.cc/6CM6-2KL9)

Socialdata (nd) [accessed March 2019] Surveys with the KONTIV® design, *Socialdata* [online] www.socialdata.de/daten/modechoice.php?lang=en (archived at https://perma.cc/9QUZ-B8MH)

Stagecoach (2017) Bus Services and New Residential Developments, *Stagecoach* [online] www.stagecoach.com/~/media/Files/S/Stagecoach-Group/Attachments/ pdf/bus-services-and-new-residential-developments.pdf (archived at https:// perma.cc/J927-WWEU)

Transport for London (2018) Travel in London, Report 11

Transport for Quality of Life (2011) Thriving Cities, *Transport for Quality of Life* [online] www.transportforqualityoflife.com/u/files/Thriving_Cities_Report_ WebFINAL.pdf (archived at https://perma.cc/V4H5-E92B)

Bus priority 11

DAVID HURDLE, G NIGEL KING AND SUSANNAH ROSENFELD-KING

Introduction

It is vital that bus services operate efficiently and are attractive to use. One important way of achieving both of these is to give buses priority over other traffic on roads. This has been happening since the 1960s in cities across the world, and this chapter explores the history and reasoning. It then describes the various types of measure, their effects and benefits; and also describes associated measures that can further improve efficiency and attractiveness. As with so many aspects of bus operation, it highlights the need for operators and local authorities to work together in partnership.

It demonstrates the valuable role that bus priorities can play in increasing bus patronage within a new environmental context of illegal air pollution and a climate change emergency. The chapter inevitably concentrates on London which has, by far, the greatest number of bus priority measures in the UK. Indeed, London accounts for 51 per cent of all bus passenger journeys in England (Department for Transport, 2019a).

Why bus priority?

Buses are very efficient users of road space. Research about 'people-moving' in London in 1990 found that during peak periods buses carried one-third of road passengers, but only accounted for 1 per cent of road vehicles (Hurdle, 1990). In terms of fuel used per passenger mile, research, again in 1990, found that a bus, half full of passengers, was about four to seven times more efficient than a car (average 1.5 persons) in urban conditions (Adams, 1990); a bus only one-third full could still be two to six times more efficient, depending on the size of the vehicles (Trades Union Congress, 1990).

Figure 11.1 The spiral of decline

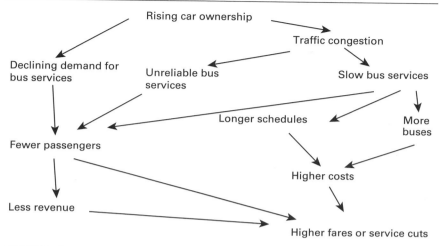

SOURCE Buchanan, 1990

The need for bus priority measures stems from the, often slow, speed of buses at peak times, and congestion that makes services irregular, unreliable, and unattractive to use. If journeys take longer this clearly increases the cost of operation. A spiral of decline arises, best explained in Figure 11.1.

Of course, road space does not belong to the bus operator; and it does have to be shared with many forms of transport. But it is a scarce resource, and if buses are efficient users of road space it makes sense to prioritize their use of it and so maximize efficient operation and attractive services. There are three other powerful reasons.

The first is environmental. Air pollution in many cities has been at illegal levels since 2010 and traffic is the main source (Carrington, 2018). In the case of nitrogen dioxide, 38 zones covering 194 local authorities exceeded legal limits in 2014 (Department of the Environment, Food and Rural Affairs, 2015). In 2015, London was 15th out of 36 major global cities in terms of overall air quality, behind other European cities such as Stockholm, Vienna and Berlin (Quilter-Pinner and Laybourn-Langton, 2016). Buses, and coaches, account for just 6 per cent of nitrogen oxide emissions from road transport compared with 71 per cent from diesel cars and vans (Begg, 2017). So, more bus use, and less car use, will contribute to reducing levels.

The second is also environmental – climate change. Following the Climate Change Act of 2008 and subsequent legislation, there is now a 'climate change emergency' and carbon dioxide emissions need to be eliminated as soon as possible. The warnings are stark – the Intergovernmental Panel on Climate Change (IPCC) has warned that:

- the world has already warmed by 1°C since the middle of the 19th century;
- warming could reach 1.5°C before 2050;
- the world is on track for a 3°C rise;
- to meet a goal of 1.5°C warming, the planet's emissions need to be 45 per cent below 2010 levels by 2030 (IPCC, 2018).

The report is the most up-to-date and comprehensive explanation of the science of climate change and the future of the Earth, compiled by 91 authors and 133 contributing authors, from 40 countries, with 30,000 assessed scientific papers and over 42,000 comments made during its review (Cool Earth, 2019).

An influential activist in 2019 put it more starkly: 'Around the year 2030 ... we will be in a position where we set off an irreversible chain reaction beyond human control, that will most likely lead to the end of our civilization as we know it. That is unless, in that time, permanent and unprecedented changes in all aspects of society have taken place, including a reduction of carbon dioxide emissions by at least 50 per cent' (Thunberg, 2019). Again, a shift from car to bus use will contribute.

The third reason is that buses are a short-term way of increasing capacity on public transport. Trains in cities can be overcrowded and it can take many years to increase capacity on railways.

So, the case for bus priority comprises:

- efficient use of road space in terms of fuel and people movement;
- air pollution and climate change dictate a significant shift from car to bus use;
- a short-term solution to increasing capacity of public transport.

History

The world's first designated bus lane was in Chicago, USA, in 1939 (American Public Transportation Association, 2007). This was also the year that the separation of buses and general traffic in London during peak periods was first proposed by the British government. An article in *The Times* in 1940 reported that the Minister for Transport was 'considering a new plan for relieving the congestion of road passenger traffic' and was proposing that 'public service vehicles and private motor cars should be kept apart' (The Times, 1940). But priority for buses, in the form of special lanes, did not happen until the 1960s. That decade witnessed considerable traffic growth, principally cars. As a Government minister observed in 1963: 'In London and the Home Counties ten years ago there were 664,000 cars. Today they number 1,815,000' (HM Stationery Office, 1963).

One suggested way to reduce congestion was parking meters to try and control on-street parking. Central London had 647 introduced in 1958: 'Local authorities were becoming increasingly aware of the value of meter-controlled parking in relieving traffic congestion'. In 1960 4,600 more meters were installed, and in 1961 another 5,700 (HM Stationery Office, 1963).

The value of bus priority was not appreciated until London's first bus lane in 1968 in Park Lane, Westminster. It was 165m long, served by 12 bus routes with 140 buses per hour, was operational between 16.00 and 19.00 on Mondays to Fridays and saved 30 seconds per bus (Collins and Pharoah, 1974). London's first lanes were introduced rather tentatively, two in 1968, a third in 1970 and a fourth in 1971 (Barker, 1990). London Transport complained: 'Although further traffic engineering schemes, clearways, parking controls and bus lanes were introduced during 1972, these useful but generally isolated measures were not being introduced boldly or quickly enough to combat the strangling effects of private cars and lorries' (Barker, 1990).

A visit to Park Lane south and northbound bus lanes and stops was made on Tuesday 8 October 2019. The southbound bus routes mid-morning between 10.45am and 11.45am were observed and the northbound bus routes 12.30pm–1.30pm.

Park Lane benefits from three traffic lanes in both directions. One of the lanes in each direction is allocated as a bus lane. It is also a London Red Route (see later in this chapter) and rules and conditions apply to ensure traffic movement (Transport for London, 2019a).

Park Lane southbound

The southbound bus stop nearest to Marble Arch Underground station interchange was a busy stop. The stop hosts 11 daytime bus services as well as four night-time bus services. The bus stop has a countdown system in place to assist with passenger information, as well as a standard bus stop shelter. Bus users can also access bus information via phone apps and texting bus stop numbers to provide additional real-time information.

However, the waiting provision on the pavement around the bus stop would benefit from enhancement as bus user numbers were often large and blocked pedestrian access for other users.

The quality of the environment for bus passengers was possibly insufficient given the number of buses and bus users at any given time during the recorded times. Whilst passenger facilities at bus stops have improved considerably over many years, a further review could now be undertaken and improvements made at popular bus stops to enhance the passenger experience.

Adjacent to the southbound bus stop (Marble Arch on Park Lane), there is a stop for Intercity coach services, and further south there is a bus stand in the bus lane for Tour Bus services. Whilst the former did not impede the flow of traffic in the bus lane, the latter blocked access and all users of the bus lane (London Buses, Intercity Coaches, cyclists, taxi drivers) manoeuvred out into the middle lane to re-join the bus lane once passed. It is fortunate that this is a three lane southbound route and is one of the widest roads in central London.

Park Lane northbound

The first stop on northbound Park lane was for tour buses. This stop was not used as a tour bus stand and therefore traffic kept moving. The TfL Buses bus stop was found opposite the London Hilton Hotel and had less passengers waiting than at its southbound counterpart, albeit this was a lunchtime observation. There was not a countdown system in place, however there was a standard bus shelter for bus passenger users.

Northbound also has three lanes of traffic, however the northbound bus lane hosted approximately 12 private hire coaches as a bus stand. Nevertheless, this, by no means impeded the flow of traffic at lunchtime.

The first lanes in Europe were in 1963 in Hamburg, Germany, when the tram system was closed and the tram tracks converted for bus travel; France followed in 1964 with one in Paris (AMTUIR, 2019). Although bus lanes got to London in 1968, the capital lagged behind other European cities. In 1970 London's three bus lanes contrasted with Milan's 35 and Paris's 83. But progress soon became rapid with totals in London of 150 in 1980, 170 in 1983, 229 in 1983 and 234 in 1990. However, the rate fell, from an average of 13 per year before 1983 to 4 per year by 1986, and two existing lanes had been withdrawn (Greater London Council, 1983). The lanes in 1990 comprised 72km, 2 per cent of total bus route length. However, this was in stark contrast to Paris's 304km, which was 12 per cent of total route length, and Tokyo's 234km, 23 per cent of route length (Hurdle, 1990).

Bus lanes had been implemented in other UK cities, over 400 in fact, by 1990. Thus, London's comprised over half. Implementation elsewhere varied considerably. For example, the West Midlands had virtually no measures, whereas Greater Manchester had 46. And bus lanes as a proportion of route length was low, eg Edinburgh's 10km of lanes was only 0.8 per cent of route length; and Leeds/Bradford's 14km just 0.6 per cent (Bushell, 1990). Glasgow introduced a lane in 1976, followed by five more, but by 1990 there had been no further progress.

A common theme in the former metropolitan counties, also London, was that since their abolition in 1986 progress had been minimal. The lack of strategic local authorities for the major cities from 1986 clearly seems to have had an adverse effect on bus priority implementation. London saw 140 lanes implemented in the 1970s; the rate dropped to 96 in the 1980s, then rose to 475 in the 1990s, and was 453 between 2000 and 2005 (Gardner *et al*, 2006).

In 1997 the central Government recognized the important role of buses by updating earlier bus priority guidance (Department for Transport (DfT), Local Government and the Regions, the Scottish Office and the Welsh Office, 1997). The guidance summed up the situation well:

> It is frequently worthwhile to introduce traffic management measures to assist the movement of buses. These can take the form of measures designed to facilitate the movement of traffic generally along bus routes, and to protect access to bus stops. They may go further and permit buses to use lanes or dedicated tracks or make movements which are denied to other traffic. Such measures can provide substantial benefits to bus passengers by allowing faster journey times and a more regular and reliable service; they can also help to attract additional passengers by eliminating unnecessary capital and operating costs by reducing the number of buses required to run the service.

Sustainable and integrated transport were now actively being talked about and progressed.

As already noted, there can be no doubt that the abolition of the Greater London Council in 1986, which eliminated a strategic, London-wide planning and transportation body, slowed further implementation. However, a London Bus Priority Initiative was set up in 1990, and the total number of lanes rose to over 500 by 1998, with programmes to reach over 700 by 2003 (King, 1998a).

Another boost to bus priority in the 1990s in London came with the introduction of Red Routes enabled by the Road Traffic Act 1991, see Figure 11.2.

This was a 483km priority system where stopping, loading and unloading was severely restricted. A key aim was 'to provide special help to improve the movement of buses' (Butcher, 2010). A 13km pilot scheme began on 7 January 1991. A final report in 1993 found that bus journeys and general traffic were considerably quicker and the variability of bus journey times was reduced by one-third; and patronage on the 43 service, which used a large length of the pilot route, had increased by 8.8 per cent at a time when there was a drop of 3 per cent in bus use in London (Wood and Smith, 1993). The scheme affecting the 43 was a 'total route upgrade' – see later in this chapter.

The 43 has gone from strength to strength! To take advantage of the better conditions, a route 43 Express was introduced (Hurdle, 1993). Then in 1999 it became the first route in London to be operated by low-floor double deck buses; and in July 2019 the first all-electric route in London.

Figure 11.2   A wide, well-marked bus lane on a Red Route (the double lines are red), Park Lane, London in 2019

London's Red Routes since 1991 have severely restricted on-street parking and helped bus flow.

Under the Greater London Authority Act 1999, responsibility for London's bus priority network passed to Transport for London (TfL). In his 2001 Transport Strategy, the Mayor of London, Ken Livingstone, stated he would do more to give buses 'real priority' and to 'effectively enforce' priority measures (Mayor of London, 2001); his innovative approach extended to a bike hire scheme and Oyster Cards. This sort of approach was continued by the next Mayor, Boris Johnson, in 2010 (Mayor of London, 2010). In 2002 a Bus Priority Team was set up within TfL.

The end of the twentieth century did rather suffer from a lack of Government policy on traffic levels and congestion. Basically, Government policy guidance was vague. Advice back in 1987 from the Secretary of State for Transport stated: 'It is not his aim to increase overall traffic levels in London' (Department of Transport, 1987). This was watered down in a 1992 Circular to – '… not increasing car commuting into or across London' (DoT, 1992). The Minister for Transport in London at the time went further, but only in response to a question about congestion at a conference: 'The DoT's job was not to increase the amount of traffic that came into the city, but actually to curtail it and, where possible, reduce it' (European Environment Bureau, 1992). But this never got enshrined in a government policy document.

But it was now the 21st century, and congestion was at last starting to be seriously tackled, at least in London, with congestion charging and Red Routes (see below). By 2017, in the UK's largest cities, congestion was 14 per cent worse than in 2012 (Greener Journeys, 2017). On current trends, the average speeds in our major conurbations are projected to fall from 27km/hour in 2016 to just 19km/hour in 2030 (Confederation of Passenger Transport UK, nd). Evaluation of schemes to reduce congestion has shown that every £1 spent on bus priority can deliver up to £8 of economic benefit (KPMG, 2015).

An important milestone in London was the introduction of the Central London congestion charge in 2003. When considering bus priority measures, it is important also to consider measures to discourage car use, such as congestion charging. A new policy shift was emerging – moving people rather than vehicles, and bus priorities not just giving existing bus passengers a faster ride but giving car users an alternative. This had three major effects on buses:

- net revenues from the congestion charge scheme were ring-fenced and largely spent on improving bus services;

- during the first year, there was a 37 per cent increase in bus passengers entering the charging zone during the charging hours;
- after one year, total traffic was down 18 per cent (Gardner *et al*, 2006).

The UK's first congestion charging zone was in fact introduced in 2002, before London's. It was for reducing traffic along a narrow street in Durham which led to the cathedral and castle. After one year, traffic during the charging hours had fallen by 90 per cent (BBC, 2003). It is of interest that proposals to expand London's Heathrow Airport include the introduction of a congestion charge (Paton, 2019).

Another way of reducing congestion is the imposition of a workplace parking levy, available to local authorities in England and Wales through the Transport Act 2000. The only city to have done this, so far, is Nottingham in 2012, though many others are considering it, eg Birmingham, Leicester, Oxford, Reading, and the London Boroughs of Camden, Hounslow, Merton and Sutton; also the Government of Scotland is planning to give councils the power (Local Transport Today, 2019a). The levy in Nottingham has raised over £44 million of revenue, which is ring-fenced by law to spend on transport initiatives. Together with other funding it has enabled the city's tram network to double in size, and provided technology for priority and late running buses at key signalized junctions. There has been a 4.5 per cent increase in bus/tram patronage since 2013/14; and the city now has the highest level of bus/tram usage per head outside London (Campaign for Better Transport, 2019).

In 2003 the Government published a report that examined the efficiency of the Red Routes and included a case study of the three-year London Bus Initiative that ran from 2000 to 2003; this group had been set up by the Traffic Director for London, responsible for Red Routes. Over that period 100 extra bus lanes were introduced, along with 50 new pedestrian crossings, 300 signalized junctions equipped with bus priority and 140 junction improvements across 27 bus routes (DfT, 2004). It found waiting times for passengers reduced by about a third, improved bus reliability, and patronage up about a fifth. Interestingly, the Traffic Director, in his initial Network Plan in 1993, had highlighted that the bus system was a valuable but underused resource which could particularly benefit from the new Red Route network (Traffic Director for London, 1993).

A key element of bus priority is traffic signal priority – see the following section for fuller details. In London this has been operating since the mid-1990s, more recently using Global Positioning Satellite (GPS) bus location systems in the application of selective vehicle detection (SVD) (Gardner *et al*, 2006).

Types of bus priority measures

With-flow lanes

These are the most common form of bus priority. They allow buses on approaches to junctions to bypass a queue of traffic. Cycling is a sustainable form of transport to be encouraged, and since 1989 the Government has recommended that cyclists be allowed in such lanes for safety reasons (DoT, 1989).

Opinion varies as to allowing other vehicles to use bus lanes. Others include coaches, taxis, minicabs, cyclists, motorcyclists, heavy goods vehicles and emergency vehicles. A study in 2017 of 14 world cities found that it was common for the first four and the last mentioned of the above to be permitted (Imperial College London, 2017). Permitting motorcyclists is becoming more common. However, it is somewhat controversial as to whether that form of travel should be encouraged or discouraged. For example, in London in 2015, motorcyclists represented 2 per cent of the traffic, but 26 per cent of all those seriously injured or killed (Mayor of London, 2018). Transport for London allows motorcycles in most Red Route bus lanes because it reduces congestion, motorcycle journey times and carbon dioxide emissions. It also contributes to the London Mayor's Vision Zero, working towards the elimination of road traffic deaths and serious injuries (TfL, 2019b).

Contra-flow lanes

These have been introduced nationwide in one-way streets. They keep buses serving passengers' objectives, and can offer more direct routeings. However, care is needed on safety grounds and cyclists are usually excluded (Armitage, 1979). Such lanes could also pose problems for pedestrians (Brownfield and Devenport, 1989).

By 1977 whereas there were 140 with-flow lanes in London and 142 outside London, there were six contras in London, but 117 outside London (National Bus Company, 1978). As of October 2019 there are 1,150 bus lanes in London, of which 1,035 are with-flow and the remainder are other types such as contra-flow, contra-flow with gate, two-way (TfL, 2019c). This is an eight-fold increase over 42 years.

Bus-only streets

The two main types of bus-only streets are those where buses use a street closed to other traffic, such as a town centre shopping street, and those where buses are able to take a short cut through a traffic system. In the 1980s there were over 100 streets in the UK where buses and pedestrians shared the space (TEST, 1987).

There has always been a debate as to whether buses should be allowed into pedestrianized streets and who should have priority – pedestrians or buses. There is no straightforward answer, as everywhere is different. However, the key feature is to get bus passengers to and from stops close to the town centre without the need for foot crossings on main roads. Buses along the pedestrianized street might be the obvious way of achieving this, but some schemes provide stops at each end of the street – though circuitous routes should ideally be avoided.

Busways and guided buses

Busways are roads built exclusively for buses. There are several UK examples. One of the most recent is the Cambridge Guided Busway, which is just over 25km long and uses former railway alignments (Cambridgeshire County Council, 2019). The earliest is at Runcorn built in the 1970s and 23km long; and there are many examples of bus corridors where part is a guided busway, such as the Crawley Fastway and Leeds' Superbus (Bus Rapid Transit UK, 2019).

Bus gates

These are often used in areas with limited road space for bus lanes. They can take the form of a spur of 'bus-only' road to a junction, or selective vehicle priority (SVP) at traffic lights. SVP extends green lights or shortens red lights so that delayed buses can pass through a junction more quickly. Light timings can also be adjusted to smooth general traffic flow. As of October 2019, London has seven sites with bus gates (TfL, 2019b).

In Hazel Grove, Manchester, SVP has reduced bus journey times by three minutes and journey time variability by 50 per cent, while cutting congestion levels for all traffic by 75 per cent (Urban Transport Group, 2014).

Turn exemptions at junctions

This could be a bus-only right turn, which may just require simple signing. A London example is the junction of the A100 Tower Bridge Road and Tooley Street. The introduction of that turn reduced a circuitous routeing by 628m, and achieved average savings of 636 seconds in the morning peak, 391 between peaks and 591 in the evening peak (Imperial College London, 2017).

Whole route treatment

This is an approach certainly adopted since 2005, although some action by London Borough Councils started in 1993, with several participating in demonstration projects then (Hurdle, 1993). A 'Green Routes' study in London in 1991 had stressed the need for such an approach (Metropolitan Transport Research Unit, 1991), and the Association of London Government (the umbrella body representing all London councils in dealing with the Government) strongly supported this approach to 'providing bus priority and other bus-boosting measures' (Hurdle, 1996).

Sometimes whole route treatments are called 'corridor management' or 'total route upgrades'. One of London's busiest bus routes, the 38, Victoria–Clapton, was chosen in 2003 as a pilot for 'Whole Route Corridor Management'. It was 12.5km long, with 25–30 buses per hour in each direction and about 7,000 passengers per hour (Spachis, nd). As well as more priority to buses, the needs of traffic, businesses, the community, pedestrians and cyclists were also addressed (Gardner *et al*, 2006).

It is very important to secure community support for schemes, so planning and implementation require careful management and consultation. A convincing case for measures needs to be presented so that communities have ownership. Liverpool is a good example, where the Combined Authority in 2019 asked people for their ideas on how bus services on key routes could be improved (Robinson, 2019). Schemes should be seen as creating choice, making buses the better way into town centres, and not being anti-car.

As well as faster, more reliable services, the whole route treatment approach should ideally comprise new vehicles, greater comfort, enhanced passenger information and marketing (King, 1998b). 'People-moving' capacity measurements need to be developed to demonstrate that more use of buses and less use of cars can increase the 'people-moving' capacity of roads. A radical approach is necessary from highway authorities, who need to provide truly comprehensive priority for buses. A total route approach should be developed in the same way as a new tram system, but at a fraction of the cost, with the aim of achieving 'I can't tell this bus from a tram' (King, 1998b)!

The 'people moving' concept is best illustrated by looking at commuting by road into central London over many years. Whilst vehicle capacity had increased from 1950 to 1993, 37 per cent fewer people were moved, and were subject to longer and unreliable journey times. See Table 11.1.

A recent example of bus lanes combined with other improvements, in this case new vehicles, is in Belfast, Northern Ireland. Lengthy bus lanes have included, since March 2019, motorway bus lanes, offering journey time savings of up to 15 minutes compared with car travel (Local Transport Today, 2019b).

Another feature of upgrading an entire route is balancing traffic control. Bus priority often focuses on specific locations rather than an entire route, and excess capacity at some locations leads to overloads at more restricted capacity sections. So, queue relocation and overall traffic control needs imposing over the entire route, which will require a much greater input from traffic signal control experts.

The Liverpool City Region Combined Authority is planning a programme to improve bus corridors, called a 'Green Bus Routes' programme. The aim will be to '...transform core commuter corridors with measures including bus priority and enhanced customer facilities' (Local Transport Today, 2019c). It is unclear if the programme will include bus lanes, as they were suspended in 2013. Similarly, Transport for the West Midlands is proposing two 'SPRINT bus rapid transit' corridors featuring numerous improvements, including bus priority measures and enhanced shelter infrastructure at bus stops (Local Transport Today, 2019d).

TfL's latest Business Plan for 2019/20 to 2023/24 includes the encouraging statement that it will: '...improve journey times and reliability by investing in bus priority measures' (TfL, 2019c). However, there are then two discouraging statements:

- It notes that to meet the Mayor's 2041 target of 80 per cent of all journeys by sustainable methods, bus patronage will need to increase by 40 per cent, then goes on to say 'This is in the face of recent trends, whereby increased congestion, particularly in central London, has led to declining speeds and contributed to falling demand'.

Table 11.1 Number of commuters by road into central London

Mode	1950	1993	% change
Bus	260,000	64,000	−77
Car	110,000	150,000	+36
Cycle	34,000	41,000	+21
TOTAL	**404,000**	**255,000**	**−37**

SOURCE King, 1998b

- Instead of whole route treatments, bus priority will be mainly '...smaller-scale interventions, such as minor changes to road layouts, extensions of bus lane operating hours and enhanced bus priority at signals, which can deliver significant benefits'.

It is very disappointing that bus speed has been allowed to fall, and that bus priority measures are going to be small-scale.

CASE STUDY   Crawley Fastway Scheme

This is a prime example of a complete package of features, covering infrastructure, vehicles and support facilities, which has enabled a dependable, high-quality local bus service to be provided.
  The key aspects are:

- a combination of guided busways and dedicated bus lanes along two core routes linking the communities and traffic objectives of Horley (Surrey), Gatwick Airport and Crawley (West Sussex);

- the ability to avoid congestion hotspots and offer faster journeys and a reliable alternative to car travel, especially for workers and passengers at Gatwick Airport;

- satellite technology providing real-time information on bus location for passengers and at stops, and giving priority to buses at junctions;

- CCTV cameras, improving passenger safety and driver awareness;

- low-floor access for mobility impaired passengers;

- environmentally-friendly, low-emission, low-noise, low-vibration buses.

The benefits and returns on this investment has produced the following outcomes:

- a £4.67 economic return for every £1 spent;

- passenger numbers increasing by 160 per cent over 10 years;

- journey times reduced by an average of 9.5 minutes;

- reliability maintained at 90–95 per cent against scheduled timings;

- passenger satisfaction found to be at over 90 per cent;

- a 19 per cent reduction in overall traffic levels between 2006 and 2013 (KPMG, 2015).

CASE STUDY   Leeds

Journeys into Leeds on one of the city's busiest commuter routes are quicker and easier following the opening of 4km of bus lanes on the Kirkstall Road. Initial monitoring showed bus user satisfaction with journey time and service reliability rose 60 per cent and 44 per cent respectively.

The improvements to the bus route mean more people have chosen to use public transport – initial surveys showed patronage up 9 per cent with further increases expected. As buses are segregated from general traffic, journeys are more convenient for car drivers at certain times of day. Lower road congestion has taken over a minute off morning peak journeys, a large reduction given the length of the bus lane.

Cyclists are permitted to use the bus lanes, contributing to a 33 per cent rise in cycle trips on the road. Six new crossings built as part of the scheme are also making the road safer for pedestrians. Changes to traffic signals are expected to deliver further benefits for all traffic (Urban Transport Group, 2014).

Traffic signals

Signal priority schemes enable buses to get a green light earlier than they would without priority. The feasibility of bus detection was proved by a Demonstration Project in 1985 in Leicester and Derby (Department of the Environment, 1985). Delays to buses were reduced, as was the range of bus journey times. And an experiment at seven junctions in Hounslow, London, in the early 1980s found that bus journey times through the junctions fell by an average of 10 seconds per bus per junction (Traffic Control Systems Unit, 1987).

Schemes may use one or more of the following methods (Imperial College London, 2017):

- early green phase (red phase cut short) – signal turns green earlier than normal when a bus approaches the red signal;
- green phase extension – extended when a bus approaches;
- phase insertion – special signal phase added on or inserted into the normal signal phase;

- special public transport phase – special signal only for buses, eg for a bus lane or bus-only turn signal;
- phase rotation – changing the sequence of signals to benefit buses.

Over 30 per cent of London's traffic signals have bus priority, although only 5 per cent of the bus network has, no doubt reflecting that much of London is suburban with lower congestion than the centre (Imperial College London, 2017). Studies in London show that, on average, each bus travelling through 'bus priority signals' saves at least two seconds (Imperial College London, 2017).

Bus stops

These are often forgotten in the bus priorities mix – but are the crucial interface between people and buses. As Chapter 17 notes, they are the shop windows for a bus route. In past highway and traffic schemes, bus stops have sometimes been moved further away from junctions and passenger objectives in order to minimize disruption to other road users. A route audit is a good opportunity to rectify this and generally review location and spacing.

As well as location, a good bus stop environment should be part of any bus priority scheme. The aims should be:

- step-free access by accurate docking at raised kerbs;
- ensuring the bus can pull in and align itself properly;
- providing information in a user-friendly format;
- comfort – shelter and seating, security.

Transport for London's (TfL's) Accessible Bus Stop Design Guidance is a valuable guide to establishing a good bus stop environment and covers location, waiting area, shelter, boarders, bays, cage markings, lighting, and kerb profiles and heights (TfL, 2017). Of London's 19,500 bus stops 13,400 (69 per cent) now have shelters (Londonist, 2019). Bus boarders are 'build-outs' from the existing kerb line and provide a convenient platform for boarding and alighting passengers. They are implemented where parking separates traffic from the kerb, reducing how far a bus must deviate to enter a bus cage.

There has been much innovation when it comes to securing level access onto buses. Before low-floor buses were considered feasible, the Swedish town of Halmstad began, in 1979, to build platforms at stops to the height of the town's buses (Wood, 1998). The Kassel kerb was tested in the German town of Kassel in the 1990s. It forms a seamless, gap-free join between low-floor vehicles and stops, and by 2001 about 16 per cent of stops in the town had been converted. It is now used in 1,200 towns and cities in Europe (ribaproductselector.com, 2019).

Birmingham provides a good example of enhancing bus routes in 1996/97 with better stops. Other features were bus lanes, bus stop clearways, Kassel kerbs, and priority at signals. As well as shelters at stops, selected ones had real-time passenger information, a bus boarder, and specially designed seats for young children. There was a 27 per cent increase in passengers (Wood, 1998). A more recent example is Middlesbrough Council's proposal in 2019 for 'superstops': enclosed stops offering improved waiting facilities, CCTV, wi-fi, new seating and electronic journey time information (Local Transport Today, 2019e).

Effects and benefits

These can be summed up as follows, for both passengers and bus operators. A study by London Transport in 1988 found that the value of the passenger benefits was about three to four times the operating benefits (London Transport, 1990):

- Faster journey times including less waiting time.

- More consistent, regular journey time reliability/punctuality.

- Higher patronage and revenue – four Quality Bus Corridors in Dublin, Eire, resulted in an average passenger increase of 61 per cent in the peak and 25 per cent off peak (Imperial College London, 2017).

- Greater passenger satisfaction from more attractive, better-quality service.

- Reduced operating costs – whole route treatments and the saving of a few seconds at numerous locations can build up to a saving of several minutes per bus journey over an entire route. This could mean fewer buses and drivers needed over the course of a day; alternatively, a higher frequency could be operated with the same number of buses and drivers, especially if patronage has risen.

- Emissions reduction – over half of London's nitrogen oxide is emitted by road transport: 24 per cent of that comes from diesel cars, 12 per cent from petrol cars, 21 per cent from heavy goods vehicles, 12 per cent vans and minibuses, 4 per cent from taxis and 26 per cent from buses (Greater London Authority, 2013). In cities outside London, the proportion of emissions from diesel and petrol cars is greater. So, in Manchester for example, 43 per cent of emissions come from cars and 11 per cent from buses (Greater Manchester Combined Authority, 2016).

- Fuel use savings.
- Less stress on drivers – bus driving has been found to be one of the three most stressful jobs, leading to health and other problems (Owen, 1998). Less stress on drivers means less stress on vehicles – engines, gearboxes, drive-shafts and suspension.

Benefits can be enhanced if bus services are improved not just by priority measures, but also in other ways, such as new buses and improved information and fare deals. There are also wider benefits:

- Safety – New York's better traffic management including bus priorities has seen a reduction in crashes of about 20 per cent (Imperial College London, 2017).
- Local planning – in Dublin, the benefits from bus priority meant that local authorities could plan higher density developments with reduced car parking; and in New York, bus priority helped to increase retail activity along a bus corridor (Imperial College London, 2017). In Barcelona, improved journey times from a neighbourhood to the city centre brought it within half an hour (Imperial College London, 2017). Where the planning process for major developments allows financial contributions towards public transport, it presents an opportunity for implementing bus priorities at the same time as the development.

Associated measures

There are many things that complement bus priority measures and contribute to encouraging greater use of public transport and more attractive services. Some have been covered above and include – congestion charge, workplace parking levy, London's Red Routes, information displays on buses and at stops, and bus tracking. Other measures include car parking charges, on-street parking enforcement, CCTV for traffic enforcement with automated vehicle registration number recognition, environmental improvements to the street-scene, and contributing to local economies.

An interesting example in London of how cutting traffic can speed up buses was a one-day taxi strike in 1967. Vehicles travelling through London's West End fell by 20–30 per cent. This increased bus speeds by 25 per cent in the afternoon, and by over 30 per cent in the evening peak period.

CASE STUDY   Chorlton, Greater Manchester

The Chorlton bus priority scheme acted as the catalyst for developing a district centre with better trading conditions, improved traffic flow and a safer, more pleasant environment. The project included installing bus lanes on the approach to Chorlton and 'built-out' bus stops to enable easier boarding and prevent buses being blocked by traffic.

At the same time, more formal arrangements for parking were introduced, along with revised traffic routeing and new pedestrian crossings. As planned, the overall package removed conflicts between pedestrians, cyclists, parking and loading activity and vehicles. In addition, redirection of cars onto strategic routes rather than travelling through the district centre meant less traffic in Chorlton and quicker journeys. Built-out bus stops meant more space for roadside parking bays and loading facilities.

All users of the street benefited. Morning peak bus journeys became five minutes faster, the number of passengers boarding buses grew by 23 per cent and congestion fell. Better crossings saw pedestrian flows across junctions increase by 7 per cent – which, along with improved parking and loading, created a more attractive shopping destination. The well-planned arrangements meant initial concerns expressed during consultation over the impact of the scheme on traffic flow did not materialize in practice.

Transport for Greater Manchester uses similar holistic approaches across its Quality Bus Corridor Programme (Urban Transport Group, 2014).

CASE STUDY   Rochester, Kent

A new bus lane on the main road into the town provided the opportunity to reduce a central reservation and increase public space on the side of the street. Trees were planted, new paving laid, guardrails removed and LED street lighting installed for the first time on a road of this type in the UK. The street-scene enhancements meant proposals for the 480-metre bus lane created minimal public objection.

Peak bus journeys through sections of Rochester are now 40 per cent faster, providing convenient access to employment and new housing across Medway. General traffic flow has also benefited, as the bus stop is now within the bus lane rather than on the road, and National Cycle Route One was improved as part of the works. In addition, the bus lane means emergency services can by-pass traffic queues at peak times.

'On the back of the bus priority scheme we were able to redesign the streetscape, creating a range of transport improvements, attractive public space and a more appropriate gateway to historic Rochester,' said David Bond, Transport Operations Manager at Medway Council (Urban Transport Group, 2014).

Conclusions

Buses need to operate as efficiently as possible and be attractive to use. And buses are very efficient users of road space in terms of 'people movement'; also of fuel. So, if buses suffer from traffic congestion, slow speeds, and are irregular and unreliable, they will be unattractive to use and costly to operate. Giving buses priority can help considerably. This has been proven for over 50 years now, ever since they were gradually introduced from the 1960s. London led the way in the UK, but did lag behind some world cities in the 1970s and 1980s.

The case for bus priority has got much stronger for environmental reasons. London and many parts of the UK have had illegal levels of air pollution since 2010, and the Government's declaration in 2019 of a 'climate change emergency' is another extremely powerful policy lever for urgent action to discourage car use and encourage public transport use. Buses are an excellent short-term way of increasing capacity on public transport. It is most encouraging that the Scottish Parliament is legislating to achieve net zero greenhouse gas emissions by 2045, five years ahead of the rest of the UK, and a £500 million bus priority fund has been pledged, to start in 2020/21 (Local Transport Today, 2019f).

There is no doubt that the abolition of the Greater London Council and metropolitan councils in 1986 slowed down the implementation of bus priorities. However, this soon changed with various initiatives – in London, a London Bus Priority Initiative group was established in 1990, followed by Red Routes in 1991; and then a Bus Priority Team within Transport for

London in 2002, and the central London congestion charge in 2003. There was also a workplace parking levy introduced in Nottingham in 2012. At last, traffic congestion hindering bus operation and attractive services was being seriously addressed.

Bus priority has clearly served as a key transport intervention in keeping people moving in London, facilitating the city's growth. The introduction of congestion charging brought about the opportunity to make step changes in the operation of London's bus network, with a renewed emphasis on the movement of people rather than vehicles.

Bus priorities take many forms – with flow and contra flow lanes, bus-only streets, busways and guided buses, bus gates, turn exemptions at junctions, bus stop location and environment, and traffic signals. But the approach commonly used since about 2005 is 'whole route treatment', a real holistic approach. This addresses many concerns, eg the needs of traffic, businesses, pedestrians, cyclists, information provision and marketing. It goes down well with communities and offers better travel choices, especially if new buses with greater comfort feature.

Many benefits flow from the implementation of bus priority measures, especially from a whole route approach. Bus operators can benefit from faster journey times, more passengers and hence revenue, lower emissions and fuel use, better driving conditions and lower operating costs. Passengers can benefit from more reliable and attractive services, quicker journeys including less waiting time at stops.

Wider benefits, depending on the mix of measures included, could be improved safety, more retail activity, environmental enhancements and acting as a catalyst for development/regeneration schemes. Car parking charges and parking enforcement will also play a role in discouraging car use and encouraging bus use. So bus priority is increasingly featuring as an ingredient in various planning and transportation activities. This is where the future of bus priority is going – not least because of climate change and the urgent need to eliminate carbon emissions.

There is a strong case now for a National Bus Strategy to harness and support all the many benefits that increased bus use could bring. This is discussed in Chapter 2. Certainly, the Government should incentivize local authorities more to work with bus operators to secure faster bus speeds and reduce unreliability, and undertake route/corridor audits, setting targets to speed up bus journey times (CPT, 2019). A strong call for such a strategy has also come in 2019 from the House of Commons Transport Committee in a report on Bus Services in England outside London (House of Commons Transport Committee, 2019). Specifically, on bus priority, it recommends:

[T]he Government should review the evidence for the effectiveness of bus priority measures across England, with a view to demonstrating the value of these measures in reducing congestion and increasing bus speeds. Local authorities must have the evidence base they need to give bus priority measures proper consideration.

It goes on to say:

Local authorities can act to improve reliability through bus priority measures, but the value for money of any such investment would be increased if accompanied by measures to reduce car use and encourage modal shift, and if the Government acted to stop the cost of public transport rising relative to the cost of motoring.

Finally, it was surprised that the DfT's guidance on bus priority measures dates back to 1997!

The DfT has responded positively to the Transport Committee's recommendations: 'As well as providing local authorities with funding to invest in bus priority measures, the government will refresh the department's guidance.' (DfT, 2019b). And all within a new National Bus Strategy for England. In February 2020 the DfT set out its plans for such a strategy, though the 2020 COVID-19 pandemic since then may well delay its progress (DfT, 2020).

So clear messages are at last coming to the fore – more bus priority, within a National Bus Strategy (such strategies already exist for roads and railways), and along with discouragements to car travel. Air pollution and climate change demand a fresh, strong action. Huge challenges lie ahead, and no other mode is better equipped to deal with increased travel demand in the short term than the bus – as long as local authorities assist.

As a researcher and writer concluded in 1991: 'By giving buses special treatment and separating them from the rest of traffic, the cities of the world have nothing to lose but their private cars' (Zuckerman, 1991).

References

Adams, M (1990) *Capital Killer: Air Pollution from Road Vehicles: An LBA Research Report*, London Boroughs Association

American Public Transportation Association (2007) [accessed 4 October 2019] 2007 Public Transportation Fact Book, *APTA* [online] www.apta.com/wp-content/uploads/Resources/resources/statistics/Documents/FactBook/APTA_2007_Fact_Book.pdf (archived at https://perma.cc/HC53-KMHK)

AMTUIR (2019) [accessed 4 October 2019] Les zones bleues et les couloirs pour autobus, *AMTUIR* [online] https://amtuir.org/06_htu_bus_100_ans/oa_1961_1970/oa_1961_1970.htm (archived at https://perma.cc/5B4N-6F8P)

Armitage, G H (1979) *Central Area Transport Infrastructure*, Paper 8 at Urban Planning and Public Transport Conference RTPI/CIT/TRRL University of Nottingham 22–23 March 1979

Barker, T (1990) *Moving Millions: A Pictorial History of London Transport*, London Transport Museum

BBC (2003) [accessed 4 October 2019] *Spotlight on Durham's charge*, BBC [online] news.bbc.co.uk/1/hi/england/2721545.stm (archived at https://perma.cc/9TS7-BXT7)

Begg, D (2017) *Improving Air Quality in Towns and Cities: Why buses are an integral part of the solution*, Greener Journeys

Brownfield, J and Devenport, J (1989) *Road Safety Issues for the Design of Bus Priority Schemes*, Transport and Road Research Laboratory

Buchanan, M (1990) *Urban Transport Trends and Possibilities*, Oxford University's Transport Studies Group

Bus Rapid Transit UK (2019) [accessed 4 October 2019] The history of BRT in the UK, *Bus Rapid Transit UK* [online] www.brtuk.com/brt-in-the-uk/ (archived at https://perma.cc/D4NU-X5XW)

Bushell, C (ed) (1990) *Jane's Urban Transport Systems*, Jane's Information Group Ltd

Butcher, L (2010) [accessed 16 September 2019] Buses: bus lanes and priority measures, *UK Parliament* [online] https://researchbriefings.files.parliament.uk/documents/SN00032/SN00032.pdf (archived at https://perma.cc/EZ7R-HEJR)

Cambridgeshire County Council (2019) [accessed 4 October 2019] The Busway, *The Busway* [online] https://thebusway.info/ (archived at https://perma.cc/H8JA-22SD)

Campaign for Better Transport (2019) [accessed 17 September 2019] A winning policy: Nottingham's Workplace Parking Levy, *Campaign for Better Transport* [online] https://bettertransport.org.uk/blog/better-transport/winning-policy-nottinghams-workplace-parking-levy (archived at https://perma.cc/DN9R-XVN7)

Carrington, D (2018) [accessed 18 September 2019] London reaches legal air pollution limits just one month into the new year, *The Guardian* [online] www.theguardian.com/uk-news/2018/jan/30/london-reaches-legal-air-pollution-limit-just-one-month-into-the-new-year (archived at https://perma.cc/YMZ5-UMS3)

Collins, M F and Pharoah, T (1974) *Transport Organisation in a Great City*, London School of Economics/George Allen & Unwin

Confederation of Passenger Transport UK [online] www.cpt-uk.org/ (archived at https://perma.cc/3JCL-9WM4)

Cool Earth (2019) [accessed 4 October 2019] IPCC Global Warming Special Report 2018, What does it actually mean?, *Cool Earth* [online] www.coolearth.org/2018/10/ipcc-report-2/ (archived at https://perma.cc/PS89-VAKN)

Department of the Environment (1985) *Bus Priorities at Traffic Control Signals*, Bus Demonstration Project Summary Report No. 1, Bus Detection

Department of the Environment, Food and Rural Affairs (2015) *Air Pollution in the UK 2014*, London

DfT (2004) *Bus Priority: The Way Ahead*, London

DfT (2019a) *Annual bus statistics: England 2017/18*, London

DfT (2019b) *A Better Deal for Bus Users*, London

DfT (2020) [accessed 20 July 2020] *A Better Deal for Bus Users*, [online] https://www.gov.uk/government/publications/a-better-deal-for-bus-users/a-better-deal-for-bus-users (archived at https://perma.cc/57K3-ADLA)

DfT, Local Government and the Regions, Scottish Office and Welsh Office (1997) *Keep Buses Moving A Guide to Traffic Management to Assist Buses in Urban Areas: Local Transport Note 1/97*, The Stationery Office, London

DoT (1987) *Pedestrian Zones: Getting the Right Balance: Local Transport Note 1/87*, HM Stationery Office, London

DoT (1989) *Making Way for Cyclists: Local Transport Note*, HM Stationery Office, London

DoT (1992) *Traffic Management and Parking Guidance, Local Authority Circular 5/92*, HM Stationery Office, London

European Environment Bureau (1992) *European Transport: The Environmental Challenge*, proceedings of a seminar, Zoological Society of London Conference Rooms, 29–30 October 1992

Gardner, K *et al* (2006) [accessed 16 September 2019] The Benefits of Bus Priority Within the Central London Congestion Charging Zone, *Massachusetts Institute of Technology* [online] web.mit.edu/11.951/oldstuff/albacete/Other_Documents/Europe%20Transport%20Conference/traffic_engineering_an/the_benefits_of_bu1329.pdf (archived at https://perma.cc/2S4Q-H7TF)

Greater London Authority (2013) [accessed 26 February 2020] London Atmospheric Emissions Inventory (LAEI) 2013, *Greater London Authority* [online] http://data.london.gov.uk/dataset/london-atmospheric-emissions-inventory-2013 (archived at https://perma.cc/T9RJ-7L88)

Greater London Council (1983) *Working for Better Transport*, London

Greater Manchester Combined Authority (2016) [accessed 26 February 2020] Greater Manchester Low-Emission Strategy, *Greater Manchester Combined Authority* [online] www.greater.manchester-ca.gov.uk/media/1276/low-emission-dec-2026.pdf (archived at https://perma.cc/2LBE-NLNT)

Greener Journeys (2017) *Tackling Pollution and Congestion: Why congestion must be reduced if air quality is to improve*, London

HM Stationery Office (1963) Publication covering transport statistics

House of Commons Transport Committee (2019) [accessed 19 September 2019] Bus services in England outside London, Ninth Report of Session 2017–19, *UK*

Parliament [online] https://publications.parliament.uk/pa/cm201719/cmselect/cmtrans/1425/1425.pdf (archived at https://perma.cc/7HXN-PKSG)

Hurdle, D (1990) *The Scope for Bus Priorities in London*, London Boroughs Association

Hurdle, D (1993) *All Aboard! Attractive Public Transport for London*, London Boroughs Association

Hurdle, D (1996) *All Change, The Association of London Government's Sustainable Transport Strategy for London*, draft

Imperial College London (2017) [accessed 16 September 2019] The identification and management of bus priority schemes, a study of international experiences and best practice, *Railway and Transport Strategy Centre* [online] www.imperial.ac.uk/media/imperial-college/research-centres-and-groups/centre-for-transport-studies/rtsc/The-Identification-and-Management-of-Bus-Priority-Schemes–RTSC-April-2017_ISBN-978-1-5262-0693-0.pdf (archived at https://perma.cc/VNC6-SVAU)

Intergovernmental Panel on Climate Change (2018) [accessed 14 February 2020] Special Report, Global Warming of 1.5°C, *IPCC* [online] www.ipcc.ch/sr15/ (archived at https://perma.cc/EDM8-NYXK)

King, N (1998a) *Roads as 'People Movers' – The Real Case for Bus Priority*, PTRC European Transport Conference, Loughborough University, 14–18 September 1998

King, N (1998b) *Physical Measures: Techniques and Innovative Systems*, PTRC course

KPMG (2015) [accessed 14 February 2020] An economic evaluation of local bus infrastructure schemes, *Greener Journeys* [online] https://greenerjourneys.com/wp-content/uploads/2015/09/Ex-Post-Evaluation-of-Bus-Infrastructure-June-2017.pdf (archived at https://perma.cc/Z5GP-6LWB)

Local Transport Today (2019a) [accessed 14 February 2020] Workplace parking levy for Scotland, *TransportXtra* [online] www.transportxtra.com/publications/local-transport-today/news/61331/workplace-parking-levy-for-scotland/ (archived at https://perma.cc/7YLG-CSSN)

Local Transport Today (2019b) [accessed 14 February 2020] Glider drives Northern Ireland public transport growth, *TransportXtra* [online] www.transportxtra.com/publications/local-transport-today/news/62280/glider-drives-northern-ireland-public-transport-growth (archived at https://perma.cc/HB5B-TC5V)

Local Transport Today (2019c) [accessed 14 February 2020] Liverpool CA prepares bus investment plan, *TransportXtra* [online] www.transportxtra.com/publications/local-transport-today/news/61364/liverpool-ca-prepares-bus-investment-plan (archived at https://perma.cc/5TD5-ULXZ)

Local Transport Today (2019d) [accessed 14 February 2020] Enhanced Partnership drawn up for TfWM's Sprint corridors, *TransportXtra* [online] www.transportxtra.com/publications/local-transport-today/news/62647/enhanced-partnership-drawn-up-for-tfwm-s-sprint-corridors (archived at https://perma.cc/Z926-N234)

Local Transport Today (2019e) [accessed 14 February 2020] Town plans bus 'superstops', *TransportXtra* [online] www.transportxtra.com/publications/local-transport-today/news/62281/town-plans-bus-superstops- (archived at https://perma.cc/RM5T-RWTV)

Local Transport Today (2019f) [accessed 14 February 2020] Scots pledge £500m for bus priority, and zero CO_2 railway, *TransportXtra* [online] www.transportxtra.com/publications/local-transport-today/news/62213/scots-pledge-500m-for-bus-priority-and-zero-co2-railway (archived at https://perma.cc/9BJW-9X2G)

London Transport (1990) Green Light for London's Buses, London Lines

Londonist (2019) [accessed 18 September 2019] How Many Bus Stops Are There In London? *Londonist* [online] https://londonist.com/2016/06/7-amazing-facts-about-london-s-bus-stops (archived at https://perma.cc/G6HQ-E7S9)

Mayor of London (2001) *Mayor's Transport Strategy 2001*

Mayor of London (2010) *Mayor's Transport Strategy 2010*

Mayor of London (2018) *Mayor's Transport Strategy 2018*

Metropolitan Transport Research Unit (1991) *Green Routes*, Report on Bus Priority

National Bus Company (1978) *Bus Priority Schemes Research Report No 19*, Marketing and Operational Research Department

Owen, J (1998) *How Bus Priorities Benefit Operators/Quality Partnerships – An Operator's View*, PTRC

Paton, G (2019) [accessed 14 February 2020] Heathrow congestion charge is expected to raise £1.2bn a year, *The Times* [online] www.thetimes.co.uk/article/heathrow-congestion-charge-is-expected-to-raise-1-2bn-a-year-wv9qn2c36 (archived at https://perma.cc/4YJQ-GMJF)

Quilter-Pinner, H and Laybourn-Langton, L (2016) *Lethal & Illegal: London's Air Pollution Crisis*, Institute for Public Policy Research

ribaproductselector.com (2019) [accessed 4 October 2019] Kassel Kerb, *ribaproductselector.com* [online] www.ribaproductselector.com/Product.aspx?ci=6218&pr=BrettLandscaping-KasselKerb (archived at https://perma.cc/5R3P-AT68)

Robinson, L (2019) [accessed 14 October 2019] Bus Services in the North of England – the case for a long term investment strategy, *Transport Times* [online] www.transporttimes.co.uk/news.php/Bus-Services-in-the-North-of-England-the-case-for-a-long-term-investment-strategy-460/ (archived at https://perma.cc/R3FW-QULP)

Spachis, C (nd) [accessed 16 September 2019] Delivery of bus priority projects – A partnership approach, *Atkins* [online] www.atkinsglobal.com/~/media/Files/A/Atkins-Corporate/group/sectors-documents/roads/library-docs/technical-journal-4/delivery-of-bus-priority-projects-a-partnership-approach.pdf (archived at https://perma.cc/86XS-LN58)

TEST (1987) *Buses in Shopping Areas*

TfL (2017) [accessed 18 September 2019] Accessible Bus Stop Design Guidance, *TfL* [online] http://content.tfl.gov.uk/bus-stop-design-guidance.pdf (archived at https://perma.cc/XJ9V-LC7N)

TfL (2019a) [accessed 7 November 2019] Rules of Red Routes, *TfL* [online] https://tfl.gov.uk/modes/driving/red-routes/rules-of-red-routes?intcmp=2192 (archived at https://perma.cc/2VUP-W9RF)

TfL (2019b) [accessed 10 September 2019] Motorcycles in bus lanes, *TfL* [online] https://tfl.gov.uk/modes/driving/red-routes/rules-of-red-routes/bus-lanes/ motorcycles-in-bus-lanes (archived at https://perma.cc/3YD4-8V9A)

TfL (2019c) Freedom of Information request, responses received 9 and 14 October 2019

The Times (1940) *Road Traffic in London Separate Route for Cars*

Thunberg, G (2019) *No one is too small to make a difference*, Penguin Books

Trades Union Congress (1990) *Transport for the 1990s*

Traffic Control Systems Unit (1987) *Traffic Control Programme for London 1988–89*

Traffic Director for London (1993) *Network Plan*

Urban Transport Group (2014) [accessed 18 September 2019] Bus priority in practice, benefiting towns and cities across the country, *Urban Transport Group* [online] www.urbantransportgroup.org/system/files/general-docs/pteg%20 bus%20priority%20brochure%20June%202014_FINAL.pdf (archived at https://perma.cc/S8XZ-D2KM)

Wood, C (1998) *Bus Stop Innovation: A Comparison of UK Trials*, PTRC, European Transport Conference 14–18 September 1998, Loughborough

Wood, K and Smith, R (1993) [accessed 14 February 2020] Assessment of the Pilot Priority (Red) Route in London, *TRL* [online] https://trl.co.uk/reports/PR31 (archived at https://perma.cc/2YZL-NWVY)

Zuckerman, W (1991) *End of the Road, The World Car Crisis and How We can Solve It*, The Lutterworth Press, Cambridge

Further reading

TfL (2019d) [accessed 18 September 2019] Business Plan 2019/20 to 2023/24, *TfL* [online] http://content.tfl.gov.uk/tfl-business-plan-2019-24.pdf (archived at https://perma.cc/FVX2-AHTE)

Planning and operating a rural bus service

12

BEN COLSON

Introduction

This chapter is about operating rural bus services. There is a growing view that keeping such routes alive is important for the wellbeing of the communities they serve, and an equally strongly held view that the way to provide transport (we now call it connectivity) for such areas is demand responsive transport (DRT) schemes.

Actually, DRT is probably not the best answer, and the reasons for this as well as alternative models with the potential to be more successful will be examined. How to measure potential demand, how to assess revenue and cost, the economics of rural bus services, elasticity of demand, fares and ticketing, operating arrangements, marketing and promotion and how to explore new market opportunities will all be considered.

First, we have to understand what is meant by the over-used word 'rural'.

What we mean by rural

Rural is an adjective meaning 'in, relating to, or characteristic of the countryside rather than the town' (Lexico, 2019). The problem is that it is binary; what is not the town must be the countryside, and therefore rural. In the last century some villages have grown into dormitories of nearby towns and cities and have lost those essential characteristics which would be described as 'countryside'; that is continuing unabated in this century, too. Examples are many, especially in the less constrained topography of the South East of England, but Kidlington, north of Oxford, is probably one of the best early examples.

In 2011 the UK government introduced Rural Urban Classifications into official statistics. This was revised and updated in 2015, and again in 2016 (Department for Environment, Food and Rural Affairs, 2016). Areas are defined as rural if they are 'outside settlements with more than 10,000 resident population'. This is better, but still lacks clarity; how is a village classified when it is so close to a town with a population greater than that, yet still has characteristics of a rural village?

The 2011 census subdivides this broad definition into six categories used to define rural (for urban areas there are four categories). These are 'town and fringe', 'villages' and 'hamlets and isolated dwellings', all of which are grouped in 'sparse' and 'not sparse' areas. Those settlements defined as 'in a sparse setting' reflect where the wider area is remotely populated. We probably all know what that means, even though it is not defined – it is something you feel about a place.

Some towns are then defined as 'hub towns', which meet statistical criteria to be considered hubs for services and businesses serving a wider rural hinterland, and their populations are considered effectively as rural in character. Hub towns have a population of above 10,000, but below 30,000. There are many such examples of smaller towns throughout the UK. As towns and surrounding commuter villages have grown, so they have ceased to be classified as hub towns as they now exceed the upper population limit, and in fact since the 2001 census, the number of people living in areas classified rural has, artificially, decreased.

In this chapter, the broader sparse and non-sparse definition will be used to apply to rural areas and associated hub towns, even if their population has grown such that they have been drawn up into the next official category, as in respect of transport connectivity, they retain the all-important role as centres for travel to work, to education, to retail, to access higher order healthcare, and to entertainment from the surrounding countryside.

How to measure demand

Demand for bus travel is a proportion of the demand for all travel in an area. It is a function of the population of the relevant area (not just a single community) and distance from the hub town. The closer to the town, the greater the demand, because everyday, rather than just occasionally used, facilities are located there, and bus travel offers greater relative advantages over using a car.

The relative proximity of competing hub towns is important. An area which is linked to just one hub will experience a high degree of association with it, aggregating demand and making the bus a more economically viable option. By contrast, where an area is surrounded by a number of hub towns, then demand is dissipated, and no matter what share of any one specific market the bus can attain, total demand will be lower and probably not viable. This is most evident where a set of communities look towards one hub town in every respect but the local education authority has allocated secondary school places in another. In this example two buses are required, one for journeys to work in the main hub and a second for students, whereas if education was provided in the same hub then transport resource and cost could be lowered as well as a more attractive link being provided for the whole community.

This relativity is important. The main hub town may be further away and yet, because it is the major centre, despite distance, draw a greater proportion of travel from the area of origin. However, the smaller hubs, because they are less distant, can draw a proportionately greater number of residents from the area of origin because journey time and cost is lower.

Understanding this dynamic is key to estimating potential demand. Take as an example a series of rural communities with a total population of one thousand. If there is only one hub town, no matter the distance, there is only one place to which those rural residents will travel. If, however, there are three, other things being equal, 330 will travel to each. That figure will be influenced either way by the range of facilities offered and distance to travel. However, what is evident is that if bus can attract a market share of typically 3 per cent to 5 per cent, then the bus potential from a one thousand population is just some 10 to 15 passengers, whereas the same population served only by one hub town will deliver 30 to 50 passengers. This greatly impacts the viability of a bus link and its attractiveness. Widespread adoption of the car, encouraging edge of town retail and hospital facilities – effectively secondary hubs – has significantly lessened the attractiveness of using the bus as a primary means of travel. There is evidence that, perhaps oddly, larger villages support fewer bus services than others simply because of this.

There is a further, spatial, factor. Rural England is topographically diverse. Population dispersal is very different in lowland compared with upland Britain.

Thus upland locations with an overall lower population density can produce better transport connectivity than higher population densities in lowland Britain, because a higher proportion of the overall lower population in upland areas is located in valley bottoms where localized densities are much higher, making those people more easily accessed by relatively direct buses. By contrast, population in areas more widely spread and with localized lower densities, makes those people less easily accessed except by meandering buses with high relative journey times and therefore lower levels of attractiveness. Cumbria exhibits the upland characteristic, and Cambridgeshire the lowland – interestingly, both have largely withdrawn financial support for bus services.

The ability to attract sufficient custom is also dependent upon the attractiveness of the product on offer. Slow, meandering buses may be the way to provide a safety-net lifeline, but is not the way to attract new users, especially younger ones with their much higher expectations. Thus, an industry which consistently scores exceptionally well on passenger satisfaction is losing its customer base.

Making a bus route attractive yet viable (whether measured socially or financially) necessitates creating routes from communities to their hub town which are relatively direct, and yet which access sufficient population for that 3 per cent to 5 per cent market share rule to still deliver sufficient use.

Assessing revenue and cost

There is a fundamental difference between urban and rural buses. Whilst urban ones are essentially engaged in delivering benefits to the local economy, rural ones are as much, if not more, about delivering social benefits to the community. Urban buses move large numbers of people to and from work and other activity in a way which the car could never do because of the demand it would place on available road space (and, increasingly, the revolt against the harmful impacts on air quality).

By comparison, rural buses tend to have more to do with ensuring students get to school and college, people have a chance to visit essential shops or hospital appointments. These are the outcomes of a more socially necessary product, and there is growing evidence that their reduction can lead to social isolation and loneliness and, especially in younger adults, translating into mental health issues.

Thus rural buses are as important as urban ones, just in a different way. Nonetheless, under the current legislation they are treated no differently from urban buses, and there is a growing body of opinion now questioning that wisdom. What is essential, however, is that there is an understanding of how to assess revenue and cost, and how both change as a result of changing volumes of output or demand. To do this, and throughout this chapter, I have created a theoretical route with a Monday to Friday bus to the major of three hub towns, the other two more local than the major one as follows. In fact, it is roughly based on the bus route from Docking to King's Lynn in Norfolk (see Table 12.1).

All but two journeys serve distinct market purposes:

- 07.30 journey to work, college, school;
- 09.30 journey to shops and health;
- 12.35 journey from shops and health;
- 13.30 journey to shops and health;
- 16.00 journey from shops, health, college, school;
- 17.45 journey from work.

To succeed, rural bus routes have to be designed to specifically meet a range of market purposes. In the above, cost could be saved – but revenue lost – if any one of the five market purposes was omitted. The key is to determine whether each is, at the margin, viable or not.

In this example, the total catchment area population is 1,500, and with three hub towns the theoretical maximum market size is 500. However, being the major town hub including the only college and hospital, it should attract a larger proportion, so say a maximum market size of 600. Applying the 3 per cent to 5 per cent bus market share indicates the likely bus market, across the entire day, will be some 25 residents travelling to and then from the hub town, so making a trip total of 50 per day.

Intuitively, just fifty passengers across eight journeys a day is a non-starter measured by financial viability, but a different picture may emerge if measured socially.

Table 12.1

Depart time from rural start point	07.30	09.30	13.30	16.50
Arrival time at major hub town centre	08.30	10.20	14.20	17.40
Depart time from major hub town centre	08.35	12.35	16.00	17.45
Arrival time at rural start point	09.25	13.25	16.50	18.35

Assessing revenue

Revenue earned is the number of people attracted to buy a ticket at the fare charged. The offer has to be attractive, but so too the fare. If the route is meandering and clocks up extra miles, it is not going to attract custom by up-pricing because of those extra miles. It may be counter-intuitive, but the better approach is to reduce the price to compensate potential users for the inconvenience of the meander.

On the route above, if all passengers pay full fare and there are no frequent traveller discounts, or for younger people, and no free pass scheme, then 50 passengers at the average fare paid will be the income earned. On this route the average fare is £4, so that indicates a daily maximum potential income of £200. However, this is not achievable. Lower fares for under 16s, return tickets priced at a discount, and especially the formula approach to concessionary (free) travel reimbursement all serve to reduce this gross income. Reimbursement for free travel is based on a national formula which produces varying results, averaging about 45 per cent of the average adult fare being reimbursed.

On this route, if 25 per cent of passengers are paying a discounted adult rate of £3.50, 25 per cent the child (half) rate, and the other 50 per cent are free pass-holders, then the total income earned per day is reduced from that £200 to just £112. This is the nub of the rural bus problem; a high proportion of those travelling will be using free bus passes or student fares and to derive sufficient income from them it is necessary to so boost the adult fare that that group is priced off the bus and into cars (or becoming isolated with the impacts associated with that).

Assessing the likely revenue derived from a route is an essential management responsibility and has to be approached realistically, rather than in a starry-eyed way. That is not to deny the importance of spotting new opportunities, or innovation and experimentation and more imaginative promotion, all of which will be covered later in the chapter.

After discussing costs generally, and specific to this route, we'll look at measures to reduce the gap between social and financial viability.

Assessing cost

The cost of operating a bus is relatively inelastic. This is because costs are increasingly determined by external forces: labour costs are a function of employment law and local labour market conditions, fuel costs a function of buying power and consumption (itself a determinant of vehicle size and type and local operating conditions), and maintenance costs a function as much of regulatory compliance as of wear and tear on units. Operators trading in the same area are active in the same labour market, they face the same fuel consumption issues and work within the same regulatory compliance regime. Where cost does vary is in the buying power of different operators and their productivity. Larger operators have greater buying power, smaller ones tend to achieve better productivity.

Driver costs

Providing drivers is individually the greatest cost factor, accounting for some 55 per cent of total cost. Rates of pay and conditions are broadly comparable between operators active in the same market, the result of a competitive labour market. That costs have risen significantly this century is less a result of staff wage rate increases but more as a result of family-friendly employment law, including longer maternity and paternity leave, pension payments and the European Social Chapter, all levelling up total labour costs towards what was historically the higher-cost employers.

As a simple rule of thumb, to the labour rate per hour a premium of some 25 per cent to 30 per cent needs now to be added to cover these additional costs, including cover for paid holiday and sickness.

Fuel costs

Much lower as a proportion of total cost at about 10 per cent, there is not much variance between fuel cost as a result of ownership. It is a fact, however, that at this early stage of their use, Euro 6 vehicles are proving more fuel efficient than earlier Euro standards, but there is as yet no full-life experience. However, larger operators can negotiate better prices and hedge their fuel costs. Hedging enables them to hold short- to medium-term fixed prices, offering benefits of certainty and stability, but later they pay the higher price, and at time of fuel price increases this creates a false sense of viability.

Alternative forms of energy, such as hybrid, electric, hydrogen, etc are all significantly more expensive and are not yet viable in urban areas, so not an alternative for rural routes where their earning capability is so much more constrained. This will potentially become a growing issue when early models are due to be cascaded from cities into the provinces.

Maintenance costs

The third major area of cost is maintenance, accounting for about 20 per cent of total cost. As a rule of thumb, some 50 per cent of materials and labour cost is a function of regulatory standards and requirements and the balance of wear and tear. The latter can be reduced through a policy of low average vehicle age, with a higher proportion therefore operated under warranty, however this is less of an option in rural areas unless the more modern vehicle can be used as a marketing tool to attract more custom – an issue which will be addressed later.

Allocating one driver to each vehicle brings reduced maintenance costs, but at the expense of vehicle productivity. It is not generally clear that the maintenance cost benefit outweighs the loss of productivity. A good compromise is to group drivers by vehicle type, so that they are accustomed to the dimensions, capability and quirks of 'their' type.

Insurance costs

Accounting for about 5 per cent of total cost, insurance costs are probably the most variable from one year to another, but generally in an upward direction only. Vehicles must be insured and the public liability element is usually fairly standard across different local authorities. Longer-term better deals are to be had by remaining loyal to one broker and underwriter combination, although short-term cost reductions accrue from constantly shifting supplier.

Larger operators self-insure, in which they put aside sufficient funds to pay accepted claims, only buying catastrophe insurance from the market in order to fund major incident payouts. Smaller operators have to submit to the market more frequently for their entire insurance need, and are thus more susceptible to changes in what is a volatile market.

Overhead recovery and profit

The foregoing indicates that about 10 per cent of total cost is available for overhead recovery and profit. Overhead includes office, management, IT, marketing and promotion, as well as other incidental costs such as vehicle licences. Generally, the overhead incurred arises from management decisions, and the lower the overhead, the greater the profit margin available.

Profit should be regarded as just a cost on the business. It is why businesses exist. Paying a shareholder for their input is essentially the same as paying a member of staff for theirs. There may be arguments as to how profit should be allocated, but it is essential that there is frequent investment in fleet renewal and upgrade, and product research and development. Modelling indicates that more than 10 per cent is required to achieve these essentials and still provide a fair dividend; currently few operators are making that sort of return on rural operations, and 6 per cent is a more realistic figure.

Putting all these figures to the test

Using the example route, with the bus being taken empty from the depot in the morning and back in the evening, the driver is working 12.5 hours a day. There may be an unpaid break, usually of no more than one hour, so 11.5 hours of cost. At a labour rate of £10 per hour, and providing 30 per cent add-on, total driver cost per day is £150 per day.

The route is 18 miles in length (13 on the empty journeys), so the bus operates 170 miles daily. At 15 miles per gallon it requires 11.33 gallons or 51.5 litres per day. After netting off VAT (which is reclaimed) and Bus Service Operators Grant (assuming it is a commercial, rather than contracted, route), fuel costs £34 per day.

Maintenance costs will depend on vehicle age, but midlife materials and labour amount to £9,000 per annum, or £36 per day. Insurance costs are £27 per day.

Total direct costs are therefore £247 per day. With overhead and profit recovery, this amounts to £262 per day. This contrasts with income of £112 per day, and a commercial business would not engage. A local authority might, on the basis of social viability – they generally measure the subsidy (£150 per day) required per passenger, so £3 per passenger trip.

Measures to improve performance

Demand-responsive transport (DRT)

Government policy makers and local authorities tend to the view that DRT is the way to provide rural connectivity and transport. The evidence is that it is not, yet policy still denies the evidence.

In June 2016, Transport Focus issued *Demand Responsive Transport: users' views on pre-booked community buses and shared taxis* (Transport Focus, 2016). It partnered with Hampshire, Suffolk and Worcestershire to look at different models of DRT. It concluded: '[V]aluable lessons can be learned about "on demand" services and we urge all decision makers to use this research as a starting point when considering the future of local passenger transport services'. It is regrettable that few local authorities have done so because the first finding is that: '[W]hilst there are overall cost savings to be made by introducing DRT there can be a significant reduction in the number of passengers when conventional services are withdrawn'.

What's more: '[T]here was consistently low awareness of DRT amongst the potential users', and when the facility was explained to them: '[Y]ounger people tend to view the service as geared for the elderly and disabled.' In effect, then, younger adults disassociate themselves from using DRT, and that can lead to their isolation and loneliness.

Two examples in Suffolk were examined in detail. In Wilford (the coastal area north of Felixstowe running as far north as Aldeburgh), when introduced in 2011/12, 8,678 passenger trips were made. Two years later, the cost had risen by some 7 per cent but the number of passengers had fallen by 20 per cent to 6,944. In the other, in the Breckland area of the county, the annual subsidy per passenger on the conventional service was £1.69 but the fall-off in passengers was so great that two years later it had risen to £21.66. This was partly because of a reorganization of commercial routes in the area.

Transport Focus concluded:

Potential users appear to be put off by the unpredictability of journey length and arrival time, particularly where they are making time-critical trips. Younger people tend to... make assumptions that journeys will be long and around the houses with frequent [long] stops.

Why these results and comments? A number of factors combine, including that – legally – free bus passes are not accepted on DRT, although an individual local authority can decide to do so. Then there is the inflexibility – it has to be booked in advance, and that involves making a phone call, which may be a considerable difficulty where there is no signal. Also there is the inflexibility of having to go out, and return, when the bus will be available, there is no choice.

Users did comment that, despite these disadvantages, compared with the conventional bus, the system was better than having nothing. But to be attractive and to fulfil its essential community importance, transport connectivity is not about providing the last resort.

DRT, like community transport, has enjoyed the benefit of a lower level of regulation, and lower regulatory costs. In 2017 the government unexpectedly started the process of removing this benefit, forcing the cost of providing these services up to close to the level of a full-sized conventional bus. That legislative and regulatory change was still ongoing in late 2019.

As will be seen below, smaller vehicles are cheaper to operate, and DRT has that benefit. If the driver is paid, as opposed to an unpaid volunteer (which will no longer generally be possible under the new regulations), then the only cost saving is fuel, and as has been seen this is a small part of the total cost anyway.

Lincolnshire's Call Connect services maybe show the best way forward. Some – but not all – run to semi-fixed routes and at pre-advertised times. The only on-demand element is to divert short distances off route to pick up pre-booked passengers with mobility issues; otherwise users congregate at points along the standard route with confidence that the bus will arrive. It means that Call Connect services do just that – connect with main road interurban buses to major hub towns at the smaller more local ones. Experience indicates that most variations of route are on return journeys from the hub town, understandable because that is when people are more likely to be laden with shopping or at the end of the working day. The system is more predictable like an ordinary bus, yet it is more responsive, and the number of those needing to book in advance is reduced to just those who really need that facility.

Using elasticity of demand

Understanding some key elasticities of demand at work in the local bus business is essential to improving performance. Elasticity of demand measures just that – how dependent demand is on any one of a range of the product features. In the case of local buses, it may be the frequency at which the bus is provided, the journey time, the fare charged and other criteria such as the attractiveness of waiting facilities.

All of these will impact demand. The higher the fare, the lower the demand – that is an inverse elasticity. The lower the frequency, the lower the demand – that is a direct elasticity. Possibly the feature most in the operator's gift is journey time – another inverse elasticity as the more meandering the route, the higher the time, so the lower attractiveness leads to lower demand. Product management requires detailed boarding point data, for if some can be sensibly eliminated so that the bus follows more closely the route a car driver would take, then the greater the likelihood of transfer from the car. Research in The Netherlands has indicated that if the bus can replicate the car journey within a one-third longer journey time, then that will create modal transfer to bus. That does not mean that it is directly applicable here, but it is probably so.

As social attitudes and personal expectations change, so elasticities change with them. There is evidence, for example, in city regions that slower buses are not necessarily undesirable if seating is comfortable with adequate leg room, and with USB, charging points and free wi-fi.

Fare elasticity of demand is perhaps the most significant, and has changed considerably in recent years, especially as a slice of the market has been removed from charging due to free concessionary travel. This has caused elasticity to rise from –0.2 or –0.3 to –0.5 or even –0.6. This means there is an inverse relationship, and for every 10 per cent the fare is increased above inflation it is now more likely to lead to a 5 per cent or 6 per cent reduction in passenger numbers over time; some years ago, it would have been a 2 per cent or 3 per cent reduction.

Frequency elasticity of demand is another simple key elasticity to understand. As frequency is increased, so that will itself attract more custom, a positive relationship. For every 10 per cent increase in frequency, a 3 per cent increase in custom will materialize over time.

All these elasticities work equally in reverse.

Using pricing levers

Demand is not uniform, and therefore a uniform set of fares is not appropriate. Income is a measure of the interaction of fares charged and the number of people attracted at that fare. It may be that discounting fares heavily at peak times will fill otherwise empty seats at those times of day, similarly between the peak times, although in practice it is not unusual for rural inter-peak buses to be busier than at peak and not appropriate for discounting. Besides, the reimbursement for free travel is based on a percentage of the adult fare, and discounting inappropriately can seriously jeopardize that income source.

To the customer the acceptable price of a ticket is increasingly based on the time taken to complete the journey, rather than the mileage the bus has travelled. As a simple rule, the younger the adult, the more important that time is compared with distance. As also indicated, the negative impact of a longer journey time can be offset by product factors such as seating comfort, USB and wi-fi access, but that is dependent upon wider digital connectivity.

In rural areas in particular, with longer average journey lengths to and from the hub town, an important factor in determining the fare is whether or not inter-peak customers would be able to visit the hub town, conclude their business, and return home in time for lunch (or vice versa in the afternoon). If this is not possible, then for them, the total trip cost will rise by the cost of lunch, so the bus fare element needs to be lower to take account of this.

Integration with school routes

Central Government calls this 'total transport', and has been running 37 trials in rural parts of England since 2015 (Department for Transport, 2019). The trials went beyond just integrating school journeys. In fact, in most rural areas these are already well integrated, and involve routeing or changing the times of a local bus service to accommodate the needs of specific school transport provision.

The above trials looked at integrating transport services commissioned by different central and local government agencies and provided by different operators, thus allowing existing resources to be allocated and coordinated more efficiently, resulting in more effective services to passengers. The sort of services were non-emergency patient transport provided by the NHS and clinical commissioning groups, home to school, and adult social care transport provided by local authorities. The results were mixed, with no 'one size fits all' solution.

The 1944 Education Act changed schooling from being local for the entire experience and split it into primary and secondary, with the latter being located more centrally, especially impacting rural areas. The Act set down then (and is still broadly applicable) that an under-11 (primary) pupil can be expected to walk up to two miles to and from school but for longer distances free transport must be provided. For over-11 (secondary) students, the distance is three miles. This has broken down to an extent as a result of parental choice and academy schools.

The sparser the area, the higher the number of school buses required, because school catchment areas are larger, but the greater is the demand for smaller vehicles.

Procuring a school bus commands a much higher competitive price, and if it can be cleverly incorporated within the local bus network, the improvement to the route's viability is both significant and positive. In the example route, if a secondary school is located midway such that the 08.35 departure from the hub town can pick students up in villages en route, and an extra journey is provided to take them home at (say) 15.30, then that could command an additional competitively bid income of maybe £200 per school day against a marginal cost of as little as £30 per day for the extra marginal afternoon trip. This price commutes to £150 per all year Monday to Friday, giving a net added value of some £120 per day. This cuts the daily loss of £150 to £30 and the subsidy per passenger trip from £3 to just 60p per passenger (assuming the students are not added to the passenger count).

The right size of vehicle

A frequent criticism of buses in rural areas is that they are oversized for the number of passengers carried. There is considerable truth in that, but even if there is a sound economic reason (such as peak loads which require the larger capacity), it looks and feels wrong for excessively large vehicles travelling country lanes with a handful of passengers.

The cost of providing a bus service is, in part, a function of the size of vehicle. The smaller the bus the lower the fuel consumption, and, of less significance, the less the body damage. Costs used for our route are based on a standard smaller sized vehicle (33 seats), but of course there are larger and smaller options available. To make a meaningful comparison a five-year-old vehicle is assumed, although there has to be caution as to the maintenance cost of the 21-seater version shown because it has not been on the market for that length of time. All figures shown are £ per day, assuming it is used five days a week (see Table 12.2).

That some of the daily depreciation costs are higher for the smaller vehicles arises from them being depreciated over fewer years, being lighter-weight

Table 12.2

	Double decker	Large single decker	Small single decker	21 seater	16 seater
Capital cost (depreciation)	50.00	39.50	44.50	47.50	47.00
Maintenance cost (incl labour)	39.50	37.50	35.50	30.00	24.00
Fuel cost for 170 miles per day excl VAT and BSOG	64.00	46.50	34.00	25.50	20.50
Insurance cost	29.50	27.00	27.00	24.00	22.00
Total vehicle cost	183.00	150.50	141.00	127.00	113.50

vehicles. However, the table does show that the smaller ones, assuming no capacity issues, have lower operation cost.

On our example route the £30 loss based on a small single decker would reduce to £16 for a 21-seater, which actually is the type of vehicle generally used on the route. If a 16-seater could be used, the route would effectively break even.

Vehicle and driver productivity

Whilst conventional wisdom is to compare revenue and cost by route, the approach taken here is to base it on the whole cost of operating the vehicle for a day and aim to recover that. It matters not from where the revenue comes, so long as it meets the total cost of operating the bus.

Thus anything over and above the core route (or school contract) can be provided at the margin. It is important to understand the difference between what economists call short-run and long-run marginal cost, and simplistically it is to ensure that the extra work is marginal in the long run, so that it will cover capital (vehicle replacement) costs.

On our route, the driver is on duty for 11.5 hours if operated from the rural starting point as described below, which means two hours of non-driving time is required to be legally compliant. Both driver and bus have some two hours non-productive time additional to this requirement, all during middle of the day 'shopping' times. There is thus an opportunity to interwork another route such that one with lower demand is added to the schedule, but only if revenue earned exceeds marginal cost. Of course, the extra journeys could be on the same route as the core, if there is sufficient potential demand.

As a general rule of thumb, it is essential that each bus deployed in a rural area provides for two morning and two afternoon peak passenger flows (to work, to college, to school) and at least two shopping routes during the day. If not, viability is impaired.

Operating arrangements

Having implemented straightforward ways of improving performance to minimize losses on the route, to make it socially viable insofar as community funding is concerned, and progressively we have reduced the financial loss from £150 per day (£3 per passenger trip) to £16 per day (32p per passenger trip). The ideal is to eradicate that loss altogether, or squeeze it to the lowest possible level.

Two further measures are possible. One is to base the bus at the rural starting point for the route, as this reduces both driver time (the greatest of all costs) and fuel used. The timetable for our route could be worked from a base at the outer end and this would reduce driver cost by one hour per day and fuel costs by 26 miles. The one hour of driver time saved will reduce the cost by £13. Based on the 21-seat vehicle, the cost of fuel will reduce by £4. Total cost saving of £17, reducing the financial loss from £16 per day to effectively breakeven.

The second is to deploy the same driver and bus each day of the week. This provides customers with confidence and certainty and, whilst there is no science to it, it is known to enhance loyalty – because it is loyalty to the individual driver, rather than the less-visible operator – and greater loyalty translates into more passengers as existing ones become the ambassador, the promoter, of the service. On top of all the other proposed measures, this would add a trickle of extra passenger trips, boosting the route from breakeven to financial viability.

Taking ownership is an important psychological facet. In the case of the actual route used for the example, the local transport authority – the county council – declined to fund the route at all, although did pursue the total transport approach to integrate as much school transport as it could. It was the parish councils which covered the losses for the first two years of service whilst the customer base was being established. They took ownership – that should be welcomed by the operator – and they promoted it through their own local outlets. It is a bit like a community rail partnership, some of which have done marvels for rural lines and stations, but at a much more grassroots level and in a less formal, structured, way. Perhaps this could include maintaining and brightening up shelters and delivering information, for example.

Building the business base: marketing and promotion

Any product needs marketing and promotion to become and stay successful. The bus is no different, and the rural bus likewise. The importance lies in understanding the way marketing and promotion work differently in rural compared with urban areas.

There are two key differences. Firstly, generally neighbours know each other in rural areas and there is a stronger sense of community, and secondly, many areas are still without adequate broadband to enable full digital access to information. These two combine to make conventional, urban-based, marketing and promotional styles inappropriate in the countryside. It is not to deny the benefit of digital promotion to attract potential out of area custom, or for where local pockets of better connectivity exist, rather that should not be the primary means of promotion.

The smaller and more isolated the community, the greater the sense of community and belonging, and this provides a rich vein of opportunity to get the message out. Whether it be parish councils, the Women's Institute, pubs, social clubs, local stores or the village newsletter or magazine, all of these are ideal outlets. The cost of advertising in village magazines is incredibly low, and putting money into the community in this way is always positive. It is essential that all these outlets are used, not only to advertise and announce changes to the bus's route, timetable or fares, but rather on a routine basis simply to keep the message fresh in residents' minds.

Wherever it is, people will want to buy a product which oozes relevance and success. The fact that it may only be necessary for a minibus to be used is not the same as assuming that 'any old van will do'. Put at its most basic, just because they live in the countryside, paying passengers don't want or expect to have to wipe the seats before they sit down. They, and especially younger adults, have expectations just as their city cousins do. That a bus is small should not take away from the basic requirements of clear destination information on the front, easy access, attractive moquette, cleanliness, and nowadays wi-fi and USB as standard.

Building the revenue base: seeking new opportunities

Any product left to its own devices will follow what marketeers call the product lifecycle, in which customer numbers grow, then plateau, then start to decline. A good business will always be seeking to refresh its products, and that does not necessarily mean constant timetable changes; it could be adding wi-fi to the vehicle or something like that.

New business opportunities will arise from new housing development, new or changed local businesses (rural businesses are remarkably stable, with new start ups at a higher rate than in urban areas) and new or changed generators of demand in the hub town to which the bus route runs.

Being aware of all of these is essential business management. Being a genuine part of the local community will open channels of information to keep managers abreast of opportunities, as will a regular route-based driver. It therefore 'pays dividends' to have these in place and well established on each and every rural route.

Conclusions

Rural bus routes are in danger of disappearing, but that doesn't need to be so. The foregoing sets out a theoretical route of 18 miles length – although actually based on a real example – and shows how the finances of a no-hoper can be made to come so close to breakeven that most authorities would want to retain it because of the social value it adds to the communities it serves.

The measures described are a mixture of revenue increases and cost reductions, all of which are both achievable and do not require the withdrawal of even the most marginal of journeys. Cutting back a service only serves to undermine the total route performance because of the impact on market purpose.

The future of rural routes may lie in the hands of their operators but it seems that increasingly communities will have a say in their own connectivity, possibly through networks negotiated under the terms of the 2017 Bus Services Act. This offers a great opportunity for regeneration so long as they are viewed as an asset, part of the infrastructure, rather than just a life-line safety net for those otherwise vulnerable from transport poverty.

References

Department for Environment, Food and Rural Affairs (2016) [accessed 6 December 2019] Rural Urban Classification, *GOV.UK* [online] www.gov.uk/government/collections/rural-urban-classification (archived at https://perma.cc/MP8S-HHQ4)

DfT (2019) *Total Transport*, feasibility report and pilot review

Lexico (2019) [accessed 6 December 2019] Definition of rural, *Lexico* [online] www.lexico.com/en/definition/rural (archived at https://perma.cc/9LZW-BG8C)

Transport Focus (2016) *Demand Responsive Transport, users' views on pre-booked community buses and shared taxis*

Further partnerships between bus operators, local authorities and employers

13

DAVID HURDLE

Introduction

This chapter explains mainly the concept of Travel Plans, a way of minimizing 'drive-alone' car use and maximizing sustainable travel. These plans have been undertaken since 1995 by any organization whose site generates travel, such as a hospital, school, housing development, or offices. They are often secured by local planning authorities when granting planning permissions for developments.

Buses can be an important element of a Travel Plan, because of a variety of actions they can provide such as improved services, fare deals, information/promotion and facilities at bus stops. But the key to their success is bus operators, local authorities and employers working together in partnership.

Types of partnership

There are many different types of partnership, such as voluntary ones between an operator and local business; for example, it is quite common to find certain journeys of a bus route extended to a business park or diverted to a school or college. Then there are formal agreements using bus legislation, which are covered in Chapter 3.

Since 1995 another type of partnership has developed, in the shape of a Travel Plan. This is a strategy for managing the travel generated by a site. It aims to combat over-dependency on cars by boosting alternatives to 'drive-alone' car use. The site can be anything from a doctors' surgery to a school, hospital, offices, place of worship, or anything that people travel to. The reasoning is that if more people walk, cycle, use public transport, car-share and work at home, there will be less traffic congestion, parking pressures, air pollution and carbon dioxide emissions; and improvements in health and wellbeing, staff recruitment and retention, and general sustainability.

Figure 13.1 shows some of the benefits to employers of a Travel Plan, and how they are linked.

Figure 13.1   Benefits of Travel Plan ingredients

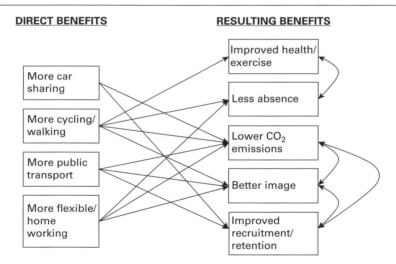

Benefits of Travel Plan ingredients

Travel Plans can be of two types:

- Voluntary: where businesses want to address their environmental ethics, improve their public image and contribute to corporate policies on, for example, carbon reduction.

- Formal: where a local planning authority may require a Travel Plan when granting planning permission for new or expanding developments.

Guidance on Travel Plans first emerged in 1995, and as central government policy in 1998. For the next ten years various guidance and details of case studies were published. Between 2001 and 2006 the government ran a 'TransportEnergy BestPractice' programme whereby businesses could receive five days of free advice from a consultant on creating a Travel Plan.

One of the key messages from travel planning guidance was that of partnership working – the need for employers' Travel Plans to be bolstered by the involvement of local authorities and public transport operators. At the end of the day an employer may identify many actions to take to achieve more sustainable travel to its site. But only some of the actions will be direct ones that it can take, such as distributing and displaying public transport information and subsidizing bus fares. It will be dependent on local authority actions, from minimizing traffic congestion to seats and shelters at the nearest bus stops, and on the local bus operators for improved services and possible fare deals for its staff.

There is no better illustration of Travel Plan partnership working than at Addenbrooke's Hospital, Cambridge. Here is a list of all their partners, including other on-site businesses (Cambridge University Hospitals NHS Foundation Trust, 2014):

On-site partners include:

- Cambridge University Hospitals NHS Foundation Trust (Lead);
- Addenbrooke's Charitable Trust;
- AstraZeneca;
- Cambridgeshire & Peterborough NHS Foundation Trust;
- Cambridge Regional College;
- Cancer Research UK;
- East of England Ambulance NHS Trust;

- GlaxoSmithKline Plc;
- Key Health (Addenbrooke's) Limited;
- Kids Unlimited;
- John Laing Plc;
- Medical Research Council;
- NHS Blood and Transplant;
- Papworth Hospital NHS Foundation Trust;
- Sanctuary Housing;
- University of Cambridge.

Community and operational partners include:

- Cambridge Cycling Campaign;
- Cambridge City Council;
- Cambridgeshire County Council;
- Countryside and Liberty Property Trust;
- Cross Country Trains;
- First Capital Connect;
- Freedom Travel;
- Go Whippet;
- Greater Anglian Trains;
- C G Myall & Son;
- Richmond's Coaches;
- Stagecoach East;
- Stansted Express;
- Sustrans;
- Travel for Work Partnership.

The remainder of this chapter discusses the growth of travel planning, outlines some of the main pieces of guidance, explains how bus operators' actions can be key ingredients of Travel Plans, and cites good examples. It ends with a checklist of 55 actions that employers, bus operators and local authorities can take.

Growth of travel planning and bus operators' roles

Nottingham led the way with Travel Plans in 1995, then called Green Commuter Plans. A resource pack specifically for the city's employers was published by Nottingham City Council, Nottingham County Council, Nottingham Green Partnership and the Transport 2000 Trust. The resource pack explained that the Partnership had been launched by the City Council in 1991 and comprised businesses, voluntary groups, the city's two universities and the public sector 'to establish through co-operative effort a comprehensive and practical approach to addressing environmental issues in Nottingham' (Nottingham Green Partnership, 1995). It is worth noting that the city is still well advanced in tackling transport issues, with a light rail system and the first example in the UK of a workplace parking levy. The light rail system opened in 2005 and was extended in 2015; it is now 20 miles (32km) with 51 stations.

Nottingham's resource pack for employers contained several public transport initiatives. These included:

- a park and ride season ticket scheme;
- discount Travelcards for staff;
- bulk purchase of day rider tickets, for staff making occasional bus journeys;
- public transport information at workplaces: the county council provided free bus and rail route maps, the city council a Journey Planner with route maps, frequency guide and information about fare/ticket bargains;
- publicity for the county council's interactive public transport information terminals at key points throughout the city.

At the time, a good Nottingham example of a major employer promoting bus use was Boots (a large UK health and beauty retailer), which operated works buses, and also subsidized over 50 bus routes. It had been providing works buses since opening at its isolated site, three miles from the city centre, in 1933.

When expanding in 1995 the council secured a Travel Plan as part of the planning permission. Today the site comprises 300 acres with about 8,000 staff (including some of other employers). Boots became one of the first organizations in the UK to begin serious travel planning. Bus-related measures have included:

- on-site installation of bus shelters;
- information displayed in the canteen and on the intranet;
- off-site bus lanes installed by the Highways Agency.

A good example of increased bus use in the city was Nottingham City Hospital, which increased bus use by its staff from 11 per cent in 1997 to 19 per cent in 2000 (Department for Transport, 2002a). Together with non-bus measures, 'drive-alone' car use to the hospital fell from 72 per cent to 55 per cent, a significant achievement. The hospital, part of the Nottingham University Hospitals NHS Trust, continues to develop its Travel Plan, which is now a supporting document to its Sustainable Development Strategy 2018–23. The Trust's main bus measures can be summarized as follows (Nottingham University Hospitals NHS Trust, 2019):

- The Medilink Bus Service, funded in partnership with the City Council and Nottingham Community Transport. It provides a link between the hospital, the Queen's Medical Centre, and two park and ride sites, for staff and the public. It transports about 1 million passengers per year.
- Discount annual passes for staff, since 2015, offered by a pool of operators. As at July 2018, 1,111 such passes are held.
- Regular communication with their staff, especially new starters, on the existing facilities, services and schemes available for public transport travel.

A travel survey at the hospital in 2016 found 49 per cent of staff drove a car on their own to work, but, given the right conditions, 25 per cent of these 'drive-alone' staff would change their travel behavior (Nottingham University Hospitals NHS Trust, 2019).

Another good example at the time of partnership working with bus operators was Pfizer's site at Sandwich, Kent. Bus use increased from 7 per cent of staff in 1998 to 12 per cent in 2001 (DfT, 2002a). This was achieved by a free shuttle bus from the railway station and town centre, contract buses and enhancement of public bus services. Pfizer has since moved to Surrey, but still provides free shuttle buses from local towns and railway stations.

BP implemented a Travel Plan in 1999 at Sunbury-on-Thames, Surrey, following a planning agreement associated with a redevelopment of their site (DfT, 2002a). Bus and rail use by staff increased significantly with a shuttle bus from the railway station (see Figure 13.2), improved local bus services, bus priority measures, and information on a leaflet, the intranet and internet. The shuttle bus is still operating in 2019 (BP, 2019).

Figure 13.2 BP's shuttle bus for staff

Research about company buses show how well they are received by employees. The key characteristics tend to be:

- a relatively small vehicle;
- a comfortable, high-quality, air conditioned and carpeted vehicle;
- a feeling of being chauffeur-driven;
- the flexibility to pick up/set down close to home;
- the facility to pre-book by phone or online;
- availability for lunchtime shopping trips;
- if charging fares, then a discount for an initial period;
- connections with trains;
- friendly drivers;
- text messaging from driver if delayed;
- a roadshow for potential users.

Soon after Nottingham's resource pack for employers came Transport 2000's *Changing Journeys to Work, An employers' guide to green commuter plans*. It included a foreword from the then-Minister for Transport, the Rt Hon Dr Gavin Strang MP:

'Green commuter plans are one way in which organizations of all sizes, and in all sectors, can make a valuable and cost-effective contribution to achieving our aspirations'; and 'I believe that employers have a duty to their organizations and staff and to the wider community to ensure that the impact of their transport patterns on the environment is kept to a minimum' (Transport 2000 Trust, 1997).

The guide included many measures that could be taken to increase bus use, and it highlighted the importance of travel surveys for identifying how routes and timetables could be more closely tailored to the needs of staff. A travel survey is the essential base for any Travel Plan; not just to find out how people currently travel but also to ascertain what things might encourage them to travel differently.

The guide cites good examples of bus measures:

- Staff at Coca-Cola in west London not entitled to a company car were given free London Travelcards;
- Derriford Hospital staff in Plymouth got a Travel Pass offering 50 per cent discount on local buses;
- Body Shop offices in Littlehampton ran a shuttle bus from a nearby railway station;
- Hewlett-Packard cut a 20-minute walk to buses to five minutes by laying a footpath across its Bristol site and opening an unused entrance;
- BAA Heathrow and the nearby Stockley Park business park jointly invested in a new, fast bus service between Uxbridge, the business park and the airport.

The above examples demonstrate the range of actions that can increase bus use. But they also highlight the need for employers and bus operators to work together.

A big central government push on Travel Plans came in 1998 with the publication of a Transport White Paper. It recognized that:

'Major employers can play their part by preparing green commuter plans which help employees to use alternatives to driving to work alone'. The government committed to working '...with local authorities to help them secure widespread voluntary take-up of green transport plans through partnership with business and the wider community. Part of this will involve local authorities leading by example and setting targets in their local transport plans'. The government also committed to '...[taking] the lead by introducing green transport plans in all Government Departments and their agencies' (Department of the Environment, Transport and the Regions, 1998).

Finally, the White Paper stated: 'We would like to see all hospitals producing green transport plans'. In fact 126 Trusts had implemented Travel Plans by 2002/03 at 322 hospital sites out of 1,200, or 27 per cent of hospitals (DfT, 2004a).

Following the 1998 Transport White Paper the government published some General Information Reports under its energy efficiency programme. One, in 2000, was specifically aimed at public transport operators – *Travel Plans, New Business Opportunities for Public Transport Operators* (EnergyEfficiency BestPractice Programme, 2000). It listed both operator-led and partnership initiatives:

- improved marketing such as information displays in workplace, personalized timetables for individual staff and timetables on company intranets;
- presentations to staff;
- information packs;
- site-specific bus services or additional stops or detours;
- altering service times and frequencies to suit better staff working hours;
- financial incentives such as season ticket loans and bulk purchase of tickets for staff at a discount from operators;
- quality of waiting facilities at stops and walking to/from them.

The report stressed the benefits to operators of getting involved in Travel Plans. It said that many businesses have a limited knowledge of a bus operator's working environment and would welcome their ideas and inputs. It cited the benefits to operators as increased patronage, targeted publicity, new business opportunities and a higher local profile. New employees were a particular group worth targeting.

From 2000 Travel Plans began to take off; as well as plans being undertaken voluntarily, more planning authorities were securing them when granting planning permissions. Accordingly, the government published an extremely comprehensive *A Travel Plan Resource Pack for Employers* (TransportEnergy BestPractice Programme, 2002). Its aim was to assist organizations to make and implement a Travel Plan. It had a section on negotiating with bus operators, which stressed the need, before meeting operators, of employers being armed with the results of a staff travel survey, plus a site assessment that had identified any deficiencies such as the lack of seating, shelter and timetable provision at bus stops. It is also a good idea for an employer to have held some focus groups after a travel survey for discussing the results, getting ideas and demonstrating employer commitment.

Two new government publications appeared in 2002 which included some case studies – *Making Travel Plans Work* (DfT, 2002a) and *Using the Planning Process to Secure Travel Plans* (DfT, 2002b). Case studies can be useful to draw upon since they cite actual activity, what it cost and what the benefits were. For increasing bus use, the 20 case studies in *Making Travel Plans Work* cited the following success factors:

- company buses;
- discount fares;
- off-site infrastructure, eg bus priority measures by local authorities;
- improved service quality, eg new buses;
- new, more frequent services;
- convenient bus stops;
- better information on tickets and timetables.

School travel is a significant subject in itself but deserves a brief mention here. More sustainable travel to schools and School Travel Plans were addressed by the government in 2003 in *Travelling to School: a good practice guide* (Department for Education and Skills and DfT, 2003). Interestingly the biggest chapter was about encouraging bus use, whether by statutory school transport, the commercial bus network or dedicated school buses. It cited a key issue: 'The challenge is for schools, local transport and education authorities, and bus operators of different kinds to work together to increase the availability and attractiveness of bus services to a wider range of pupils'.

A further government Transport White Paper, in 2004, included a target for all UK schools to have Travel Plans by March 2010 (Department for Transport, 2004b). By then about 2,000 of England's 25,615 schools already had Travel Plans (Hurdle, 2004a), and about 1,200 workplaces did (Hurdle (2004b). Rather oddly, no target was set for the 'work run', a far greater problem than the 'school run' which only accounts for 10 per cent of traffic on urban roads between 08.00 and 09.00 (DfES and DfT, 2003).

Despite the 1998 government White Paper advocating that local authorities should have their own Travel Plan to lead by example, progress was slow. By 2001 the number of authorities in England and Wales implementing their own Travel Plans went up from 3 per cent to 24 per cent. However, a survey by the author in 2005 found, ironically, limited progress among shire districts; the very ones who were planning authorities and granting planning permissions requiring Travel Plans, so should be setting an example (Hurdle, 2005). It could be argued that it was hypocritical for a local planning authority to secure Travel Plans through the planning process when it had failed to implement its own exemplary one. The proportion of authorities implementing their own Travel Plan in 2005 was:

- shire districts: 53 per cent;
- counties: 95 per cent;
- English unitaries: 89 per cent;
- metropolitan boroughs: 86 per cent;
- London boroughs: 84 per cent;
- Welsh unitaries: 67 per cent.

In London, a survey by the Centre for Independent Transport Research in London found that only one of the capital's 33 local authorities had a Travel Plan, and only half were preparing one (Hurdle and Rajesparan, 1997). Only nine offered interest-free season ticket loans to staff, and only nine provided public transport information.

Ten years later, in 2007, London had its own Travel Plan guidance. Transport for London published *Encouraging sustainable commuting, A guide for London's local authorities in delivering effective Travel Plans*; it was prepared on behalf of Transport 2000 and funded jointly by both organizations (Hurdle, 2007). The three purposes were to encourage London's 33 authorities to secure Travel Plans through planning permissions; to actively encourage the take-up of voluntary ones; and to have their own plans in place, thus leading by example.

The guide included a survey of the 33 authorities' practices on Travel Plans; all 33 responded to the survey. Results were better than in the above 1997 survey. It found that:

- 19 offered their staff season ticket/Travelcard loans.
- 17 provided public transport information to their staff.

- 20 had a Travel Plan for themselves in place; nine had drafts they were developing, and four had not prepared one.

- Of six who had done 'before' and 'after' Travel Plan surveys, all reported increased bus use, particularly in inner London – 11 per cent of Camden's staff used buses before the Travel Plan, which went up to 18 per cent afterwards. In Southwark, it was 10 per cent before and 19 per cent after.

- 559 Travel Plans had been secured through the planning process, an average of 27 per responding authority.

- Some authorities had secured car-free housing through the emerging concept of Residential Travel Plans. This had been pioneered by Camden Council since 1997.

As already noted, data from a travel survey and a site audit are vital when preparing a Travel Plan. Indeed they are the base for one. This is confirmed in government guidance in 2008: *The Essential Guide to Travel Planning* (DfT, 2008); they are also 'a good basis for dialogue with public transport operators'. Company intranet sites are good places to put travel information, as long as the site is in regular use by staff as part of their work routine; printed information will still be necessary for staff not office-based, and for visitors.

Again the guidance supports these actions, as well as outlining the exemptions from tax and National Insurance for certain bus measures:

- works buses provided by the employer which have more than nine seats;

- public bus services subsidized by the employer, including free or discounted fares for staff, but only where the employer has a contract with the bus operator;

- passing on discounts for bulk-purchased tickets to employees;

- interest-free loans (up to £5,000 per year) to buy season tickets.

One has to ask whether the plethora of guidance about Travel Plans since 1995 was reaching bus operators, and were they taking notice? A survey by the author in 2003 of public transport operators in England found inconsistency (Hurdle, 2003).

Table 13.1 shows the survey results, from major bus groups and train operators.

Since then bus operators have certainly been more proactive. Typical measures are illustrated in the checklist on pages 234–41, drawn from many implemented Travel Plans.

Table 13.1 Survey of bus operators about Travel Plans

Question	Yes	Comments
Do you take the initiative and approach major employers, offering assistance with developing their Travel Plans?	10	One bus company advertises in local business publications
If not, do you assist if approached by an employer and/or local authority?	18	
Do you provide 'fare deals' for employees of businesses doing Travel Plans?	16	
If so, what type?		
(i) Discount seasons/passes bought in advance	13	One bus company offers a scheme of free travel to
(ii) Discount books of tickets bought in advance	4	employees in return for a negotiated payment from their
(iii) Discount upon showing photo ID	4	employer to pay for additional
(iv) Free 'try the bus/train' week, vouchers or similar	5	buses/drivers. One scheme in operation, another starting soon
Do you provide stocks of timetables, other material or information packs to businesses doing Travel Plans?	17	
Do you offer individual employees of a business tailored travel information for their journeys to/from work?	6	Some refer people to websites or Traveline
Do you provide notice boards/leaflet racks or other displays of information for workplaces?	7	
Do you brand any buses/trains with a business's name/logo?	3	Subsidy usually involved
Can you provide examples of:		
(i) New/extended/diverted/more frequent services or additional bus stops as a result of Travel Plans?	11	
(ii) Bespoke services just for employees of businesses doing Travel Plans?	5	
(iii) Participation with local authorities and businesses in commuter forums/travel clubs?	7	

(continued)

Table 13.1 (Continued)

Question	Yes	Comments
(iv) Talks/presentations given to employees in their workplaces?	9	
(v) Increased use of services as a result of Travel Plans?	7	Difficult to measure; often linked with service revisions. Travel surveys by businesses more useful
Do you have a specific person with responsibility for working with businesses on their Travel Plans?	8	
Do you have a copy of the publication in 2000 by the DfT's TransportEnergy Best Practice Programme (TEBPP) – *Travel Plans, New Business Opportunities for Public Transport Operators*?	5	
Do you have a copy of the DfT's *A Travel Plan Resource Pack for Employers*?	4	
Do you receive *Travel Plan News* published by TEBPP?	2	
What do you run?		
(i) Buses	15	
(ii) Trains	4	

SOURCE Hurdle, 2003

Travel Plan bus measures checklist

This checklist section begins with a few general comments before listing the sort of inputs that can be made by employers, bus operators and local authorities.

General comments

Before listing measures, some words of explanation. The checklist is broken down by the likely implementer, either an employer or bus operator; or local authority, of which there are usually three different levels. But some measures may be the responsibility of one of these in one area but another elsewhere, or may be addressed jointly. So partnerships will certainly come into play again. Indeed, this was stressed regarding information provision in some Department of Transport (DoT) guidance back in 1996, *Better Information for Bus Passengers, a Guide to Good Practice*. It states:

'Local authorities and operators need to work together to produce the best results'. And it notes that 'The (bus) industry has not always done enough to promote bus services and to think through a co-ordinated strategy for information provision. Spending on marketing as a proportion of turnover is far lower than in many comparable industries' (DoT, 1996).

Stagecoach's co-founder Brian Souter said at a conference in April 2004 that the industry had failed to spend enough time and energy on marketing (Transit, 2004). It does seem odd how little information about bus services comes through letter boxes yet every empty seat is a lost opportunity. The author remembers his boss at London Transport on his first day there, saying 'We are not in business to run buses. We are in business to carry passengers.'

The above guide, despite publishing in 1996, is still highly relevant as much of the advice is common sense; such as lists of departures at bus stops instead of full timetables. Another commonsense measure is for a list of destinations displayed at bus stations, which bus service goes there, and then which stop to walk to for the bus to that destination. But some readers will know of bus stations where this does not happen.

Worth noting in the guide is some research carried out in 1993/94 which revealed that despite the efforts of many authorities to publicize information, only a minority of people seem to know what is available, or who provides it (Transport and Travel Research, 1994). This was confirmed in 1998 by further research that found that 'Much of the information currently provided is very little used by the public, because they are unaware of it, cannot easily obtain it, or cannot understand it' (Balcombe and Vance, 1998). However, despite the above negativity there are some excellent examples of good information provision.

Let's explore publicity and promotion before looking at the contributions the various parties can make. Publicity provides and displays information whereas promotion relates to marketing, which can be more than just publicity. It is about encouraging use. And a golden rule of marketing is that you must have a good product to market! Unreliable, late-running buses are not worth promoting. Hence why local authorities need to 'pave the way' for buses. Indeed Section 18 of the Traffic Management Act of 2004, which applies to English Local Traffic Authorities, gives a Network

Management Duty to 'Where necessary … work with the relevant parties, including Traffic Commissioners and bus operators, in formulating and implementing improvement plans for bus punctuality' (DfT, 2004c). Operators should grasp this opportunity to work with their traffic authority and identify places where buses are delayed by traffic, parked cars (legally and illegally), delivery vehicles. Once operators have a good product they can promote it!

Let's look into local government, as they are becoming increasingly complex. In England there are metropolitan boroughs, London boroughs, unitaries, and (non-metropolitan) counties with districts; also parish/town councils. There are also Combined Authorities (eg Cambridgeshire and Peterborough, Manchester, Sheffield), some of whom have elected Mayors, which were created voluntarily; they allow a group of local authorities to pool appropriate responsibility and receive certain delegated functions from central government in order to deliver transport and economic policy more effectively over a wider area. In Wales there are city, county and county borough councils plus community councils; in Scotland there are unitaries plus community councils; and in Northern Ireland just district councils.

Finally, there seems to be inconsistency across the country in what is being implemented. As other chapters show there are success stories but they stand out rather than being the norm. Brighton is one such area where bus journeys increased 45 per cent between 1993 and 2003, an average increase of 5 per cent a year (DfT, 2004d). Partnership working played a big part along with high profile marketing and promotion.

Figure 13.3   Sign in hospital to buses

Employers' input

Employers can:

- Conduct a site audit, with local authority, of walking to/from stops, crossing types or lack of them, pavement conditions – width, obstacles, litter, parking on, landscaping; traffic – safety, proximity, speed, volume.

- Oversee waiting conditions at stops: seating, shelter, timetables, lighting, security, illegal parking.

- Give evidence to operators, making the case:
  o results from travel surveys and focus groups;
  o mapping of bus services and staff home postcodes – eg consider using Mapline to see how many staff live on and near bus services (Mapline, nd);
  o banding together with other local employers (strength in numbers).

- Highlight the benefits of the bus over car travel to staff:
  o they are able to relax, read and work;
  o it is often cheaper than the real cost of the same journey by car;
  o no need to find a parking space;
  o it represents a chance to socialize;
  o it's safer than car travel;
  o fewer cars on the roads aids bus travel;
  o it's good for health as more walking at each end of the journey;
  o there is less carbon dioxide emitted.

- Install on-site signs to stops, such as the example in Figure 13.3.

- Provide bespoke information. A good example was the *Public transport to Stepping Hill Hospital* leaflet by the Stockport NHS Foundation Trust, which featured frequencies/days of week for all services, journey times from places along the routes, walking times from local rail stations, a map showing bus stops in relation to departments/clinics and walking routes between them, information about different types of ticket, advice on how to get the leaflet in large print or on tape, and telephone enquiry numbers, including a service for textphone users. DfT's 2005 *Travel information leaflets for healthcare facilities* in 2005 is still relevant and applicable to other sites, and listed the following ideas for inclusion on public transport (DfT, 2005):
  o services to the site and the nearest stops;
  o services using low-floor, accessible buses;

- o nearest rail station(s) and train services;
- o whether services are accessible to the impaired;
- o bus services from the rail station including journey times and fares;
- o telephone enquiry numbers and websites for information;
- o location of 'real-time' information – at stops, in reception areas, on websites;
- o Dial-a-Ride, community transport schemes, patient transport and the reimbursement of transport costs.
- Provide prominent information displays in reception areas/canteens.
- Provide a travel office.
- Provide information in job application packs and at induction training.
- Offer season ticket loans.
- Encourage staff to arrange meetings to avoid peak hour travel.
- Provide public transport information in correspondence to visitors.
- Offer later appointments to visitors having to travel the furthest, so they can avoid morning peak period travel.
- Offer later appointments to older and disabled people so they can use their concessionary bus passes/railcards.
- Encourage public transport use for business travel.
- Publicize operators' improvements.
- Set up dialogue with local authority and operators on Travel Plan issues, eg traffic congestion.
- Explore running a company bus.
- Publicize actions in the local media.
- Participate in station travel plans, which are drawn up with various partners to secure more sustainable travel to/from railway stations.
- Link Travel Plans with other related corporate policies. Examples of policies to which Travel Plans should be linked are shown below. Such linkages will help to embed the Travel Plan in an organization's corporate policies and business objectives, and enhance the plan's status and commitment to it:
  - o corporate social responsibility;
  - o work–life balance;
  - o environmental management;

o occupational health, wellbeing;

o equal opportunities;

o 'Investors in People' accreditation;

o efficiency;

o health and safety;

o Comprehensive Performance Assessment.

Bus operators' input

Bus operators can:

- Offer fare deals. People love discounts; employees are no exception. Not surprisingly surveys of staff travel attitudes always show this to be a very attractive option. Discounted weekly, monthly, quarterly and annual tickets could be offered, and free 'taster' vouchers.

- Put on roadshows/presentations at workplaces.

- Reroute or extend service or certain journeys nearer to the site; aim to stop as close as possible. A good example is the Royal Marsden Hospital, Sutton, where buses enter the site via a bus and ambulance-only lane and stop right at the main entrance.

- Increase frequency.

- Extend peak period frequency, eg for hospital staff finishing a shift at 20.00.

- Extend a service terminating nearby.

- Retime existing journeys to fit working hours.

- Network with other employers; approach five largest in area/along bus corridors. Stagecoach Devon first became involved in Travel Plans in 1997 with Wonford Hospital, Exeter (Energy Saving Trust, 2005a). It found that Travel Plan agreements with employers helped to enhance its reputation, increase awareness of services and contribute to increased patronage and profits. It regarded Travel Plans as an opportunity to generate new business and retain a competitive edge, and worked in partnership to promote bus travel by discounts on annual tickets, information leaflets, 'taster tickets' and roadshows. The bus company also found that local business forums were an excellent way to establish links and build relationships.

- Use bus branding and flashes on stops.

- Provide easy-to-understand promotional material.
- Introduce one or more additional stops.
- Include a site as a timing point in timetables so people can immediately see the service goes there.
- Depict the National Rail symbol in timetables where buses serve stations. This symbol was introduced in 1999, is helpful to people and is also used on road signs.
- Publicize that fold-up bikes can be conveyed on buses.
- Provide, and publicize, real-time bus information on website.
- Provide modern buses with high-quality seating, free wi-fi and USB charging points.
- Participate in local communities, eg presentations to Chambers of Trade, working with transport campaign groups and schools, supporting local charities, attending stakeholder events, joining working groups for improving town centres and preparing Neighbourhood Plans.
- Set up a forum to get passengers' and employers' views.
- Keep an eye out for expanding or relocating businesses, as councils may require Travel Plans when granting planning permission.
- Respond to council consultations, eg on their Local Plans.

Local authorities' input

These measures may fall under county, unitary, district, or community/parish/town councils. And some may overlap with some listed above, eg timetable provision at stops may be an operator in one area and the county council in another; or a council may provide timetables in part of its area but not in another; or provide a timetable frame but not the actual timetable. Similarly, with shelter provision which may fall to lower tier councils. Sometimes seating and shelters can be part financed by local businesses.

Local authorities can:

- Introduce bus priorities, eg bus lanes, bus-actuated traffic signals, stops nearer passengers' destinations/road junctions, build-outs at stops or raised kerbs to ensure level access onto low-floor buses. Chapter 11 deals with bus priorities in detail.
- Introduce highway, traffic management and parking schemes to improve traffic flow and reduce delays to buses.

- Carry out tree lopping to prevent damage to double deckers.
- Review all planning applications and require Travel Plans for large developments. In 2004 the DfT suggested a development employing more than 50 people should be required to draw one up (DfT, 2004e).
- Add pedestrian crossings.
- Add seating and shelters. Community/Parish/Town Councils may have finance, or may part-finance with sponsorship from local businesses. Henley-on-Thames Town Council in Oxfordshire subsidizes some local bus services (Campaign for Better Transport, 2018).
- Offer real-time information.
- Add additional stops to serve a site or reduce a long gap between stops.
- Provide off-site signs to stops.
- Provide cycle parking at main bus stops.
- Involve operators in very first stages of major developments, eg new housing area, masterplans.
- Provide encouragement, getting everyone together.
- Set up a local Travel Plan Network.
- Introduce a workplace parking levy. The Transport Act 2000 gives authorities in England and Wales the power to introduce such a parking levy, revenue from which has to be used on local transport. The only authority so far to implement a levy is Nottingham City Council, which raises £9 million a year (Campaign for Better Transport, 2018).

Change is possible!

These examples show the proportions of, usually, staff using buses.

Hospitals

Hospitals are big generators of travel, about half of which is by staff. Addenbrooke's Hospital, Cambridge:

- staff in 1993 travelling by bus: 4 per cent;
- staff in 2013 travelling by bus: 27 per cent;

- patients/visitors in 1993 travelling by bus: 3 per cent;
- patients/visitors in 2013 travelling by bus: 11 per cent (Cambridge University Hospitals NHS Foundation Trust, 2014).

Derriford Hospital, Plymouth:

- staff in 1995 travelling by bus: 8 per cent;
- staff in 2001 travelling by bus: 15 per cent (DfT, 2002b).

Norfolk and Norwich:

- staff in 2002 travelling by bus (including park and ride): 12 per cent;
- staff in 2016 travelling by bus: 23 per cent (Norfolk and Norwich University Hospitals NHS Foundation Trust, 2006 and 2016).

Nottingham City Hospital:

- staff in 1997 travelling by bus: 11 per cent;
- staff in 2000 travelling by bus: 19 per cent (DfT, 2002b).

Universities

Universities and colleges are also big generators of travel. In some cases, the increase in bus use has been due to the university running their own bus.

Lancaster University:

- staff in 2003 travelling by bus/coach: 10 per cent;
- staff in 2015 travelling by bus/coach: 23 per cent;
- students in 2006 travelling by bus/coach: 57 per cent;
- students in 2015 travelling by bus/coach: 71 per cent (Lancaster University, 2017).

Newcastle University:

- staff in 2004 travelling by bus: 17 per cent;
- staff in 2014 travelling by bus: 24 per cent (Newcastle University, 2015).

University of Bristol:

- students in 2008 travelling by bus: 4 per cent;
- students in 2015 travelling by bus: 16 per cent (University of Bristol, 2018).

University of Sussex:

- staff in 2001 travelling by bus: 12 per cent;
- staff in 2015 travelling by bus: 22 per cent;
- students in 2001 travelling by bus: 27 per cent;
- students in 2015 travelling by bus: 54 per cent (University of Sussex, 2016).

Private companies

AstraZeneca, Macclesfield:

- staff in 1997 travelling by bus: 2 per cent;
- staff in 2001 travelling by bus: 7 per cent (DfT, 2002b).

BP, Sunbury:

- staff in 1998 travelling by bus: 4 per cent;
- staff in 2001 travelling by bus: 15 per cent (both included rail) (DfT, 2002b).

Orange, Bristol:

- staff in 1999 travelling by bus: 3 per cent;
- staff in 2001 travelling by bus: 8 per cent (DfT, 2002b).

Wellcome Trust, Genome Campus, Cambridge:

- staff in 2004 travelling by bus: 17 per cent;
- staff in 2009 travelling by bus: 28 per cent (Hurdle, 2012).

Zurich Financial Services, Cheltenham:

- staff in 2002 travelling by bus: 5 per cent;
- staff in 2003 travelling by bus: 10 per cent (Energy Saving Trust, 2005b).

Local authorities

Buckinghamshire County Council:

- staff in 1998 travelling by bus: 5 per cent;
- staff in 2001 travelling by bus: 10 per cent (DfT, 2002b).

The way forward

There is a large variety of measures that can be taken by employers, operators and all levels of local authorities to increase bus use. Travel Plans are one way. They are now well established and it has been ably demonstrated they are an ideal 'vehicle' for increasing bus use. Much guidance on doing them has been produced by central and local government since 1995, as well as ample evidence of what they can achieve. The need for travel planning is even stronger nowadays given the urgency to reduce carbon dioxide, also air pollution, some of which is at illegal levels; and to secure less car travel.

The key feature of Travel Plans is that they are partnerships; an opportunity to work jointly – employers, bus operators and local authorities of all levels working together. An employer can only do so much, eg offer season ticket loans to staff. Other measures such as good facilities at bus stops, reliable, punctual buses, information, and attractive fares and ticketing are matters for local authorities and operators.

There are some excellent examples of partnership working on Travel Plans and getting more people using buses. Increases in use have certainly been achieved, but activity varies. Everywhere is different, but generally there would seem to be scope to do more. From employers approaching their local bus companies and bus companies approaching local employers; to county/unitary authorities doing audits of bus routes with operators to improve reliability; to planning authorities securing, and then monitoring, Travel Plans secured through planning permissions, and community/parish/town councils providing bus shelters and seating.

The above checklist in this chapter totals 55 actions and provides a very wide range of 'food for thought' on what to aim for and what can be achieved; and will hopefully prompt more action. Some actions are very cheap and simple to do, others are more challenging. It is a question of weighing up not just the costs, but also the benefits, even if some may be difficult to quantify. The above actions are all actual examples that have all been done somewhere. Because everywhere is obviously different, it is not a question of doing all of them but just those appropriate to a particular area.

The 'essentials' of a good Travel Plan are travel survey results – not only about current travel, but what incentives might encourage different travel – then focus groups to discuss the results and get ideas, and site and local area audits. An employer then has the evidence to make the case to operators and local authorities. Working with other local employers should bolster their case. Typical criticisms by survey respondents about bus services are lack of a direct bus, slowness, infrequency and unreliability (Watts and Stephenson, 2000); clearly matters for local authorities, not just operators.

Meanwhile, bus operators should engage more in the communities they serve, by:

- participating in local forums and groups, eg Chambers of Trade, Local Enterprise Partnerships, council consultations on plans and highway / traffic / parking / pedestrianization schemes;
- monitoring large planning applications;
- approaching local employers;
- marketing as well as publicizing their services.

Operators should also do audits with highway authorities to reduce congestion and on-street parking to improve bus flow and save time. This should result in a more attractive and marketable service and improve operating efficiency.

Community/parish/town councils can be a valuable source of funding for shelters and seating at stops, as might local businesses willing to sponsor such facilities.

References

Balcombe, R J and Vance, C E (1998) *Information for bus passengers: a study of needs and priorities*, prepared for Department of the Environment, Transport and the Regions, Transport Research Laboratory

BP (2019) [accessed 16 August 2019] Travelling to BP International Centre for Business & Technology, Sunbury-on-Thames, *BP* [online] https://apps.bp.com/link/maps/docs/ICBT_Directional_Map.pdf (archived at https://perma.cc/8SGS-JEPP)

Cambridge University Hospitals NHS Foundation Trust (2014) *Caring for our Campus Commuters: Access to Addenbrooke's Plus*

Campaign for Better Transport (2018) [accessed 25 June 2019] Three stages to better bus services using the Bus Services Act, *Campaign for Better Transport* [online] https://bettertransport.org.uk/sites/default/files/research-files/bus-services-act-guidance.pdf (archived at https://perma.cc/YRG8-QD4S)

Department of the Environment, Transport and the Regions (1998) *A New Deal for Transport: Better for Everyone (Cm 3950)*, The Stationery Office, London

DfES and DfT (2003) *Travelling to School: a good practice guide*, London

DfT (2002a) *Making Travel Plans Work*, case study summaries, London

DfT (2002b) *Using the Planning Process to Secure Travel Plans*, research report, London

DfT (2004a) *Smarter Choices – Changing the Way We Travel*, final report, London

DfT (2004b) *The Future of Transport, a network for 2030*, The Stationery Office, London

DfT (2004c) *Traffic Management Act 2004*, Network Management Duty Guidance, London

DfT (2004d) *Smarter Choices – Changing the Way We Travel*, case study reports, vol. 2

DfT (2004e) *Making Smarter Choices Work*, London

DfT (2005) *Travel information leaflets for healthcare facilities*, London

DfT (2008) *The Essential Guide to Travel Planning*, London

DoT (1996) *Better Information for Bus Passengers, A Guide to Good Practice*, London

EnergyEfficiency BestPractice Programme (2000) *Travel Plans, New Business Opportunities for Public Transport Operators*, General Information Report 73, Didcot

Energy Saving Trust (2005a) *Stagecoach Devon makes business with travel plans*

Energy Saving Trust (2005b) *Zurich Financial Services: travel plans for major office sites*

Hurdle, D (2003) *Travel Plans – Getting Public Transport Operators on Board survey*, presentation to PTRC Second UK Transport Practitioners Meeting, Aston University

Hurdle, D (2004a) Improving health sector travel, *Health Estate*, 58 (9), pp 29–32

Hurdle, D (2004b) Introducing Travel Plans at Business Parks, *Journal of the Institute of Logistics and Transport*, 6 (8), pp 39–41.

Hurdle, D (2005) Shire districts fall short on travel plan proposal, *Planning*, 2 December, p 9

Hurdle, D (2007) *Encouraging sustainable commuting, A guide for London's local authorities in delivering effective travel plans*, Transport for London and Transport 2000 Trust, London

Hurdle, D (2012) *Engaging with Public Transport Operators, Advisory Note 9*, Business in the Community, London

Hurdle, D and Rajesparan, Y (1997) *Green Commuter Plans – London Boroughs' Progress*, Centre for Independent Transport Research in London, London

Lancaster University (2017) [accessed 13 December 2018] Travel Plan, third edition, 2017–2022, Lancaster University [online] www.lancaster.ac.uk/media/lancaster-university/content-assets/documents/facilities/TravelPlan2020.pdf (archived at https://perma.cc/VHT3-NMHA)

Mapline (nd) [online] https://mapline.com/ (archived at https://perma.cc/9H9H-U8VC)

Newcastle University (2015) [accessed 13 December 2018] Travel Plan Update July 2015, *Newcastle University* [online] www.ncl.ac.uk/media/wwwnclacuk/sustainablecampus/files/nu-travel-plan-update-2015.pdf (archived at https://perma.cc/TM39-RGSP)

Norfolk and Norwich University Hospitals NHS Foundation Trust (2006 and 2016) Personal communication

Nottingham Green Partnership (1995) *Green Commuter Plans, A Resource Pack for Nottingham's Employers*, Nottingham

Nottingham University Hospitals NHS Trust (2019) [accessed 26 September 2019] Executive Summary to the NUH Travel Plan 2018–2023, *Nottingham University Hospitals NHS Trust* [online] www.nuh.nhs.uk/download. cfm?doc=docm93jijm4n5063.pdf&ver=10317 (archived at https://perma. cc/69ZZ-QKN4)

Transit (2004) Souter calls on bus operators to be more innovative, *Transit*, **233**, p 5

Transport 2000 Trust (1997) *Changing Journeys to Work: An employers' guide to green commuter plans*, London

Transport and Travel Research (1994) *Bus passenger information study*, Oxford

TransportEnergy BestPractice Programme (2002) *A Travel Plan Resource Pack for Employers*

University of Bristol (2018) [accessed 13 December 2018] Combined Travel Plan 2018–2023, *University of Bristol* [online] www.bristol.ac.uk/media-library/sites/ transportplan/documents/university-of-bristol-travel-plan-2018-% 20to-2023.pdf (archived at https://perma.cc/2UAC-B9P4)

University of Sussex (2016) [accessed 13 December 2018] Travel Plan Final Report, *University of Sussex* [online] www.sussex.ac.uk/webteam/gateway/file. php?name=university-of-sussex-travel-plan-22022016-for-website. pdf&site=442 (archived at https://perma.cc/AXZ8-K9VL)

Watts, E and Stephenson, R (2000) Evaluating an Employer Transport Plan: Effects on travel behavior of parking charges and associated measures introduced at the University of Sheffield, *Local Environment*, **5** (4), pp 435–50

The bus industry in Wales 14

STUART COLE

Introduction

The first section of this chapter shows how the Welsh Government's transport vision has evolved since about 1990 in how it sees the requirements of the travelling public. The second section sets out those requirements from research in Wales, and how TrawsCymru (the national bus network) increased demand, reversing the national trend.

Section 1: Government policy and legislation – Wales diverges from England

The bus industry in Wales has the same format as in Scotland and England. The deregulation legislation in the 1985 Transport Act has resulted in a mix of commercial and tendered bus route services with reasonably good urban frequencies Monday–Saturday 07.00 to 18.30 but with lower frequencies or no bus service outside those times and in rural areas.

The common legislation also allows for non-statutory quality bus partnership schemes and quality bus contract schemes.

House of Commons, 1984

The general view in Wales (though in the main not of the bigger bus companies) was set out by the House of Commons report into public transport in Wales (House of Commons, 1984) as a competitive franchising basis for bus operations. This has essentially been the objective of the Welsh Government since its creation 13 years later.

Transport Act 2000

The Transport Act 2000 (sections 124–34) did move to a position where the deregulated market could be suspended in a specific area through a competitive tendering process. This was however constrained because the local authority had to show it was 'the only practicable way' of implementing their bus strategy.

Transport (Wales) Act 2006

The 2006 Transport (Wales) Act became the first indicator of how the recently (1997) formed Welsh Assembly Government would like to see bus operations in Wales develop. It provided powers for Welsh Ministers to: 'provide/subsidize public passenger transport services they think are necessary and that would not otherwise be provided commercially' within or near to Wales (reflecting the winding nature of Offa's Dyke/Welsh border). This was extended by the Local Transport Act (UK) 2008 to include a 'service quality' criterion.

The repeal of Part 2 of the 1985 Transport Act in respect of Wales and its replacement with Wales-only legislation was seen as an essential prerequisite to an integrated transport policy. During the 2004 Draft Transport (Wales) Bill's parliamentary stages, bus regulation and policy was supported by the joint National Assembly and House of Commons committee but opposed by the Westminster Government (an important exclusion from the 2006 Act), (House of Commons, 2004; National Assembly for Wales, Economic Development and Transport Committee, 2004).

Under the 2017 Wales Act, the Welsh Government acquired enabling powers for bus registration.

Bus and Coach Legislative Competence Order (National Assembly for Wales, 2008)

This ambition moved one stage further with the publication by the National Assembly of a Legislative Competence Order (LCO) (the Westminster equivalent of a Bill) proposed by Huw Lewis, AM (a government minister):

'The LCO provided for more control over bus services in Wales and gained cross party support in the National Assembly (called the Senedd from January 2020). The key issues were the need for an integrated transport system which brought together bus quality, safety, service frequency, timetables and ticketing. This required, as a pre-requisite, powers over the operations of buses, trains and coaches in Wales, and "franchising as an important part of the toolkit" (Deputy First Minister, Ieuan Wyn Jones AM). The underlying social and economic objectives were increased accessibility to employment, health and education for those families (up to 70 per cent of the total in parts of Wales) without cars.'

'The cause of this dichotomous position lay not in the concept but in fears by bus companies that services they have built up into profitable operations may be lost if there is a supply side competition and their representative body the Confederation of Passenger Transport UK (CPT) has suggested a debate is required on whether "franchising is theft"' (Sir Brian Souter).

The Local Transport Act provided the Secretary of State for Transport (in London) with powers to appoint and direct through a Senior Commissioner, the Traffic Commissioners (TCs) who no longer have a specific area (eg Wales) responsibility. This went against the views expressed by the House of Commons Select Committee on Welsh Affairs, the National Assembly Economic Development and Transport Committee and by CPT Cymru Wales, the bus companies' representative body.

The Commission on Devolution in Wales (Silk Commission)

The Silk Commission's second stage report (Commission on Devolution in Wales, 2011) on specific areas of governance included an analysis of the transport responsibilities required by the Welsh Government to achieve its objectives of an integrated transport system. For buses, the Commission recommended powers covering bus regulation and the TCs' bus responsibilities as a major step forward. But public transport policy generally should also be transferred to the Welsh Government, so creating a stronger framework for bus, rail and taxi services. It would be logical for any powers conferred on local authorities in previous legislation to also be ascribed to the Welsh Government.

There will need, of course, to be a commensurate transfer of additional financial provision via the Welsh block grant and a strong rationale for all these transfers based on benefits to travellers, making travel easier and more affordable.

The Silk Commission's recommended transfers of responsibilities have a logical rationale and are essential to maximize the transport system's economic potential and fiscal responsibility, without waiting another ten years to achieve agreement from Westminster.

Bus Services (Wales) Bill: Rationale

The rejection of the Bus Services Act 2017 by the Welsh Government as inappropriate for Wales resulted from the policy developments over thirty years set out above. These led to a Government White Paper Improving Public Transport (Welsh Government, 2018) which included (alongside new rail responsibilities) proposing legislation for reforming the planning and delivery of local bus services plus licensing taxis and private hire vehicles. The Bus Services (Wales) Bill seeks enabling powers which the Government believes will improve bus services and increase passenger numbers.

The Government sees three key areas of bus policy which provides a new route (pun intended) for bus operations underpinning the rationale to achieve Welsh Government buses policy and its vision of an integrated public transport system:

- information sharing;
- local authorities to operate bus companies;
- enhanced forms of partnership.

Information sharing

There are 80 bus companies in Wales of varying sizes who operate commercial routes; and with tendered services through 22 local authorities. Getting agreement between all parties has proved difficult. Two bus services from two separate companies operating into a bus station hub failing to agree to coordinate timetables, tickets or other factors such as fitting with a school closure time is not uncommon.

Persuading these organizations to share information has generally failed mainly for commercial reasons, even with a confidentiality guarantee. There may also be technical information on vehicle maintenance and operating procedures/events which could reduce a risk to the general public. This has prevented integration and maximizing efficiency in terms of public subsidy. Powys County Council, covering about a quarter of Wales' land area, does operate full-cost contracts and takes the revenue risk, and has better information sharing.

The Government's proposal is to create a legal requirement and formal mechanism to cover the concerns of all parties.

Local authorities to own/operate bus companies

The Welsh Government position since 2012 has been to encourage continued and new ownership of local buses by local authorities. There had been a history of municipal bus services in valley towns, though not in western industrial centres such as Llanelli, Swansea and Bridgend. These, and much of Wales, have been dominated by private local companies, the BET Federation or Tilling subsidiaries which became the National Bus Company and subsequently Arriva, First Cymru and Stagecoach.

There is a discussion to be had for/against Cardiff Bus, Newport Bus and Monmouthshire Public Transport remaining in local authority ownership when they face financial challenges. Indeed, many small private or municipal operators have sold out to the 'big three' operators or their predecessors.

However, the bigger government concern lies in rural Wales where the number of companies able to run bus services is reducing. Parts of Wales may have already become a monopoly, leading to fewer bidders, the lack of competition for bus service tenders pushing up subsidy costs and tendered services for which there are no bidders. It is in these areas the Government is encouraging local authorities to operate buses themselves.

Enhanced forms of partnership

This can be of two types: Quality Contract Schemes (QCSs), and franchising.

The provision in the Transport Act 2008 (applicable identically in Wales as in England) for statutory quality bus partnerships (SQBP) and statutory quality bus contracts (SQBC) gives an opportunity for local authorities to 'make' (set up) a SQBP/SQBC on any route or in any geographical area. Any new operator on a route or in an area has to meet these standards, and an existing operator has to improve service standards to the defined level for that scheme. Those not doing so can have their registration declined or removed by the Traffic Commissioner who has a key role in the process and in enforcement.

Local authorities are empowered to make a SQBP/SQBC scheme under provisions contained in the Transport Act 2000 (as amended by the Transport Act 2008). These are made on a route commercially operated by a bus company and which receives no subsidy from the Welsh Government or local authorities.

These go part of the way to helping Government achieve integrated public transport, but the Government suggests a more robust and efficient process is required. Welsh ministers consider the current QCS process to be: 'overly complex and resource intensive and no QCS has been developed in Wales. The Government's preferred option is bus franchising (by the government or joint transport authorities) which is suitable for Welsh circumstances' (Welsh Government, 2018).

The Welsh Government's rationale for franchising to achieve its buses policy is as follows.

Perception 1: Deficiencies in the current arrangements
The current provisions could be argued to have the following deficiencies:

- Any subsidized service is prevented from competing with a commercial service.
- Commercial services are generally cherry-picked.
- Bus companies choose to operate profitable sections/times/days.
- Non-profitable sections or times of day and Sundays are subsidized by county councils.
- The lack of cross-subsidy means that counties' expenditure is increased.

Perception 2: Consequences
Damaging consequences to passenger services and the travelling experience and ease of travel have frequently followed from the 'free market provides' philosophy of the 1985 Act:

- Instability in the market (no control of timetable changes).
- Competition facing Welsh small and medium-sized (SME) companies from large bus operators with dominance in a local market make the latter more able to spread the risks of a contestable market and reduce opportunities for Welsh SMEs. Changes in the economics of bus operation may see changes in this position, but supply-side competition will still remain the preferred means of operating for many SME companies.
- No coordination of timetables.
- No cross-subsidy.

Part of the National Transport Plan's implementation of the first TrawsCymru route between Carmarthen and Aberystwyth (Service T1) was delayed for two years (2011–13). This provides an example of the unacceptable consequences of the current arrangements, which the Welsh Government wishes to replace.

Bus franchising (or enhanced form of partnership)

The Welsh Government's intention is to bring benefits to bus passengers – integrated tickets, fares and timetables, increased frequency, reliability, punctuality, convenience, predictable journey times, improved evening/Sunday service/frequencies, park and ride facilities at key bus stops (in parallel to the railway), and sufficient capacity on peak journeys.

It considers the evidence points to a statutory model more proscriptive than a SQBC, as the market has shown a reluctance to change service provision. It also enables a government, already funding up to 60 per cent of bus users through various concessionary fares, to pursue a low fares policy (Cole, 2008).

Solutions

Arriving at the solution of the problem entails consideration of the question of who should own and/or control public transport in Wales with the author's delivery perception (Cole, 2018).

Delivery

This will be the role of Transport for Wales (TfW), a limited by guarantee company owned by the Government (National Assembly for Wales, Economic Development and Transport Committee, 2019) and local authorities, either individually or more likely as Joint Transport Authorities (JTAs). The intention is for TfW to move into bus operations, extending beyond its current role in developing the Wales and Borders rail franchise with Keolis Amey – operating as TfW Rail Services.

The TrawsCymru contractual arrangements are to be transferred to TfW during 2020, and developed into a franchised operation. The TrawsCymru network and brand, initially created by Professor Stuart Cole, is owned by the Welsh Government.

Although the Government proposes that local authorities will determine the most appropriate model, a regional approach using JTAs provided by the Transport 2006 (Wales) Act would be its preference. These would then work with TfW to link the national bus and rail network with local bus services.

The introduction of a national ticket for use on all bus, tram, tram–train and rail services would follow. This could take the Netherlands Chipkaart or the London Oyster card as a basis.

The 4Is (Cole, 2000) could then become the basis for bus services provision:

Information + Interchange + Investment + Imagination = Integration

Section 2: Where do passengers want bus services to be?

An underlying criterion in determining where subsidy or capital expenditure on buses or bus infrastructure should be placed is the evaluation basis. HM Treasury (Westminster) has introduced the Five Case Model, where the strategic, economic and financial cases are directly relevant to the allocation of funds. The objective is to provide a value-for-money guide for achieving the most effective projects.

The output measure is the benefit/cost ratio (BCR); the Treasury is only prepared to accept schemes with a BCR of over 2:1 but this gives priority to densely-populated areas. Connectivity in rural areas will therefore always be a lower priority under this criterion. Of course, ministerial decisions may always overrule this process, and the use of BCR alone may be changed to one where the strategic case output becomes a more important decision-making factor.

This has been the view put forward by James Price, Chief Executive Officer of Transport for Wales (EISC, 2016), who suggested that the southeast (of both Wales and England) have been higher up the investment priority list, to the detriment of rural Wales.

It reflects the position of Ken Skates, the Minister for Economy and Infrastructure (including transport), who said in 2019 that we have to consider: '...connectivity especially between the rural west of the country and our capital city Cardiff, and major markets in England. Public investment to achieve that would not receive priority using BCR alone but the rural and small-town economy in Wales is as important to our economy as is the south east capital region.'

The Welsh Government has considered research (inter alia, ABMUHB, 2015; Cole, 2014; Cole, 2008; Welsh Government, 2018) into what travellers want from their bus service. A 2014 Federation of Small Business (FSB) Cymru survey of business travellers (both commuting and in business travel) identified the incentives from the public transport industry which would persuade them to change from car to bus/rail. As in all the case studies referred to, travellers, particularly commuters, regard reliability and predictable journey time as the essential bus travel quality factors which would encourage transfer from their car. This relates to the need to arrive at work at a specific time.

A most important individual factor to encourage is lower fares (FSB Cymru, 2014), but leading bus companies have indicated reliability and timekeeping as the criteria they have identified. The importance of lower fares as a bus travel incentive is greater for those on lower incomes, and for those comparing travel cost by car. However, for the FSB respondents reflected in Figure 14.1, factors such as integrated ticketing and timetables, frequency and wider area of route coverage (seen often as convenience) are almost equal as criteria for modal change.

Affordable/lower bus fares

The UK Government has sought mechanisms (Welsh Government, 2018) whereby the cost of bus travel can be reduced to improve employment

Figure 14.1 Factors affecting modal transfer from car to public transport

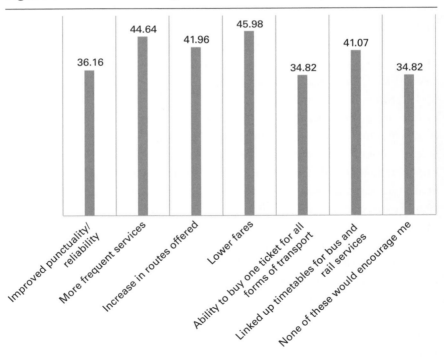

SOURCE FSB Cymru, 2014

horizons, accessibility to other services, meet social objectives and increase demand as a means of reducing car usage and consequently contribute to air quality targets. Currently its schemes are:

- Concessionary free travel for residents 60 or over, or for those with disabilities, which has resulted in 40–50 per cent of passengers on any one service being holders of free passes.
- Discounted travel for young people. This has had a limited impact on numbers but success has varied between counties. Carmarthenshire had the highest take-up, which they say reflects the level of promotion activity.
- TrawsCymru free weekend travel.

As it provides free travel for 60 per cent of bus passengers, it is considering the possibility of free travel throughout Wales. The Estonian Government decision in 2018 to provide free national travel for residents and low-price visitor fares (Cole, 2018) is a useful impact comparator for Wales. Its policy is also reflected in the reduction in train fares in the upper Cardiff and Newport valleys and in north Wales by 10 per cent in January 2020, compared with an increase in England of 2.5 per cent.

In addition, commercial discount price schemes with a yield management base through market segmentation are a popular demand targeting technique which has generated revenue and passenger demand.

Fares therefore have a role to play in influencing modal split between car and public transport, but should only be considered in an overall context of service quality, in particular reliability, predictable journey time and frequency. Only then do travellers consider, for example, wi-fi or comfortable seating for long journeys.

Reversing the bus passenger numbers trend in Wales – TrawsCymru a case study

There has been a downward trend in bus passenger numbers since about 2010. However, there are operations which have reversed that trend. One of these is the Welsh Government-owned TrawsCymru national bus network.

Figure 14.2 shows how, from its previous collection of TrawsCambria routes, it has grown demand by five times over its six years of existence.

In 2008, the Government commissioned research into new forms of rural transport provision, which reported to Ministers in 2009/10 (Cole and Hall, 2010), establishing a national bus network, TrawsCymru. In 2012 this took over on a quite different format from the declining TrawsCambria services.

Figure 14.2 TrawsCymru total network annual patronage trends, 2007/08 to 2018/19

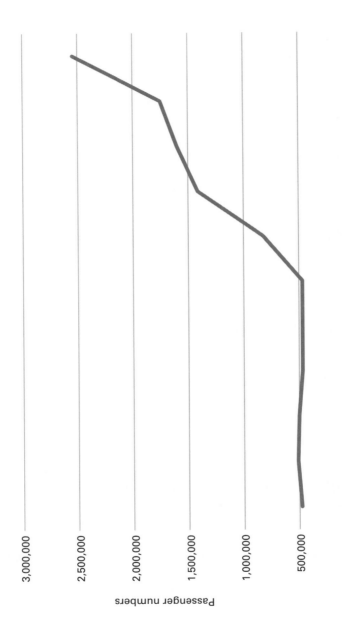

	2007/08	2008/09	2009/10	2010/11	2011/12	2012/13	2013/14	2015/16	2016/17	2017/18	2018/19
Total Pax	477,639	511,871	501,282	469,318	469,318	469,318	823,410	1,411,940	1,600,700	1,751,827	2,544,699

From several research studies and reviews (TrawsCymru, 2011; Cole *et al*, 2017; Winkler, 2013; TrawsCymru, 2019), the criteria for the network's success has been identified as follows.

Base criteria:

- Detailed market research to determine demand.
- An affordable subsidy level determined to assess the Welsh Government's ability to invest in the services.
- Each route researched for growth.
- Development and management of a consistent, high-quality brand, comprehensive and recognized all over Wales.
- Giving travellers what they want within budget limits (based on fare revenue/subsidy).
- Profitability on some routes – however, fares policy is based upon the Welsh Government's economic, environmental and social criteria.

Market criteria:

- Reliability in operating vehicles and timetable.
- Frequency and clock face timetable.
- Quality of vehicles – new, comfortable, leather seats, next stop information audio/visual (not old, tired buses) designed as a hybrid between bus and coach, within an available budget.
- Longer routes serving a wider range of communities (size and geographical spread).
- Connectivity with rail (linked into Wales and Borders rail franchise) and other TrawsCymru/National Express/Megabus operations for longer-distance journeys and local bus services.
- Availability of TrawsCymru network day tickets at a competitive price for travel to many parts of Wales.
- Hubs at Aberystwyth and Brecon for other TrawsCymru services.

Conclusions

Government policies have long gestation periods even when only one government is involved – bus deregulation took six years, and rail privatization ten years. Little wonder therefore that with two different governments in the

UK and in Wales, one for free market competition and the other for social and economic wellbeing, delays have occurred.

The initial proposal for competitive franchising was put forward in 1984. It was recommended by the UK government's Silk Commission in 2014 (30 years later), and is not likely to be implemented under the present UK government's free market regime.

The outcome is to create an integrated transport system where all buses and trains in Wales operate within one national and several regional networks. It brings connectivity between services, one national ticket (as with the London Oyster or Netherlands's Chipkaart) and consequently ease of travel, higher frequencies on one ticket and convenience as a demand-determining factor for public transport, an increase in demand resulting in fewer cars.

In Wales, Cardiff City Council's ambitious public transport development plan aimed at reduced pollution and road congestion will not fully achieve these objectives without the Welsh Government achieving its legislative goals.

References

ABMUHB (2015) *Abertawe Bro Morgannwg University Health Board*, Staff Travel Survey

Cole, S (2000) *Journey to Success: The Transport and Tourism Debate*, English Tourist Board

Cole, S (2008) *Public v Private – who should own and/or control public transport*, International Conference on Transport System Studies, University of Mumbai, India

Cole, S (2014) Moving Wales Forward, Federation of Small Business Cymru

Cole, S *et al* (2017) *TrawsCymru Free Travel Weekend Trial – Impact Assessment Study*, Wavehill Social & Economic Research, Aberaeron

Cole, S (2018) *Targeted Discount Bus Travel and Traffic Management – on key services/corridors affected by congestion and/or poor air quality*, Welsh Government

Cole, S and Hall, D (2010) *TrawsCymru Operational Options for Welsh Government*

Commission on Devolution in Wales (Silk Commission) (2011) *Second stage report*, Wales Office (UK Government), London

Economy, Infrastructure and Skills Committee (2016) *Evidence to the Economy, Infrastructure and Skills Committee*, National Assembly for Wales

FSB Cymru (2014) *Survey of members travel to work – reasons for modal choice*

House of Commons (1984) *Public Transport in Wales,* Committee on Welsh Affairs. Special Adviser: Professor Stuart Cole

House of Commons (2004) *Welsh Affairs Committee, HC 759, Draft Transport (Wales) Bill.* Special Adviser: Professor Stuart Cole

National Assembly for Wales (2008) *Proposed Provision of Bus and Coach Services Legislative Competence Order*, consultation paper. Special Adviser: Professor Stuart Cole

National Assembly for Wales, Economic Development and Transport Committee (2004) *Draft Transport (Wales) Bill.* Special Adviser: Professor Stuart Cole

National Assembly for Wales, Economic Development and Transport Committee (2019) *The future development of Transport for Wales*

TrawsCymru (2011) *TrawsCymru market research into T1 Aberystwyth to Carmarthen service*

TrawsCymru (2019) *Review of TrawsCymru weekend free travel initiative*, Strategic Research and Insight, Cardiff

Welsh Government (2018) *Improving Public Transport*, consultation document

Winkler, V (2013) *Review of TrawsCymru*, Bevan Foundation for the Minister for Economy, Science and Transport

Further reading

Ministry of Results (2017) Research for Traveline Cymru, Cardiff

Working with the public

15

DAVID SIDEBOTTOM

Background

Passengers, customers, guests… call them what you will. Without them there would not be this book, largely because there would not be a bus industry! When you boil it all down, anyone associated with the bus and transport sector will say that the 'passenger is at the heart' of their business, investment or policy development. But, how many decisions, operational or policy based, are wholly based on the needs of the travelling public?

Is that because costs and politics get in the way of decision making, or because we (the collective 'we') do not really know enough about the current experience of the travelling public, what they believe are the key priorities for improvement and how the bus sector can build enough trust amongst current bus users and those that need to be convinced to give the bus a go, to either make more bus trips or start using the bus for the first time ever or for a number of years?

Let us take one organization very much at the heart of this matter.

Transport Focus

At Transport Focus it is our role as the independent, statutory consumer body to speak up for current and future users of buses. Thus, this is probably the good time to get the dull, stuffy 'who are Transport Focus?' bit out of the way.

As the independent watchdog for transport users, Transport Focus is working hard to make sure user needs are built into all the decisions and investment made on their behalf. It aims to be useful to those who make decisions about transport, and to help them make better decisions for the user.

Annual surveys

Every year Transport Focus speaks to more than 100,000 passengers and road users through large annual surveys and ad hoc research including:

- The National Rail Passenger Survey: The largest published rail satisfaction survey in the world. Twice a year, in January and June, it gives scores for factors including value for money and punctuality.

- The Bus Passenger Survey: Around 50,000 passengers give their views on a range of factors, from value to cleanliness.

- The Strategic Roads User Survey: This reflects the experience of all drivers – whether in cars, vans, lorries, coaches or on a motorbike – across a range of issues.

All work is published at www.transportfocus.org.uk, including a data hub to make exploring the results easy. Our staff are based throughout the country, helping us get a regional picture as well as a national one as we hold the industry to account.

The role of Transport Focus

In April 2008, the Secretary of State for Transport announced plans to widen the role of Passenger Focus (as Transport Focus was once known) to include bus passenger representation in England, outside London. The Local Transport Act 2008 amended the Transport Act 2005 to allow our remit to be extended through secondary legislation. This received Parliamentary approval as the Passengers' Council (Non-Railway Functions) Order 2010.

Since 2010 Transport Focus has worked hard to better understand the needs and experiences of bus passengers as well as the future, potential users of bus. This is done through robust and clear, evidence-based consumer research to help build clear policy messages and communications. Aligning this body of research to active engagement on behalf of passengers with the bus industry, politicians, media and other relevant stakeholders, Transport Focus strives to help decision makers and funders to focus on the factors that will make the biggest difference for the bus passenger of today and tomorrow.

Bus passenger survey

The first piece of major work we wanted to deliver was a benchmarked, comparable view of bus passenger experience across our statutory remit area – England, outside of London. With a pedigree in similar research on behalf of rail passengers, we developed the Bus Passenger Survey. In developing the methodology for this survey, we worked closely with those that would use the results. This included a range of bus operators, transport authorities, Department for Transport (DfT) and other key stakeholders.

A pilot methodology was developed and tested in 2009 across six geographic areas of England. As with our work for rail passengers, we wanted passengers to rate the journey they had just taken. To do this, we have a field force of market research agency staff boarding buses to distribute a detailed, self-completion questionnaire to passengers. In more recent years we have also offered an electronic questionnaire to passengers who prefer to complete the survey online. Again, passengers are steered down the route of rating their last journey.

The survey was designed to reflect the profile of bus passengers aged 16 and over. In each authority area, the survey took account of three key variables:

1 operator market share within the authority area;

2 service frequency;

3 the proportion of passengers who are 'fare paying' versus those using concessionary tickets.

These features of the passenger profile have been ensured through a combination of the sample design itself, and weighting of the resultant data.

It is important to receive as much 'actionable' information as possible from passengers so that bus operators and authorities can use it to make future services better for passengers. That is why we want the passenger to focus on the trip they have just completed. In addition, we also ask a lot of questions of passengers. In fact, feedback has suggested that our survey is something more akin to a tax return! However, the completion rate over the years has held up incredibly well despite what may be perceived as a more dated method of collecting survey responses. I think the ability to explain to a passenger that their response is being used by the independent passenger watchdog carries more weight than just another survey by the bus operator or local council.

The first annual Bus Passenger Survey took place in the autumn of 2009. Results were published in late spring 2010. Around 19,000 bus passengers gave us their views on bus services across 14 different areas of England outside of London. This first survey was entirely funded by Transport Focus.

Since this first work in 2009, the Bus Passenger Survey has grown tremendously. Over the years bus operators, local transport authorities and governments have all seen the usefulness of the results of the survey in their planning. In fact, the 2019 survey will have been the single largest survey undertaken in our statutory remit area of England outside of London. Nearly 44,000 passengers will have taken part across dozens of geographic and operational areas. In fact since the first survey in 2009 we have sought the views of over 400,000 bus passengers across Great Britain. This growth has been achieved by significant funding contributions from bus operators, local transport authorities and governments. In fact, in 2019 the financial share contributed by Transport Focus was around a quarter of the overall cost. The remaining 75 per cent has been largely split equally between bus operators and transport authorities.

A great example of a great product that has found a place in a market and makes a difference! In fact, we have been asked to undertake survey work in Wales and Scotland, all fully funded by governments, operators and transport partnerships, to get a better picture of bus user experience and to benchmark local experience to other areas of Great Britain.

Results

So, over the ten years (2009 to 2019), what has the survey told the bus world? Well, overall bus passenger satisfaction has largely remained high. Typically, in response to the question: 'Overall, thinking about your journey, how satisfied were you?', around 85–90 per cent of passengers, on average, said they were fairly or very satisfied with their most recent trip.

Transport Focus manages its annual survey across bus users such that it not only gives strong evidence of the views expressed about particular operators, but offers intelligence on the bus business as a whole. As with any industry and service, an understanding of the detailed requirements and aspirations of customers is vital.

The most recent results, published in March 2018, even in summary, offer just a taster of the data and evidence available for operators, along with (importantly) their partners, such as local authorities, to work upon.

The survey for 2018 embraced 48,971 passengers across England (outside London) and Scotland. An immense amount of data was gathered, with Derbyshire, new to this survey, coming out top with an overall 95 per cent passenger satisfaction level. East Sussex showed the highest level of passengers 'very satisfied' (at 62 per cent), whilst Swindon had the lowest in this category at 34 per cent. But Swindon had achieved the biggest overall improvement in satisfaction – from 78 per cent in 2017 up to 93 per cent. Cornwall had a similar positive message, with overall satisfaction rising from 86 per cent to 90 per cent over the same timescale. Worcestershire remained the location of lowest level of satisfaction, resting at 75 per cent.

In terms of value for money, as expressed by passengers, Swindon reported 81 per cent fairly to quite satisfied, but with declines in other areas including Essex, Greater Manchester, Worcestershire, West of England and York. Importantly, punctuality remains a challenge for almost all operators with, for example, an average of 73 per cent of passengers in metropolitan areas satisfied, although this drops to as low as 60 per cent in some other areas. A slightly better picture arises with the rating of 'on bus' journey time. Cornwall, which had suffered a decline in the previous year, had recovered to 85 per cent satisfied in 2018. In metropolitan areas, this particular result averaged 84 per cent.

Information was available concerning the main impacts on journey times, with congestion being the most significant. Second to this was the time it took for passengers to board, followed by waiting too long at stops (perhaps to use the jargon of some operators 'to regulate the service'), poor weather conditions and a few cases of drivers taking the journey slowly.

In terms of operators, Trent Barton, along with Oxford Bus Park & Ride, Stagecoach South West, Stagecoach in Nottinghamshire and Midland Classic in Staffordshire, all achieved 90 per cent or more in overall satisfaction. Diamond Bus in Worcestershire came lowest at 60 per cent. In all, despite the issues raised by passengers, 88 per cent were satisfied with what was offered, although there was an immense amount of evidence upon which to address issues and apply solutions.

Finally, as a simple headline, what makes a great journey? Almost half (41 per cent) said the driver with a further 22 per cent looking to the overall environment of the vehicle and the comfort it provided. Look after drivers – bus, train, coach – and support them... and they will look after your customers, make them happy and grow your business!

Bus passengers' priorities for improvement

While the annual Bus Passenger Survey provides a nationwide 'in the moment' rating and benchmarked ranking of bus passenger experiences, other regular work from Transport Focus seeks views from passengers to better understand their general priorities for improvement.

Aligning current bus passenger experience and what drives satisfaction, alongside the views about what passengers want to see improve as a prioritized set of factors, brings together a focus on where best to deploy valuable resources.

This picture should help governments, bus operators and transport authorities where to best invest their time, effort and funding to deliver the best improvements in services for passengers. This should not only improve experiences for today's users, but also make the bus a more attractive proposition for the potential users of tomorrow.

In February 2020, Transport Focus published the third of its *Bus Passengers' Priorities for Improvement* studies completed over the past ten years. This work sought the views of 5,000 people across England, outside of London, who used the bus at the time of the survey at least once every three months. This research, carried out in spring 2019, looked at improvement priorities for three main groups: bus users, non-users of buses, and young people.

Looking specifically now at the views of current bus passengers, Transport Focus asked users to rank their priorities for improvement in all aspects of their local bus services. This research asked bus passengers where they felt most need for improvement in their bus service, selecting from a list of more than 30 individual options across these groupings:

- the bus itself;
- tickets and payment;
- bus information;
- the service and driver;
- the bus stop;
- the bus network.

Getting the basics right has never been more important to bus passengers. Bus passengers now want services running more often and going to more places that are on time at their bus stop. Better value for money is still important, as is buses arriving at their destination on time. Tackling antisocial behaviour, faster journey times and next bus displays are the other items that need attention. Through the Transport Focus Bus Passenger Survey, we know that the single most important factor that delivers a satisfactory journey for passengers is the timeliness of the trip.

Improving value for money is also important. This could be tackled through fare deals to match the more flexible way we live and work now;

meet the demands of those who simply do not all travel five days per week. Improving the quality of service provided and the basic cost for distance travelled would also help. Aligning what we know from this latest work on bus passengers' priorities for improvement, and what we already know drives up levels of bus passenger satisfaction, it is clear that now is the time to really focus on getting the basics of a punctual and reliable service right.

Improving the bus network is by far the biggest priority. A clear and consistent need, it informs four of the top five priorities. Passengers want buses to run more often, go to more places, be on time at the bus stop and more bus journeys on time.

Outside the 'top five', tackling antisocial behaviour leads the longer list of priorities for improvement, reflecting a concern seen in previous years. This is followed by faster journey times, an improvement that's particularly important to young people. More 'next bus' displays as well as better quality information at bus stops were the next most important features for passengers. More space for wheelchairs and buggies completes the 'top ten' priorities. Maintenance of bus stops and driver communications were felt to be least in need of improvement.

Overall, different types of bus passenger share the same improvement priorities. However, convenience is king and there are differences in the relative priorities expressed by users, non-users and young people, as shown in both the ranking and index scores. Time is key for commuters who are most concerned with frequency and punctuality. Young people's top priority is the number of places buses go to, and faster journey times also makes the top five for this group.

Opportunities to increase bus use

More than half of all bus passengers have access to a car most of the time, and almost two-thirds travel by car at least a few times per week. The bus is their most used means of public transport, with just 13 per cent of bus passengers also regularly travelling by train or tram.

Commuters are the passenger type with least car access while leisure passengers have most. Those aged 25–34 years were most likely to be able to access a car some of the time, while older age groups were more likely to be able to access a car all the time. Bus passengers with a disability were less likely to have access to a car.

Those two-thirds (62 per cent) of bus users who often travel by car as well as by bus estimate that around a fifth of their car journeys could be made by bus instead. Commuters and younger passengers are most likely to feel this way. However, they have stronger views: 'I only use buses (instead of other means of transport) if I have to', and: 'People like me don't use buses'. This is a challenge for bus companies and local transport planners to address the convenience and negative perceptions of the service.

The conditions exist to grow bus use among users. A majority of passengers (68 per cent) say they 'wouldn't mind making more journeys by bus'. A little over half of the survey respondents believe buses could play a 'large' or 'reasonable' part in reducing air pollution; male, older users and less frequent users are more likely to hold this view. On the other hand, just over two in five bus passengers think buses have only 'some' or 'no' impact in reducing air pollution. There is a clear opportunity for bus operators and authorities to educate people on the environmental and associated health benefits of taking the bus.

The future – growing the market

Throughout the ten years that Transport Focus has been tracking bus passengers' satisfaction with their journeys, the group of passengers who have solidly remained the least satisfied is ironically the single largest current user group – young people! Not a great business model, having the largest section of your customer base being the least satisfied.

To better understand what really drives the levels of satisfaction across young people (aged 14–19 years old), Transport Focus commissioned both quantitative and qualitative research in 2017. This research 'got under the skin' of what young people want from bus travel, what they want to see improve, and, ultimately, what would entice them to continue being tomorrow's long-term bus passenger.

This work reinforced what we have learned from other Transport Focus research: improving value for money, punctuality and reliability are constant priorities. The industry – bus operators, local authorities and government together – need a relentless focus on delivering these basics.

Getting the essentials right, alongside a more effective and targeted approach to customer retention, will help build trust and loyalty to make using the bus a viable long-term proposition for young people. As part of this new research we also took the opportunity to capture the experiences and needs of young people under the age of 16, an age group that our current Bus Passenger Survey work does not cover. This new work contributes to understanding what the important 14–19 age group needs and wants from bus services today to encourage them to be tomorrow's bus users.

So, what are the key messages?

Building confidence

Young people are starting to travel to more places spontaneously and independently. As a result, they are using different transport options that can offer welcome independence and freedom. However, this also brings anxiety about 'getting it right' – a key concern for young people. They don't want to be embarrassed in public or in front of their friends, so they may be reluctant to interact with the driver or other passengers. At the same time, they appreciate the reassurance of the journey going as expected, to build their confidence.

Many of the concerns young people have come from a lack of confidence or not understanding 'the system'. For some, using the bus seems like a club where they do not belong. This impacts all the stages of a young person's journey. For example, they don't necessarily know where to go to find information, and then at the stop young people may worry about what they should do if the bus is late, drives past or does not turn up at all. They also want to be sure they know which stop to get off at. Real-time information is a key requirement to provide reassurance. The experience of boarding the bus can be a stress point too. These concerns are largely focused around the interaction with the driver: Do I know where I am going, and will the bus driver understand what I am asking for? Do I have enough money, the right change or will my pass work?

Young people worry that if they get this bit wrong, they might be asked to get off the bus. A fifth of young people in our survey have additional needs, classifying themselves as having a disability – which may be hidden – where they may need even more support. We also found that even if they do use the bus for school, this does not seem to teach young people the skills they need to catch the bus at other times. Sometimes the experience of the school bus is unpleasant, and these negative memories can carry into their wider experience of using a bus. Young people need encouragement to give the bus another go.

Get the basic service right

The journey experience starts at the bus stop. Punctuality is a big issue, with a quarter of regular bus users in our survey claiming the bus is late all or most of the time. The environment here makes a big impact and young people really notice poor quality. Young people shared their negative experiences of bus stops that were dirty, littered with rubbish, poorly lit and displaying timetables that were unreadable. Young people – like all passenger groups – want a proper shelter with somewhere clean and comfortable to sit rather than just a pole and a sign. While on the bus, young people were strongly negative towards litter and dirty seats, which made them feel uneasy.

Information is an important requirement at the stop, both paper timetables and live bus running times. Young people are not used to waiting and do not want to waste time standing at the bus stop. They would prefer a system that gives them the bus times in advance, so that they can plan to get to the stop just in time. This ease of use is important for infrequent and non-bus users as well. For a comfortable experience on the bus, young people want to sit with their friends. They can feel quite uncomfortable on an overcrowded bus and do not like it when 'randomers' sit next to them. The bus driver is also key to how young people feel about the journey; a friendly approachable driver makes young people feel relaxed when they board and helps to set the tone for the journey. Young passengers want to use their time effectively and not feel bored. For them this means listening to music, using social media, browsing the internet and chatting to friends.

Wi-fi is needed to support many of these activities – and it must be fast and reliable. When asked to rank improvements, this was young people's second highest priority. Equally important was the provision of charging points at seats, particularly when they feel their journey is longer than a short hop.

Use technology to engage

Using mobile apps is a familiar way to access services for young people. However, space on young people's phones is limited and, therefore, valuable. Apps must first stand out as interesting enough to download and must then prove their worth through relevance and usefulness to earn a permanent place – they must also be designed well and easy to use.

Young people like using Google Maps, which comes ready installed on most smartphone devices; it does the job well, pulling different transport options together, and is seen as reliable. Young people are reluctant to download additional apps that do the same thing. Therefore, there may be more merit in collaborating on a single source or integrating functionality into Google Maps.

There is additional value too in an app-based solution to minimizing interaction with bus drivers and other passengers. This would help younger passengers avoid the anxiety of being 'shown up' in front of friends or other passengers when things go wrong.

Many systems young people are familiar with – such as apps to book cinema tickets – offer an easy-to-use interface, downloadable tickets and tailored offers and discounts. These apps are supported by good customer service that offers individual deals and options, and that put the consumer in charge with little interaction with staff. By contrast, young people don't feel that they have any relationship with bus operators, nor do they see that offers are targeted at them, or have them in mind.

Reliable, real-time information is key to helping young people feel confident when using the bus and improving their journey experience. They want easy-to-use, centralized and streamlined information. Young people want visual mapping and the ability to personalize their journey, across modes and operators. They want systems to 'hold their hand' through the experience and create a sense of understanding and familiarity. This includes fares shown with journey plans and at bus stops, clear information on discounts and easy ways to pay such as through smart and contactless. They also want information that updates along the journey, especially during delays, to give the cause, revised journey times and connections, supported by announcements and screens on board. Information is key.

While the basic needs for information and support are much the same for most bus passengers, is the industry doing enough to differentiate its offer to young people? Young people want to be engaged in the process of improving services and facilities. They want to be involved by decision-makers through social media, pop-up surveys within apps, short questionnaires on board and incentivizing responses through prize draws or money-off deals.

Simplify fares, make them consistent and reward loyalty

Although there are lots of discounts and special offers available for young people, there is limited awareness of these. Around half of young people did not understand the different discounts or special fares offered, including just under a fifth who were not sure these existed at all. Young people also don't feel like promotions are targeted at them. Only 42 per cent agreed that buses are the cheapest way of getting to places. In addition, 35 per cent pay for fares from their own pocket money or earnings, so feel the expense more keenly. Among young people, as in all age groups, value for money is the top priority for improvement.

Eligibility for reduced fares for under-16 or under-18-year-old passengers is not well understood. Young people are confused about what they are entitled to and when. 'Can my bus pass that gives half fare for travelling to education during the week be used for weekend travel?' 'Why do I have to pay adult fare if I am under 18 and travelling to college?'

It is felt to be particularly unfair to have to pay an adult fare under 18 when the school leaving age has been raised to 18. And with no national scheme for a young people's concession, there are confusing inconsistencies between bus operators and areas. Young people would like to see a reappraisal of bus fares for young people, applied consistently across areas and operators, with action to ensure they are not missing out on the best fares, to encourage greater use and make this a real and affordable option for them.

So, in summary, and in many respects, young people want the same from their bus journey as their fellow passengers, ranking value for money, punctuality and reliability highly as priorities for improvement. There are however key differences that young people want to see addressed:

- They do not feel services are designed with them in mind, or that enough is being done to encourage them and make them feel valued.

- Not knowing how the system works or what to do is a barrier and a source of anxiety about 'getting it right'.

- Improving the journey experience is important; young people notice poor quality provision.

- There is a need to design systems better, learning from other industries in the way they appeal to young people.

- Fares for young people are confusing and inconsistent. This work provides valuable understanding of young people's needs and aspirations for bus services.

Conclusions

These recommendations should be read as a checklist for action and a catalyst for bringing the industry together, working in collaboration towards making buses better for the users of tomorrow. In closing, I would best sum up my call to bus operators, transport authorities and governments as follows:

- Keep a relentless focus on delivering the basics of a punctual, reliable and value-for-money bus service.

- Bus drivers deliver the 'great journey' for passengers. Look after them, and they will look after your business.

- Think about your customers of tomorrow – young people. As one young person said to me 'make using the bus as easy as ordering a pizza'. Achieve that, and it will be easier for you to keep your current customers satisfied as well as attracting new business.

Finally I would like to finish by mentioning Bus Users UK, an independent charity that resolves complaints and seeks improvements for bus and coach passengers.

Bus Users UK

Bus Users UK is an independent, registered charity that aims to bring people and communities together through socially inclusive transport. It promotes high standards of urban and rural transport planning and service delivery, raising awareness of social exclusion caused by a lack of adequate transport, and working to make public transport inclusive and accessible to everyone.

It acts on behalf of passengers to resolve their complaints and improve services, and is an approved Alternative Dispute Resolution (ADR) Body for bus and coach passengers and the body which deals with complaints under the European Passenger Rights Regulation (outside London). A programme of local Your Bus Matters events aims to give passengers a voice, and bring communities together with the people responsible for running their services. Bus Compliance Officers in Scotland and Wales hold operators to account and help improve services for everyone. Bus Users UK works with bus and coach operators ensuring the needs of communities are at the heart of service planning and delivery. By understanding and responding to the needs of their customers and building healthy customer relationships, it supports operators to realize the business benefits of putting passengers first.

The value of the bus to society 16

CLAIRE HAIGH

Introduction

This chapter emphasizes the vital role that buses play in our society. The bus presents a major underexploited opportunity to reduce emissions, grow our economy and support everyone in our society. However, despite the enormous social value of the bus, patronage is declining. The impacts of the decline in bus patronage on society are severe and include increased social deprivation, damage to local economies and greater pollution.

The chapter investigates where we are now, where we want to be and how we will get there. We need a long-term bus investment strategy if we are to reverse the decline in bus patronage and maximize the role of the bus in tackling air pollution and carbon dioxide reduction, supporting jobs, growth and productivity, and providing essential access for millions in our society.

Where are we now?

Buses are the backbone of our public transport system, accounting for 59 per cent of all public transport journeys (Department for Transport, 2018a). However, bus patronage is declining. DfT bus statistics for March 2016 to March 2017 showed an average annual fall of 1.5 per cent across England (DfT, 2017). Quarterly figures show this trend continuing, with falls of 1.2 per cent in London and 1.7 per cent in England outside of London.

Scotland and Wales have fared even worse, with falls of 5.8 per cent and 3.7 per cent respectively (DfT, 2018b). This is part of a long-term trend. The number of bus services has shrunk every decade since the middle of the last century, from a high of 13,000 services in the mid-1950s to fewer than 5,000 in 2018.

The impacts on society of the continuing decline in bus patronage are severe. There is a clear quantified link between access to bus services and levels of social deprivation (University of Leeds Institute for Transport Studies, 2016a). Buses provide crucial assets to employment, education and essential services. 77 per cent of job seekers, and 87 per cent of 16 to 24-year-old job seekers, have no access to a car and are dependent on bus services (University of Leeds Institute for Transport Studies, 2013a). Buses are the primary means of access to city centres, facilitating 29 per cent of city centre expenditure (University of Leeds Institute for Transport Studies, 2013b). The decline in bus patronage damages local economies and leads to worsening congestion and pollution.

Many factors are contributing to the decline in bus patronage

These factors include rising congestion, increasing bus journey times and fares, disruptive changes, including more online shopping and delivery vehicles and private hire vehicles, the relatively low costs of motoring compared to public transport, and structural changes in the economy, including more part-time commuting, flexible working and home working. A study by KPMG found that the 7 per cent decline in bus patronage in Scotland 2012–16 was caused by higher car ownership, growth in online services, rising congestion and journey times and fare increases. The study showed that of the net reduction of 27 million trips in Scotland, 3.2 million were the result of changes to the structure of the economy and the labour market (KPMG, 2017a).

Congestion is both a major impact and cause of the decline in bus use, and congestion is worsening pollution. Buses are affected more detrimentally by congestion than any other mode. Since the 1960s congestion has been causing bus speeds to slow down by on average 10 per cent per decade, causing bus patronage to decline by 10–14 per cent, and costing 5,000 jobs per year (Greener Journeys, 2016). The latest figures show that this trend is worsening, with traffic congestion in the UK's largest cities 14 per cent worse than it was five years ago (Greener Journeys, 2017a).

Slower traffic speeds cause emissions to rise. Halving average city traffic speeds leads to a 50 per cent increase in harmful nitrogen dioxide emissions from larger vehicles (Low Carbon Vehicle Partnership, cited in Greener Journeys, 2017a). In nose-to-tail traffic, tailpipe emissions are four times greater than in free-flow traffic (Bell, M, cited in Greener Journeys, 2017a).

One of the factors behind slower traffic speeds is a change in the composition of traffic. In 2016 vans made up 15 per cent of all traffic, compared with 9 per cent in 1985 (SMMT, cited in Greener Journeys, 2017a). The change in the composition of traffic reduces the self-regulatory effect of rising congestion. With cars, lower speeds make it less attractive to drive. With vans, lower speeds mean more vehicles are required to maintain service levels. There may no longer be a floor to traffic speeds, and vehicles travelling at walking pace will become the norm unless action is taken.

The decline in bus patronage is linked to disruptive changes and is part of a world-wide trend. Buses have been hit hard by the impact of online retailing. The increase in delivery vehicles is worsening traffic congestion which impacts severely on bus services. Bus patronage is also suffering because people are increasingly shopping online and making fewer trips to the high street. Uber, Lyft and other 'ride-hailing' car services are also luring people away from buses. Studies show at least a third of ride-hailing trips would have been taken by public transport. American Public Transportation Association (APTA) figures show that the number of public transport journeys has fallen in the USA for each of the three years, 2016–18 (APTA, 2019).

The cost of public transport compares unfavourably with the car. Analysis for the RAC Foundation has shown that cost inflation for cars (which includes fuel as well as insurance) has been lower than bus or train ticket inflation over a ten-year period. The 2018 RAC *Annual Report on Motoring* showed that drivers' dependency on the car has increased, with 33 per cent more dependent on their cars and a quarter of these blaming a deterioration in public transport (RAC Foundation, 2018).

Increasing costs for road users is politically difficult, which is why fuel duty has been frozen since 2011, at a time of historically low oil prices and austerity. As the direct result of the freeze in fuel duty the price of fuel at the pump is 13 per cent lower than it would otherwise have been. This has caused traffic to grow by 4 per cent since 2011, an additional 4.5 million tonnes of carbon emissions and an additional 12,000 tonnes of NOx, and up to 200 million fewer bus journeys (Greener Journeys, 2018).

The potential of the bus to support local economies is not being realized

There is a lack of funding for local transport. This is despite local bus journeys forming a huge majority of public transport journeys and enabling people to access work, education and training, healthcare and social activities. Funding tends to be weighted in favour of capital expenditure with inadequate revenue support, which impacts particularly heavily on bus services. Moreover, buses have consistently lost out when tough decisions have been made on transport funding (Greener Journeys, PTEG & Campaign for Better Transport, 2015). Cuts to local authority budgets have severely impacted bus funding. Over the period 2010–18 there has been a 45 per cent reduction in funding for supported services; 3,347 services have been reduced or withdrawn (Campaign for Better Transport, 2018).

The potential of the bus to support local economies is not being realized. Investment in bus is not part of strategic economic plans. Cities are unable to plan effectively, and lack the funding and structures needed to develop integrated strategies for transport, employment and housing. Moreover, city and local leaders must bid for many different competitions, which provide a short-term funding stream and place a significant strain on the limited revenue available for transport planning (Urban Transport Group, 2018).

Funding for urban transport has not kept pace with other transport funding. While progress has been made on the interurban corridors and international gateways, investment in urban transport outside of London lags behind. This is in spite of the fact that urban transport networks underpin commuter journeys that create deep labour markets and enable people to access cultural and leisure activities (National Infrastructure Commission, 2018).

Infrastructure cannot drive growth alone, but lack of infrastructure can inhibit growth. Most major cities in the UK are behind national productivity levels, in contrast to large cities in many other European countries, which add to their country's productivity (Centre for Cities, 2016).

Where do we want to be?

We need to reverse the decline in bus patronage and deliver modal switch from car to bus and other forms of sustainable transport. This will help to support UK manufacturing and create jobs, alleviate congestion and improve air quality, support the decarbonization of transport, reduce social deprivation, support our major capacity challenges, and increase productivity and support local economies.

Buses can deliver many wider benefits to society

Buses support UK manufacturing and create more jobs. British bus manufacturing is already a success story. At least 80 per cent of urban buses sold in the UK are built in the UK, compared with just 13 per cent for cars (SMMT, cited in Greener Journeys, 2017a). Putting bus at the centre of investment and plans for local transport would further support UK manufacturing and create more jobs. Already more than 170,000 people are employed by the bus and coach industry. Through its supply chain the bus industry creates a further 83,000 jobs. The bus sector spends £2.5 billion in its supply chain (Greener Journeys, 2012).

Buses should be a major part of the solution to air pollution and congestion. Air pollution has been linked to 40,000 early deaths a year (Royal College of Physicians, 2016). Real-world testing of modern diesel buses demonstrates a 95 per cent reduction in NOx emissions compared with previous models, and a double decker bus can take 75 cars off the road. A modern diesel bus produces fewer emissions overall than a modern diesel car despite having 15 to 20 times the carrying capacity (Greener Journeys, 2017a). Government support for bus retrofitting provides 15 times better value for money per kilogram of NOx saved than car scrappage (Greener Journeys, 2017b).

Buses can play a central role in the decarbonization of transport. The bus sector already has the highest penetration of low carbon emission vehicles of all modes and types of transport. We have seen a revolution in clean bus technology – with more than 7,000 low carbon emission buses in operation. Buses are also leading the way on the road to zero. In 2018 4.2 per cent of new buses registered in the UK were zero emission at the tailpipe, compared with just 0.6 per cent of pure battery electric cars. Modal switch from car to bus will be key to meeting our carbon reduction targets. If everyone switched just one car journey a month to bus, there would be a billion fewer car journeys on our roads and a saving of 2 million tonnes of carbon dioxide every year.

Buses can play a major role in tackling social exclusion and deprivation. Nearly one in four people in the UK is at risk of social exclusion, and a quarter of households have no access to a car (KPMG, 2016). Half of all workless households have no access to a car. A 10 per cent improvement in local bus service connectivity can deliver a 3.6 per cent reduction in social deprivation. In the 10 per cent most deprived neighbourhoods in England, this reduction in deprivation is equivalent to 9,909 more people in work, 22,647 people with increased income, 7,313 more people with adult skills, and an improvement of 2,596 years in total life expectancy (University of Leeds Institute for Transport Studies, 2016b).

Concessionary bus travel for older and disabled people delivers real and significant economic and social benefits. Taking away the bus pass could cost the UK economy considerably in excess of £1.7 billion a year due to a decline in volunteering and poorer health and wellbeing amongst older people. The bus pass delivers a huge range of wider benefits to the UK's society and economy. Every £1 spent on the bus pass delivers over £3.80 of wider social and economic benefits. The bus pass enables older and disabled people to take part in activities that would not otherwise be accessible or affordable (KPMG, 2017b).

Buses have an important role to play in creating a fairer and more inclusive society. Bus travel supports education, training and employment and opens up opportunities for all. More than 50 per cent of students over 16 are frequent bus users (University of Leeds Institute for Transport Studies, 2012). Bus also strengthens the fabric of society and helps tackle loneliness. Two-thirds of bus users say that the bus creates strong community ties (Mindlab, 2015). A third of people in the UK have deliberately caught the bus in order to have some human contact (ComRes, 2018).

Improvements in bus services support training, employment and increase productivity. More people commute to work by bus than all other forms of public transport combined, and those bus commuters generate £64 billion in goods and services (University of Leeds Institute for Transport Studies, 2012). As a direct result of bus services, 400,000 workers are in better, more productive jobs and the additional economic output they produce is worth £400 million (University of Leeds Institute for Transport Studies, 2012). A 10 per cent reduction in bus journey times would mean 50,000 more people in work (University of Leeds Institute for Transport Studies, 2014).

Maximizing the potential of the bus to support local economies

Planning and investment in local bus networks will help unlock the value of new housing (KPMG, 2018). New developments in urban centres can stimulate 50 per cent more economic growth than similar developments located at the fringe, but these benefits will be diluted if traffic congestion cannot be controlled. Bus investment delivers significant returns for local economies. The bus facilitates 29 per cent of city centre expenditure, and 22 per cent of town centre expenditure (University of Leeds Institute for Transport Studies, 2013b). Typical capital schemes generate £4.90 per £1 invested, and high performing schemes such as the Crawley Fastway and Hampshire Eclipse generate returns of up to £8.10 per £1 invested (KPMG, 2017b).

We need to harness disruptive changes to encourage a switch from car to bus and other forms of sustainable transport. The pace of change in the UK's mobility landscape is arguably the fastest ever. Disruptive changes include bike share, car share, driverless cars, pods and buses, electric bikes and scooters, delivery drones, lorry platoons and delivery robots. These innovations need to be harnessed and channelled through platforms such as Mobility-as-a-Service to reduce car dependency.

We must ensure that the role of the bus is maximized in local economic plans. Local decision makers need to set out more coordinated plans for optimal outcomes across housing, transport, skills and productivity. Local transport authorities outside London should have stable, devolved infrastructure budgets, comprising five-year settlements, as Highways England and Network Rail have. These budgets should secure adequate provision for investment in local bus infrastructure.

Cities must have the powers and funding they need to pursue ambitious, integrated strategies for transport, employment and housing. Appropriate authority to make decisions on how to invest devolved urban infrastructure funding will usually be one that already exists: a Mayoral Combined Authority, Combined Authority or Unitary Authority. Where cities have no urban infrastructure authority of their own, Government should put appropriate arrangements in place.

How will we get there?

We need a long-term bus investment strategy with a funding commitment from central Government, and a commitment from bus operators and local authorities to work together to maximize the wider social, economic and environmental benefits of bus services. The strategy should focus on linking desperately needed new housing with areas of significant employment to help support the wider local economy. It also needs to be linked to demand management as the only real way to tackle traffic congestion and pollution.

The strategy should include:

- **Revenue support for bus services**. Local bus journeys form the huge majority of public transport journeys and provide essential access to work, education and training, healthcare and social activities. Revenue funding for bus services must be protected. The economic, social and environmental benefit for each £1 spent on bus revenue funding ranges from £2 to £3.80 (KPMG, 2017b).

- **Increased funding for urban transport.** The next wave of major transport upgrades should focus on transport within cities, to be provided to local transport authorities via stable, devolved infrastructure budgets, which must ensure adequate provision for local bus infrastructure. Buses need to be fully aligned with local plans for growth, land use planning and new housing, and plans to tackle air quality, carbon reduction and congestion.

- **Increased investment in local bus infrastructure.** Expenditure on bus capital projects is shown to generate considerable wider economic, social and environmental returns. Expenditure on bus capital projects generates £4.90–£8.10 of wider social, economic and environmental benefits for every £1 invested (KPMG, 2017b).

- **Modal switch from car to sustainable transport.** Bus operators, technology firms and local authorities need to form alliances to encourage service and product innovations, and to encourage the development of platforms such as Mobility-as-a-Service to reduce car dependency.

- **Demand management measures to reduce traffic.** Building new roads will not reduce traffic congestion. Typically, new roads lead to new journeys quickly filling up the additional space (Duranton and Turner, 2011). The only solution is to make better use of existing road capacity through measures such as road pricing, workplace parking levy and city centre entry restrictions.

A national strategy focused on maximizing the benefits of bus would support central Government priorities such as the Industrial Strategy Grand Challenges: Clean Growth and Future of Mobility, the Clean Air Strategy and the Road to Zero, as well as efforts to tackle the housing crisis, to reinvigorate our towns and city centres, even to tackle loneliness. It would strengthen local economies, reduce pollution and congestion, tackle social exclusion and build more cohesive communities.

A national strategy focused on maximizing the wider benefits of bus would support devolution by providing local transport authorities with the necessary funding and powers to invest for inclusive and sustainable growth in their local areas. It would help decision makers identify the costs, benefits and risks associated with different interventions. It would provide a framework for local decision makers to make the most of the powers in the Bus Services Act 2017 to maximize the wider benefits of bus.

A national bus strategy will also help the bus sector ride the wave of change in the new fast evolving urban mobility landscape. The emergence of countless new players providing new dynamic on-demand services brings both challenges and opportunities for traditional bus services. In a radically changing environment, public transport needs to be not just operations-cultured but needs to bring new products and services to market that will enhance customer experience. The strategy will need to create an environment where innovation can thrive.

The strategy will need to focus on addressing factors contributing to the decline in patronage. Some of these factors, such as long-term structural changes in the economy and labour market, increases in online shopping and other disruptive changes, may be beyond the scope of transport policy. However, factors such as rising congestion, increased bus journey times and fares, increased private hire vehicles, and the relatively low costs of motoring compared to public transport will need to be addressed.

If a national bus strategy is to be effective in reversing the decline in bus patronage, it must necessarily complement wider transport policy. Bus policy cannot sit in isolation to policies for roads, parking, traffic management and fiscal measures. Turning the tide will require a major refocusing of Government priorities. Currently all the price signals point the wrong way. The freeze in fuel duty since 2011, for example, has caused a 4 per cent increase in traffic and 200 million fewer bus journeys (Greener Journeys, 2018).

Conclusions

The bus presents a major underexploited opportunity to grow the economy, reduce emissions and support everyone in society. Investing more in local bus networks supports job creation and improves productivity. Expenditure on bus capital can generate £8 of wider economic benefit for every £1 invested (KPMG, 2017b). Buses can play a key role in reducing congestion and air pollution. A modern diesel bus produces fewer harmful NOx emissions overall than a modern diesel car despite having 15 to 20 times the carrying capacity (Greener Journeys, 2017a). Buses help create a fairer and more inclusive society. A 10 per cent improvement in bus service connectivity is associated with a 3.6 per cent reduction in social deprivation (University of Leeds Institute for Transport Studies, 2016b).

However, despite the vital role of the bus in supporting the economy, reducing pollution and congestion, and providing access for many to work, education and essential services, bus patronage is declining. Bus networks are suffering from a perfect storm of rising congestion, increased bus journey times and fares, the effects of disruptive changes including online shopping, more delivery vehicles and increase in private hire vehicles, structural changes in the economy and labour market; and the relatively low costs of motoring compared with public transport.

The impacts of the decline in bus patronage on society are severe and include increased social deprivation, damage to local economies and greater pollution. The decline comes at a time when it is more important than ever that the potential of the bus is harnessed to tackle our air quality crisis and reduce carbon emissions and congestion.

We need a long-term bus investment strategy if we are to reverse the decline in bus patronage and maximize the role of the bus. The strategy should include:

- support for bus revenue funding;
- increased funding for urban transport, provided through stable, five-year and secure devolved budgets;
- increased investment in local bus infrastructure;
- the use of new technology platforms to reduce car dependency and encourage modal switch;
- demand management measures to reduce traffic congestion.

It is time we had a national strategy for buses. All other forms of transport, including even walking and cycling, have national strategies. A national strategy for bus would create a policy framework to help decision makers at all levels to maximize the very considerable wider benefits to society of the bus.

References

APTA (2019) [accessed 27 September 2019] 2019 Public Transportation Fact Book, *APTA* [online] www.apta.com/wp-content/uploads/APTA_Fact-Book-2019_FINAL.pdf (archived at https://perma.cc/9UCC-PKRH)

Campaign for Better Transport (2018) *Buses in Crisis 2018*, London

Centre for Cities (2016) [accessed 13 February 2020] Competing with the continent, *Centre for Cities* [online] www.centreforcities.org/publication/competing-with-the-continent/ (archived at https://perma.cc/X3ZF-RESC)

ComRes (2018) *Survey for Greener Journeys*, 2002 British adults interviewed 19–20 September 2018

DfT (2017) *Annual Bus Statistics Year Ending March 2017*, London

DfT (2018a) *Annual Bus Statistics Year Ending March 2018*, London

DfT (2018b) *Quarterly Bus Statistics January to March 2018*, London

Duranton, G and Turner, M A (2011) The Fundamental Law of Road Congestion: Evidence from US Cities, *American Economic Review*, **101** (6), pp 2, 616–52

Greener Journeys (2012) *Bus Policy: A Five Point Plan for Growth*, London

Greener Journeys (2016) *The Impact of Congestion on Bus Passengers*, London

Greener Journeys (2017a) *Tackling Pollution and Congestion: Why congestion must be reduced if air quality is to improve*, London

Greener Journeys (2017b) *Improving Air Quality in Towns and Cities*, London

Greener Journeys (2018) *The Unintended Consequences of Freezing Fuel Duty*, London

Greener Journeys, PTEG & Campaign for Better Transport (2015) *A Fair Deal for Bus Users*, London

KPMG (2016) [accessed 14 February 2020] A study of the value of local bus services in society, *Greener Journeys* [online] https://greenerjourneys.com/wp-content/uploads/2016/10/Greener-Journeys-Value-of-Bus-to-Society-FINAL.pdf (archived at https://perma.cc/B58J-Y35U)

KPMG (2017a) [accessed 14 February 2020] Trends in Scottish bus patronage, *Get on Board with Bus* [online] https://getonboardwithbus.scot/wp-content/themes/minimum/doc/Trends_in_Scottish_Bus_Patronage.pdf (archived at https://perma.cc/2ZVQ-7BJN)

KPMG (2017b) [accessed 14 February 2020] The 'true value' of local bus services, *Greener Journeys* [online] https://greenerjourneys.com/wp-content/uploads/2017/07/Greener-Journeys-Value-for-Money-Update-FINAL.pdf (archived at https://perma.cc/5SMN-F8XL)

KPMG (2018) Sustainable Transport: the key to unlocking the benefits of new housing, *Transport Knowledge Hub* [online] https://transportknowledgehub.org.uk/wp-content/uploads/2018/05/CRT090572_Sustainable-Transport_Housing_FINAL.pdf (archived at https://perma.cc/F73A-5E52)

Mindlab (2015) *University of Sussex research for Greener Journeys*

National Infrastructure Commission (2018) *National Infrastructure Assessment*

RAC Foundation (2018) [accessed 14 February 2020] RAC Report on Motoring 2018: The frustrated motorist, *RAC Foundation* [online] www.rac.co.uk/pdfs/report-on-motoring/rac10483_rom-2018_content_web (archived at https://perma.cc/Y22X-WD3A)

Royal College of Physicians (2016) [accessed 14 February 2020] Every breath we take: the lifelong impact of air pollution, *Royal College of Physicians* [online] www.rcplondon.ac.uk/file/2912/download (archived at https://perma.cc/E6L8-EVKP)

University of Leeds Institute for Transport Studies (2012) *Buses and Economic Growth*

University of Leeds Institute for Transport Studies (2013a) *Survey of bus use amongst the unemployed*

University of Leeds Institute for Transport Studies (2013b) *Survey of town and city centre expenditure*

University of Leeds Institute for Transport Studies (2014) *Buses and the Economy*, ii Task 3

University of Leeds Institute for Transport Studies (2016a) *The value of local bus services*, Task iii Technical Report Econometric Analysis

University of Leeds Institute for Transport Studies (2016b) *A study of the value of local bus services to society*

Urban Transport Group (2018) [accessed 14 February 2020] Policy Futures for Urban Transport, *Urban Transport Group* [online] www.urbantransportgroup. org/system/files/general-docs/UTG %E2%80%93 Policy futures for urban transport 2018 FINAL web.pdf (archived at https://perma.cc/C9BZ-CC8M)

Further reading

Low Carbon Vehicle Partnership [online] www.lowcvp.org.uk (archived at https:// perma.cc/5RDY-B2GM)

RAC Foundation [online] https://racfoundation.org (archived at https://perma.cc/ NS3J-TZ6M)

Presentation 17

ROGER FRENCH AND RAY STENNING

Introduction

How bus services are presented is not just about a commanding livery or an attractive timetable leaflet. It's about communicating a brand ethos which, as far as possible, sums up what the company is all about and, in a customer-centric business, emphasizes excellent customer service. This must be at each and every touchpoint of the business: whether that's conversations with drivers or other customer-facing staff; how letters, phone calls, emails, tweets and social media are answered; how timetable, ticket information and promotional collateral are presented and distributed; how the bus is presented both externally and internally. A brand covers all these points and needs consistently to convey the same customer-centric message.

Managers need to be obsessed with giving exceptional customer service. There must be a 'wow' factor to each journey so that a passenger is already looking forward to their next journey before they leave the bus. It's all about creating a desire to travel by bus.

To believe our job is merely getting human cargo from A to B at minimal cost is to seriously not understand both the nature of running a bus business and what a proper customer-focused business should be all about in the 21st century – how to build a strong business with clout.

Let's knock into touch the nonsense about 'bus companies are not retailers'. What complete nonsense. People pay money and get goods and or services in return. That's retail, whether it's a pair of Jimmy Choo shoes, a pound of spuds or that bus ride to the shops.

Marks & Spencer doesn't just sell sandwiches, ready meals and underwear, John Lewis doesn't just sell bedding, curtains and cutlery, Amazon doesn't just sell everything. They are a lifestyle choice, and provide a pleasurable experience that their customers love and keep coming back to experience again and again because it was so pleasurable (note – not just satisfied with).

The best retailers draw you in and seduce you with enticing goods beautifully displayed, with contemporary design, clever lighting and arresting interior decor, so much so that it would be churlish not to spend money with them. Compare that to unenlightened bus companies who offer a sea of battleship grey, harsh strip lighting, bland wipe-clean surfaces and a surly driver stuck behind an anti-terrorist Perspex screen – welcoming it is not.

Imagine turning up at a hotel as a guest. The hotel won't have third-party adverts covering the major part of its frontage, including one for its competitor up the road. The paintwork's unlikely to be damaged, scratched or even scuffed. The hotel is likely to have the correct name over the front door (wrong route branding on buses is endemic in some parts of the country). In the hotel reception, it's unlikely you'll find the receptionist welcoming you from behind a Perspex screen. They'll smile warmly, pass pleasantries and make you feel welcome and inspire confidence. How does the hotel decor make you feel? Is it stylish and contemporary or flat, grey and depressingly bland? Do the walls, doors and windows rattle? Is there dirt accumulating around chair legs and in corners? Are there dead flies and debris in the light fittings?

In your room is the upholstery and bedding worn, faded and stained? Is the bed comfortable and can you fit in it, including your feet? You booked a room with a sea view. Can you see it? Are the windows clean? Can you see out of them, or are they covered with grime or, worse, contravision so you can only see a fuzzy, blurred, dim view of the sea as it advertises some other product back to front. Look around the room. Does it have (poorly-arranged) adverts reminding you about health and wellbeing?

We don't, and should never assume that we do, have a captive market or we have an inalienable right to that market. In this day and age, everyone has choices. And with the internet and Skype, sometimes the choice can be not to travel at all. Even commuters can jump on their bikes, cadge a lift or work somewhere else, if what you offer them is not to their liking.

The mindset must be all about keeping the market and growing it. There's a constant churn due to customers changing their travel patterns, moving away, changing work or education, shopping elsewhere, aside from societal shifts including online shopping and regionalization of medical facilities. There's also a tendency for some to regard bus travel as a last resort mode of travel, a distress purchase. Something for those sad people who don't have a car or access to a lift in one.

There's no place for such a defeatist attitude. Buses must be presented as an aspirational purchase for savvy travellers not wanting to be encumbered with a metal box on wheels, which they have the stress of driving and then finding somewhere to park when they reach their destination, often at considerable cost too. Increasingly, there are sound environmental reasons why bus travel is a much more appropriate mode than private car use as awareness of climate change and calls for action grow louder. Advances in propulsion technology means buses are often less polluting than cars, even before the relative capacity for passengers is taken into account.

But it's naive to think motorists will be won over simply by running an electric or gas-powered bus. That is unlikely to make much impact in its own right – it's more of a 'feel good' reassurance the correct decision has been chosen to take a more efficient and sensible way of travelling due to other factors.

The best businesses, including bus companies, are the ones that have the right products and know how to create desire for those products, and how to make buying them an absolute pleasure. The customers keep coming back, and new ones are attracted. Personal recommendations even follow. One reason major retailers have failed in recent years (eg BhS) is that they lost touch with their customers and weren't selling what those customers really wanted, and made it all a pretty drab experience to boot.

Sometimes you don't have to change your product, just how you present it. Previously, Lucozade is what people bought to drink when they were recovering from an illness. It came in a large screw-top bottle with orange cellophane wrapped round it. Sales were declining, so they repositioned it in the market as a youthful energy drink for athletes and wannabe athletes. Sales soared.

You don't go to a nice restaurant merely to eat. You go because you're hungry, of course, but you choose it for the atmosphere, the ambience, the company, the decor, the buzz, the service and all sorts of things. This same thinking is needed in selling bus travel. Let's make people really desire taking a bus journey.

Understand the local market

Understanding the market is an essential first step to marketing a bus service. And this means understanding that each local market is different. The market for bus travel in Brighton is different to Blackpool and different again to Bridlington. Some towns and cities are characterized by high student populations and a vibrant night life. Others may have traditional industrial estates. Others still have a strong leisure market based on a coastal location. Some have a major out-of-town shopping centre which sucks trade and vibrancy from the traditional high street; others have invested in their town centres and are enjoying a renaissance despite the challenges facing the retail sector. The locations of schools and health facilities, hospitals and leisure destinations are also very much local influencers.

Bus company managers must ensure they know all about the markets of which their network of bus services forms part. The presence of competition from other bus companies or a local train network as well as local authority policies on car parking can have a major impact. All these local factors determine how buses and bus routes are presented. A bland corporate image and presentation just doesn't cut it when each local market is so different.

Livery

Few businesses have the luxury of displaying their brand so prominently to customers and potential customers as a bus company. Buses are on display all over our towns and cities, including right through busy centres where footfall is at its highest. Other commercial businesses would pay dearly for such high profile awareness; indeed, they do, on 48-sheet billboard posters, or (ironically) on the outsides of buses. It's always puzzled us why some bus companies forgo the opportunity to exclusively promote their own brand values, and instead subjugate these in favour of a third party in return for payment.

Great care is needed to ensure a livery conveys the brand values of the company and is professionally designed to acknowledge the shape and lines of each type of bus body to great advantage. Specialist marketing agencies who understand this and are well experienced in designing liveries with attention to detail are recommended. A livery designed by a well-meaning, but misguided, bus company director who fancies themselves as an amateur designer or a design agency with no experience of buses is usually all too obvious.

Many areas have a long association with buses being painted in a certain colour; this goes back to days of proud municipal ownership or long established locally based private companies well before nationalization in the 1960s. It might make sense to acknowledge such traditions in designing a livery for the modern age, as it shows a bus company being in tune with local heritage – but not if that earlier tradition is now regarded in a very unfavourable light.

Livery variations can be a very effective way of differentiating different products within a bus network. A number of bus companies use colour-coded route branding to highlight their most frequent and popular bus services, and crucially do so within an overall brand which emphasizes the network as well as individual routes. Reading Buses and Nottingham City Transport have been doing this for some years to great effect, as does neighbouring Trentbarton, which was an early adopter of individual route brands for its network of bus routes across Nottinghamshire and Derbyshire. It makes for a bright, attractive and colourful bus scene across these counties, and it's interesting to compare the vibrancy of the city network in Nottingham to the more staid and less exciting image created by Arriva's corporate brand in Derby.

Other bus companies have used variations of a livery to differentiate the type of service being offered. Stagecoach have developed a Gold brand to indicate higher-quality interiors and Arriva have used Sapphire and Max for similar objectives, while Travel West Midlands have adopted a Platinum brand.

It's important not to try to convey too many messages within a livery. There's a limit to how much can be taken in from a cursory sighting of a moving vehicle as it passes by and it's best to identify the key positive features of the route or network and concentrate on these.

For over two decades Brighton & Hove Bus Company have followed a tradition of naming each bus in their fleet after local deceased people who made a significant contribution to local or national life during their lifetime. The name is carried in a prominent space on the front of the bus. This project has proved to be an excellent way of associating the bus fleet with the local area, giving each bus a personality and raising local interest – most of the names have come from suggestions submitted by local people and it's now regarded as quite an accolade for a deceased person to be acknowledged in this way; akin to a blue plaque.

On the inside

Once a livery has successfully enticed customers to step aboard and take a journey, it's important that the design of the interior maintains the same brand values providing a seamless transition from outside to inside. The choice of seat, seat fabric, floor and wall covering and the overall colour scheme chosen together with lighting effects are key decisions. These need to be taken by managers who understand the local market and are well versed in the company's brand values and designed with the help of experienced experts in this field.

We want, and passengers deserve, a cool, swish, stylish travelling experience that is enjoyable rather than merely endurable; why not inspirational too? We need to look at every aspect of the interior and exterior to make it not just fit for purpose, but enticing, an object of desire that makes a journey something you want to do again and again. Why not? The better end of the retail trade and just about every urban cafe worth its salted caramel latte understands this. If you think a bus is merely a conveyance for human cargo, come into the 21st century and beyond.

Indirect lighting, as pioneered by Optare several years ago, is just one example of a lovely touch that makes bus travel better – why do we persevere with harsh (although slightly diffused these days) overhead strip lighting? You wouldn't have it in your living room at home.

There may be technical reasons why on some buses, there are often uncomfortable, hard, and sometimes forward-tilted seats at the rear or over wheel arches, but we should be looking at ways to eliminate these offences. A great example of this can be seen on the stylish buses used on Transdev Blazefield's flagship route 36 where the rearwards facing seats downstairs have been replaced with a useful table-like shelf and small luggage stowage areas for those in the rear row. The rear cramped five across seats have been replaced by a more spacious four-across layout. This has transformed the rear downstairs to be a prize place to sit, a piano nobile in architectural terms, rather than the least favourite.

When people pay money to get on a bus, they have paid to get from A to B but, just like in a bar or restaurant, they are giving up a fair number of minutes of their life to you, so those minutes should be as enjoyable as bus companies can economically make them. The ambience they are in, the seats they sit on, the surrounding features they are seeing or able to make use of, should all be so superb and enjoyable that they want to pay more money to do it all over again, and again, and again. Note the word 'want', not 'have to'. Functional just won't cut the mustard any more with our discerning customers of the future.

Why should a bus journey too often be the moving equivalent of the worst NHS waiting room? Why, as an industry, do we view good design with such suspicion? It's not a bit of superficial froth, it's an essential business tool that can improve the bottom line.

Many bus companies fit wi-fi and USB sockets as standard to each seat in recognition of changing lifestyles and priorities; some are now including litter bins with segments for recycling. However, the benefit of wi-fi can be nullified by a complicated sign up procedure, poor signal, or limited use before being cut off. This soon turns a positive into a negative, particularly if expectations have been raised by prominent signage.

Despite the obvious benefits of next stop displays and announcements, some bus companies have resisted adding this hugely useful facility, especially appreciated by strangers and tourists in an area, let alone those with sight or hearing impediments. Such aids are now standard on new trains and should be so on buses.

Websites

A bus livery is a great way to share a bus company's brand values with everyone walking the streets of a local area, but a website gives a bus company a global audience. Its design and functions must be carefully considered. It's likely to be the main touchpoint for the majority of potential customers who've yet to actually take a ride. The design and layout must be instantly recognized as being 'on brand' and the homepage should clearly identify the main pages used by those visiting the site.

Bus times, information about prices of fares and tickets, and maps are key pages to highlight. Many websites give prominence to journey planners; some bus companies use the Traveline resource which provides travel information for all operators and across modes, while others restrict the results to their own services. The downside of the latter is that passengers can be given incomplete information; it's understandable why bus companies should want to promote their own services through a journey planner, but it makes no sense to conceal options for passengers to take. Concealing the truth is perceived as telling a lie.

Two downsides of journey planners are, firstly, in some cases, for the data file to work, passengers need to be able to correctly specify the name of the bus stop they're aiming to travel to or from, which may be unknown and, secondly, on infrequent services, passengers may not be aware that a journey runs just before the desired departure time they specify and think they have a considerable wait rather than be able to travel just slightly earlier. That's why journey planners are no substitute for traditional presented timetables and a map.

There are some excellent websites for bus companies – many for smaller companies, or those in the Go-Ahead Group. The problem for Arriva, First Bus and Stagecoach is they are trying to present local information on a national website. This can make for a clunky and confusing experience.

Printed timetables and maps

Many passengers now obtain information about their bus services online and some bus companies misguidedly believe this removes the need to produce printed timetables and other promotional literature. It's absolutely essential to make available an attractive printed timetable leaflet or booklet which can act as a sales document to encourage travel as well as providing information. In addition to the timetable itself, information should be provided about fares and tickets, a map and locations of key bus stops, as well as reasons to catch the bus route or network, such as local attractions and places of interest served.

Having the information online is no substitute for the necessity for printed literature. Can you imagine being seated at a table in your favourite restaurant, and the waiter says they've ceased producing menus as it's all online, and you have to use your smartphone (if you have one) and hope there's a mobile signal or wi-fi? It wouldn't impress, and neither does it impress when bus companies don't offer printed timetables.

It's very much down to local circumstances to decide whether to produce a timetable book providing comprehensive coverage of all bus routes in a local network or individual route leaflets for each bus service. Bus companies in tourist areas find a timetable book is popular with passengers, as it provides the full picture of what's available and encourages travel right across the network. Examples of excellent booklets produced twice a year are for the Lake District, Isle of Wight, Dorset and Cornwall. There's a long-standing Bus Times magazine-style timetable which has been produced twice each year since soon after deregulation in 1987 by Brighton & Hove. This also includes the timetables and information of all bus operators in the area (who contribute towards the cost) and is an excellent example of providing a useful timetable which is highly valued by passengers.

It's important to include a 'valid until' date as well as a 'starts from' date on a timetable book so passengers can be reassured the contents are up to date and correct. If bus companies follow the discipline of having two or three fixed dates each year on which changes are made to bus routes, it naturally follows that a timetable book can be produced for that period and everyone knows where they are.

One benefit of producing individual route leaflets is they don't need reprinting if the contents haven't changed, but from the passenger's perspective they may not be reassured that the leaflet they may have in their possession is up to date and correct. There's also less opportunity to cross-promote other bus routes in a network, and passengers may only be aware of the route they use regularly or occasionally.

Good quality network and bus route maps are an essential ingredient of a timetable book or leaflet. There's no better way of graphically demonstrating where a bus route goes, and its relationship with other routes in a network, than on a coloured geographic style map. Route 'Underground style' diagrams are never so good for an even slightly complex network; they may work for track-based systems, but seldom do for road transport based routes. A professional cartographer is highly recommended as it's important to convey the information in a clear and easy to assimilate way, including the use of colour, how routes are shown grouped together, bus stops served and terminal points.

It is simply incongruous that Transport for London ceased producing a bus map in 2016, including online. There have been many changes to bus routes across the capital since then yet, other than a map produced independently by a bus enthusiast, there's no official representation of where bus routes go as a network across London. A quite extraordinary state of affairs, and the best example we know of how not to run a bus network. Even more bizarre is that TfL produce printed and online maps for the Underground (a much simpler network) and in many different versions too, including showing walking times, availability of toilets, sections under and over ground and much more.

Sadly, a number of country councils have also ceased producing maps and where parts of the network are run by a disparate collection of smaller bus operators it is simply impossible to find out where bus routes go. No wonder passenger numbers are falling, it's impossible for any new passengers to be attracted with such a dire lack of information.

It goes without saying that timetables and maps, when produced, need to be made freely available. There's one bus company which places timetables in leaflet racks in their Travel Shop, with notices restricting customers to only take one copy. This is a quite extraordinary policy – can you imagine a pizza take-away restaurant having a similar rule for its take-away menus? With notable exceptions, bus companies are very poor at making promotional literature widely available. Stagecoach in Cumbria is one of those who excel making its Lake District timetable book available in hopper units at many high profile places throughout this busy area, including rail stations and supermarkets. Bespoke units containing the books are also built into every bus and are always kept topped up with copies. That's how you encourage bus travel.

Bus stops

If you had a shop, and the council came along and dug up the pavement in front of it so that people couldn't get in – and left it like that for days, or months – you'd rightly be up in arms. So why, when a council no longer has enough time, money or manpower to maintain bus stop infrastructure and information, do some bus companies either not notice or just shrug their shoulders?

Bus stops are the shop windows for a bus route, and bus companies are lucky to have such a prominent place to display details of their services where passers-by can see it. Other businesses would be delighted to have such promotional opportunities for their products on the street. In those areas where local authorities insist on taking responsibility for maintaining bus stops and the information displayed, it behoves bus companies to take a keen interest that such information is presented well and is up to date. If it's lacking, then bus companies should be relentless in ensuring action is taken, and not give up until it's sorted.

In other areas, bus companies themselves look after the display of information, and in such cases there's no excuse for any shortcomings. It's important that bus stop flags and timetable cases are kept clean and present an excellent impression.

The information presented needs to be easily understood. Some scheduling systems purport to be able to churn out roadside information, but these are often designed by techy people who fail to understand how things need to be presented from a customer viewpoint. The information is too often data driven, not customer focused. For example, if there is a 'field' for a route number and it's only a number 16 that goes from that stop, that number is repeated on every departure time, an unnecessary visual fidget that compromises quick understanding of the information. Likewise, those awful chronological lists that make you have to look elsewhere to see if the 10.46 number 203 goes to where you want it, or if you have to wait for the 216 at 11.05. And if only final destinations are listed on the separate route list, how do you know if it goes to your intermediate destination?

There's a golden rule that you should never make customers have to keep cross-referencing different bits of information or, worse, make them do mental arithmetic to work out the actual time the bus departs.

One reason that it is sometimes woefully bad in some areas is that people working within the company's office don't get out and about anywhere near enough on their own (and others') buses to see what it's like on the ground and out in the field.

Social media

Years ago, it was a huge challenge for bus companies to be able to communicate instant information effectively with customers. If services were being disrupted due to adverse weather or congestion issues, it was virtually impossible to let passengers know what was happening. Now, thanks to social media channels, it's easy to communicate to tens of thousands of potential customers and keep them informed, as well as others who are just taking an interest in how a company is performing.

It behoves bus companies to make sure their social media is up-to-the-minute and effective. Many bus companies have embraced this opportunity and have built an audience of many tens of thousands of followers who appreciate the information and the ability to communicate two-way with someone at the bus company who is in touch with what's happening on the road. Sadly there are some appalling examples from some well-resourced (international) bus groups who choose to centralize their social media comments, such that the result is ineffective and often embarrassing. Worse still, when there might be widespread disruption, some banal marketing message or an inept attempt to engage with the audience (which may be automated to be sent out at a particular time) completely misses the mark, and makes the company look out of touch and foolish.

Conclusions

It really can be the details that make the heart-warming difference; the touchpoints rather than the grand gestures. So, the comfort of the seat can have a greater impact on a customer's positive relationship with the bus company more than the fact that it's a Euro 6 engine (although do promote that as well); the warm, welcoming smile from the driver on a miserable day means an awful lot more to a customer than the corporate message about how much bus companies spent on buying buses.

And, likewise, the reassurance offered by stylish presentation of accurate, easy-to-understand, easy-to-read, helpful information at bus stops, in bus stations and by the roadside is invaluable. Bus companies simply can't afford not to do it.

The future and new technology

18

TONY FRANCIS

Introduction

Evidence suggests that the bus and coach business can have a secure, long-term future in making an even more significant and positive contribution towards society. Support for this comes from the growing awareness and concern for action to mitigate climate change, linked with the need to improve air quality, along with offering a high standard of mobility for everybody.

This requires addressing the overuse of highways, growing urban pollution, congestion which so adversely affects bus operations, complex journey needs and ensuring the ever-changing mobility requirements of the population are properly met. Addressing isolation of those living in remote areas is also a matter being earnestly debated. Although such issues have long existed, the combination of these environmental and social pressures generate a climate in which expeditious action is hopefully likely to occur.

The harnessing of ever-developing IT products to support public transport is likely to be a vital cornerstone of this future scenario. Such products need to support customers, staff and operations; applied accurately they will lead the business forward.

It has been encouraging to note that one of the industry's leading organizations, the Confederation of Passenger Transport (CPT), targets an increase in bus use by almost a quarter over the period to 2030, but only with working with other, allied parties (CPT, 2019). CPT offers improved and more attractive ticketing and new ultra low/zero emission buses, in return for measures that put bus travel 'at the heart of local and national government planning'.

Partnering

Through the many options in the Bus Services Act 2017, but also with previous legislation, work between operators and local authorities has shown such co-operation can provide improved bus services.

Recent examples include NE Bus which acknowledges the economic benefit of bus services and is also addressing the need to identify bus preference measures which can offer a positive return. Similar work in the Liverpool City Region aims to offer a comprehensive bus system throughout Merseyside. There have been other, now long-established arrangements throughout the country, upgrading bus services and providing highway measures to improve the conditions in which they operate.

These have provided the foundations upon which future, wider partnerships are likely to arise, involving other bodies with an interest in the community. They may be, for example, local and national employers, health and social service organizations, along with utility providers.

Buses meet local needs, and thus it is vital that knowledge and intelligence is secured to influence the network of services provided. Information on the social and economic situation, the challenges faced by people making local journeys and the various business and social activities need to be fully understood. Given the concerns being expressed over the future of the planet and the need for sustainable lifestyles, the bus (and in many cases the coach as well) offers an ideal solution.

Buses are part of the totality of ingredients offering quality mobility; we will look at the standards which the business can and will almost certainly aspire to. But before doing so, let us also examine the foundations of a successful public transport system, which are found in the planning.

Transport and land use planning

There is a realization that greater attention needs to be given in planning both residential and commercial developments to the travel needs of people. Equally, there is the growing acceptance that this must be done sustainably; ensuring human activity does not adversely affect the climate, thus safeguarding the future of the planet. The provision of transport which contributes to such objectives is a key matter that is now acknowledged.

With operators and their representatives working closely with developers and local stakeholders, proper provision for bus operation, balanced alongside cycling, walking, commercial and private transport should be achieved.

Road pricing, paying for the use of highways as they are used, has been the subject of debate since the 1960s. This could now be an alternative tax raising option for government as fossil fuel consumption reduces. Importantly, it could be applied to ensure only optimum use was made of highways, thus eliminating uncontrolled congestion which adversely affects public transport provision.

Vehicles – propulsion

It is difficult to determine whether all electric, battery electric, diesel electric hybrid, hydrogen, bio-fuelled or even some conventional diesel engine buses will dominate vehicle fleets in the longer term. It is possible that a variety of systems will apply along with methodology that has yet to appear. Already the Low Carbon Vehicle Partnership, through its Bus Working Group, has been pursuing a cleaner bus fleet throughout the country (Low Carbon Vehicle Partnership, nd). Initially this has concentrated on a 30 per cent reduction in greenhouse gas emissions, but there is now an acceptance that zero emissions should be the target. Transport for London (TfL) plans to ensure that from 2020, all new single deck buses operating on their network will be emissions-free (TfL, 2019). All TfL contracted routes should be provided with zero-emission buses by 2037.

Nearly all buses delivered nationwide into service in 2018 already incorporated fuel saving devices; significant numbers of diesel-hybrid buses are operating along with zero-emission buses. As older vehicles come up for replacement, their successors will be of the latter variety.

Where different fuels and propulsion systems are used (such as all electric), there will be impacts on power supply, garaging and potential extra costs in maintaining a fleet economically, which could also affect land use and street design issues.

Vehicles – autonomously driven or not

Already the concept of minimizing the requirement, if not totally dismissing the need, for a bus driver has been almost proven. A bus can be safely driven without a human at the wheel albeit, under controlled conditions. Technology is already applied to monitor and support drivers whilst working, especially to ensure fatigue does not compromise safety. It is conceivable that on corridors (such as exclusive busways) where the bus has exclusive use, the driver can assume a more supervisory role, but further developments are likely to be applied to improve safety, efficiency and the overall quality of service to passengers.

The driver will remain but assisted through further technology to provide an even safer and more comfortable journey for passengers.

Vehicles – interior design

Already current bus and coach design takes increasing account of customer needs, especially around safety, information and amenities. With increasing knowledge about a community's needs, especially those with disabilities, others accompanying children and luggage, plus students and the business community, the opportunity can and may well be increasingly taken to adapt the interior layout to meet such requirements.

Passengers and their buses

A long identified obstacle to using buses had been the challenge of actually finding out about them. Information and publicity standards vary, with little uniform system of presentation, so a potential user may not easily (if indeed at all) establish what is on offer. If any partnership is to succeed in making more use of buses, then there is likely to be greater concentration of effort in this field. There is a need for a debate between paper versus electronic information, to ensure which is right (or is it both?) to reach the potential passenger, as well as the present customer base.

There is an acceptance that the shop window of the industry needs uplifting; be that of the humble bus stop along with the vehicles themselves. Good presentation is seen (including clear destination indicators) as important along with further driver and staff training. Again these are likely to be matters of importance as part of any partnership. Presentation is discussed fully in Chapter 17.

Paying for the journey

The cashless transaction, using bespoke prepaid cards or contactless bank cards, is rapidly becoming the norm. What next? Predicting accurately is difficult, but facial recognition, although currently potentially infringing on privacy matters, may be one option to identify individual passengers and ensure they were debited with the required fare. Alternatively, some authorities may look to offer more free travel by bus to encompass a greater share of travel needs.

It will be incumbent upon operators to be aware of other IT developments in this field and take advantage, ahead of any rivals.

Bus and coach services

Scheduled bus

There has been a decline in daily commuting, perhaps inevitable with the ability to communicate and correspond remotely, along with an adverse effect on shopping travel into town centres. However, attempts are being made to revive high streets especially with new recreational activities. Understanding these upheavals and recasting services requires working in collaboration with others in the community to determine the future role of local public transport. The emerging partnerships will be an important basis of this identification.

Quite probably, conventional, local bus services, working to a fixed schedule with fixed picking up and setting down points will continue. These will be based in urban areas, running along main corridors linking towns and city centres via adjoining suburbs and secondary centres. The frequency and capacity of such services will depend upon not only the legislative framework applicable to the area but a variety of other commercial and social pressures. The pattern of services within an area such as London and possibly elsewhere, where one authority may determine the network, may be different to one where commercial considerations of operators are commercially influenced. However, the involvement of partnership working will potentially influence network design.

There is growing recognition that rural areas equally require public transport; but with greater imagination on how they are secured for the longer term. Over 25 per cent of bus users in England and outside the capital are mainly made in rural dominated areas; thus there is still a not insignificant market.

There is much potential in the greater application of 'total transport' or where one vehicle is deployed for a variety of tasks, ranging from home to school transport, a social service link to a care centre, non-emergency patient transport to hospitals, and then a bus link between villages and the adjacent regional centre/market town. Again this requires local knowledge and co-operation (through partnering) with other public agencies and with local intelligence, as to exactly what is required by way of bus links that will gain maximum use.

On-demand bus

The growing application of demand-responsive services, based generally on the use of shared minibuses operating in or near a defined area, are the half-way house between a conventional bus and a taxi. They still require a sig-nificant and constant demand and a number of them have existed for a fairly short period of time.

Some of those that continue may evolve into a largely fixed route sched-ule, although more frequently adjusted than the conventional network. This is an excellent example of how the industry is attempting to meet people's needs with an ability to adjust services accordingly.

Community transport

Additional to the conventionally provided bus network, as summarized above, the role of community transport could potentially provide an en-larged role. This might be, especially in the combined travel business, meet-ing the needs of specialist groups, as well as offering rural bus links and services to those living in less densely populated suburban communities.

Conclusions

Buses, coaches and the services they provide will certainly not disappear; they are essential. But they need to be provided to a high quality, with con-sistency and relevance to the community. Easy-to-access information on ser-vices and making it easy to pay for them will remain priorities, along with continuing to ensure they are available to all, regardless of disability. But buses can only be successfully delivered as part of a team comprising all the other stakeholders with an interest in improving the quality of life in any community.

Indications show these are being acknowledged and followed.

References

CPT (2019) *Moving Forward Together*, London

Low Carbon Vehicle Partnership (nd) [online] www.lowcvp.org.uk/ (archived at https://perma.cc/BW4W-ZZUF)

TfL (2019) [accessed 5 December 2019] Improving buses, *TfL* [online] https://tfl. gov.uk/modes/buses/improving-buses (archived at https://perma.cc/ XX7U-HF82)

Further reading

Buses Magazine [online] www.busesmag.com/ (archived at https://perma.cc/ VC7T-RJ77)

Omnibus Magazine [online] www.mercedes-benz-bus.com/en_GB/brand/omnibus-magazin.html (archived at https://perma.cc/XNP5-F6UW)

Passenger Transport (nd) [accessed 21 February 2020] The Magazine, *Passenger Transport* [online] www.passengertransport.co.uk/the-magazine/ (archived at https://perma.cc/HAE2-SVYF)

Focus Magazine (Chartered Institute of Logistics and Transport) [online] https:// ciltuk.org.uk/News/Focus-Magazine (archived at https://perma.cc/NAL7-6DWF)

UK Bus Awards [online] www.ukbusawards.org.uk/content/index.php (archived at https://perma.cc/JKL4-JRG7)

APPENDIX I: REGULATION OF ROAD PASSENGER TRANSPORT IN THE REPUBLIC OF IRELAND

Cyril McIntyre

Historical background

Following the establishment of the Irish Free State in 1922, pre-existing legislation governing railways and road traffic remained in force. Subsequent new legislation in these sectors was enacted along similar lines to that of the United Kingdom. For example, the Railways Act 1924 amalgamated all railway companies within the State to form the Great Southern Railways, excluding those operating cross-border lines into Northern Ireland.

The Road Transport Act 1932 introduced a licensing system for bus and coach services similar to that of the UK Road Traffic Act 1930. The Road Transport Act 1933 facilitated the acquisition of many independent operators by the statutory railway and tramway companies, with provision for compulsory acquisition by Ministerial order, including arbitration on compensation, in cases where voluntary agreement could not be reached.

The Transport Act 1944 created Córas Iompair Éireann (which translates literally as 'Transport System of Ireland') by amalgamating the Great Southern Railways and the Dublin United Transport Company. Under the Transport Act 1950, CIÉ was amalgamated with the Grand Canal Company and nationalized, becoming a statutory state-owned commercial body. In 1958 that part of the Great Northern Railway (Ireland) operating within the Republic was absorbed by CIÉ; the Northern Ireland operations of the GNR(I) became part of the then-Ulster Transport Authority.

Over the years since 1973, when Ireland became a member of what was then the European Economic Community, now the European Union, all relevant EU Directives and Regulations governing road transport have been duly transposed into Irish law. EU legislation governs the requirements to hold a Road Passenger Transport Operator's Licence, driving hours, organization of working time and licensing of international services.

The basis for general road traffic legislation is the Road Traffic Act 1961, which has been amended and updated by a succession of Road Traffic Acts over the years. Under this legislation, the Road Safety Authority (RSA) implements the Driver Licensing system, the issue of Road Passenger Transport Operator's Licences and the Vehicle Roadworthiness Testing system. The RSA is also responsible for enforcement of driving hours regulations, in conjunction with An Garda Síochána (the national police force). An Garda Síochána is also responsible for issue of public service vehicle licences.

The Public Transport Regulation Act 2009 repealed the Road Transport Act 1932 and transferred responsibility for licensing bus and coach services from the Department of Transport to the National Transport Authority (NTA).

The National Transport Authority

The NTA is a statutory non-commercial body, operating under the aegis of the Department of Transport, Tourism and Sport. It was established in 2009 under the Dublin Transport Authority Act 2008, originally as a transport authority for the Greater Dublin Area (GDA). It was renamed the National Transport Authority in the Public Transport Regulation Act 2009.

In 2010, the role of the NTA was extended to include the provision of integrated information schemes for public transport in the cities and counties of Cork, Galway, Limerick and Waterford, and the neighbouring areas of those counties.

Since 2011, the NTA is responsible for regulation of the small public service vehicle sector, in accordance with the Taxi Regulation Act 2003.

The NTA objective is to develop and implement key strategies that will ultimately provide high-quality, accessible, sustainable transport connecting people in communities across Ireland.

NTA's role in public transport

At the national level, NTA's role is to:

- procure public transport services by means of public transport services contracts;
- provide integrated ticketing, fares and public transport information;

- develop an integrated, accessible public transport network;
- license public bus passenger services that are not subject to a public transport services contract;
- manage the Rural Transport Programme and the successor structure of Local Link offices;
- provide bus infrastructure, fleet and cycling facilities;
- develop and implement a single public transport brand;
- develop and maintain a regulatory framework for the control and operation of small public service vehicles (taxis, hackneys and limousines) and their drivers;
- prepare submissions in relation to statutory land use plans;
- collect statistical data and information on transport;
- enforce EU passenger rights in rail, maritime and bus and coach transport;
- validate EU authorizations and journey forms in relation to bus and coach travel, in accordance with EU Regulation 1073/2009;
- operate as the national conciliation body for electronic toll service providers;
- regulate vehicle clamping operations.

Within the Greater Dublin Area, the NTA has additional roles to:

- undertake strategic planning of transport;
- secure the provision of public transport infrastructure;
- develop the effective management of traffic and transport demand.

In addition to its statutory functions, the NTA undertakes a number of functions on behalf of the Department of Transport, Tourism and Sport on a non-statutory basis. These include:

- planning and funding of sustainable transport projects in the regional cities of Cork, Galway, Limerick and Waterford;
- administration of the Smarter Travel Workplaces programme;
- management of the Green Schools Travel programme;
- provision of accessibility funding to transport operators and other relevant bodies;
- advancing Ireland's transition to a low emissions transport system.

Transport for Ireland

Transport for Ireland (TFI) was developed by the National Transport Authority as a single unified brand to promote and coordinate the provision of public transport in Ireland. Detailed information on each individual transport operator is still available on their own websites.

TFI is a 'one-stop shop' for public transport information, helping public transport users access information on all aspects of travel by using the following apps:

- TFI Journey Planner – helps people plan their journeys, using public transport, walking or cycling;
- Real-Time Passenger Information – gives real-time information for train, bus and tram services throughout Ireland, including Dublin Bus, Bus Éireann, Go-Ahead Ireland, DART, Iarnród Éireann and Luas;
- TFI Leap Card – a convenient way to pay for public transport in Ireland, available in Dublin, Cork, Galway, Limerick, Waterford, Athlone, Sligo and Wexford;
- information on taxis, walking and cycling in Ireland.

Bus and coach licensing

Under the Public Transport Regulation (PTR) Act 2009, the National Transport Authority is responsible for the licensing of public bus passenger services, often referred to as 'commercial bus services', as they are operated without any public subsidy from the NTA.

The PTR Act 2009 defines public bus passenger services:

- Each journey is used by members of the public.
- A charge or charges are paid in respect of each passenger.
- Save where the NTA otherwise determines:
  - the service is provided on a regular and scheduled basis;
  - carriage is provided for passengers between specified terminal points or a specified route, or otherwise in accordance with a published timetable.

Bus services which do not require a licence under the PTR Act 2009 include:

- those provided solely for the transport of children to or from school, excluding third level education;
- those that are subject to a public services contract with the NTA, entered into under the Dublin Transport Authority Act 2008;
- international services (authorized under EU regulations).

Anyone who has a valid Tax Clearance Certificate may apply for a licence. Applicants who do not hold a Road Transport Operator's Licence may apply once they can prove that they have the capacity to provide the service. When a completed application is received and validated by the NTA, it is considered in line with the requirements of the PTR Act 2009.

These requirements include taking account of:

- the demand or potential demand that exists for the public bus passenger services, to which the application refers, by considering the needs of consumers;
- any existing public bus passenger services on or in the vicinity of the route to be served by the proposed public bus passenger services;
- the impact the proposed service would have on public passenger transport services that are subject to a public transport services contract on or in the vicinity of the proposed route.

Licence categories

There are currently five categories of public bus passenger service licence.

1. Regular service licences

This category provides for the regular transport of passengers on a predetermined route, with predetermined pick-up/set-down points. Services of this nature could include:

- Interurban services: services linking major towns and cities. Such services may be further categorized as:
  - express services – with no immediate stops or limited intermediate stops at major towns or cities on the route. For example: Cork to Limerick to Galway;

- multi-stop services – with multiple intermediate stops between terminal points.

- Commuter services: services to centres of employment or education (not a bus service solely for carrying children to or from school), which are provided to match the travel patterns of commuters, predominately in the peak travel periods.

- Rural services: services linking two or more small towns, villages, or rural areas.

- Urban/suburban services: includes the majority of services that operate within urban and suburban areas.

Licences in this category are valid for three years and are renewable under section 16 of the PTR Act 2009. Licences can be for an all-year-round service or for seasonal services; for example, summer months or academic terms.

2. Specific targeted services (including tours, social events, etc)

This category applies to operations providing dedicated services specific to groups such as tourists or social event attendees.

There are two categories of specific targeted services:

- city or regional hop-on/hop-off tourist services;
- services for people attending specific social events, which may serve one destination or may include intermediate stops.

Licences in this category are valid for three years, and are renewable under section 16 of the PTR Act 2009.

3. Event- or venue-specific licences

This category applies to provision of services to:

- events: such as a festival, race meeting, concert, etc;
- venues: all events for a period of twelve months at a specific venue.

Licences in this category are not renewable; future applications are considered without any entitlements arising from previous licences held for a particular event.

Licences in this category are valid for the period of the event or for twelve months for a venue with a number of events.

4. Temporary services

This is a special category of licence to facilitate provision of bus services in exceptional circumstances.

5. Demand-responsive services

Services authorized to have optional routes that reflect specific demands; for example, a service that addresses the specific needs of particular people living in relatively remote locations, normally provided for passengers who have booked in advance. Licences in this category are valid for one year, and are renewable under section 16 of the PTR Act 2009.

International services

International Service Authorizations are issued by the NTA under the provisions of Regulation (EC) No 1073/2009. If a proposed International Service includes pick-up and set-down of passengers solely within the Republic of Ireland, a National Licence may be required in addition to the International Authorization.

Further information

Department of Transport, Tourism & Sport [online] www.dttas.ie (archived at https://perma.cc/R4UU-TAQ3)

Irish Statute Book [online] www.irishstatutebook.ie (archived at https://perma.cc/M46B-NRZ9)

National Transport Authority [online] www.nationaltransport.ie (archived at https://perma.cc/A8AS-5RKP)

Road Safety Authority [online] www.rsa.ie (archived at https://perma.cc/EW2F-F74Z)

Transport for Ireland [online] www.transportforireland.ie (archived at https://perma.cc/ZM2F-P895)

APPENDIX II: SCOTLAND'S BUSES

Gavin Booth

Scotland's national transport agency is Transport Scotland, an executive agency of the Scottish Government. Its stated aims are:

- to provide the environment for the bus to act as an effective economic enabler by providing competitive, high-quality public transport;

- to enable the bus to provide an effective alternative to the car by improving reliability, average bus speed and encouraging improvements to the quality of services and infrastructure;

- to encourage investment in more efficient vehicles that produce less greenhouse gases and contribute to the targets in the Climate Change (Scotland) Act 2009;

- to link communities, people, places of business and employment and essential services through encouraging the maintenance and development of the bus network in Scotland.

The majority of bus services in Scotland are operated on a commercial basis by private bus companies. Some 80 per cent of vehicle kilometres are on commercial services, and this figure has remained fairly steady over the period 2010–20. Vehicle kilometres per head of population works out at 61.4 – Scotland's population is around 5.4 million; the equivalent figure for Great Britain, with a population of over 64 million, is considerably lower at 36.7.

The principal operators are First, with a significant presence in Aberdeen and the greater Glasgow area; Stagecoach, with bus and express coach services throughout Scotland, from Orkney to Dumfries & Galloway; West Coast, with local services as well as its Glasgow Citybus and Borders Bus operations; council-owned Lothian Buses, with its Edinburgh city fleet and expanding services in the Lothians; McGill's, operating in Glasgow, Paisley, Greenock and along the Clyde coast; and National Express, which provides the urban services trading as Xplore Dundee.

The number of public service vehicles in Scotland sits at around the 4,000 mark, which represents a 10 per cent drop since 2015. The average age of the bus fleet is 8.5 years.

The number of passenger journeys made on buses in Scotland has declined from over 400 million annually in 2016 to 380 million in 2019; of these, more than a third were made under the National Concessionary Travel Scheme. The greatest drop in passenger numbers has been in the Highlands, Islands and Shetland, where numbers have fallen by 20 per cent in five years. The lowest drop over this period, just 3 per cent, has been in the south-east – Edinburgh and the Lothians, Fife, Central Scotland and the Borders.

Local or Central Government funding for the Scottish bus industry totalled £300 million in 2017/18, while passenger revenue was £385 million. Local transport authorities can provide subsidy for services that are not provided on a commercial basis, but this is entirely a matter for the local authority.

Following eight rounds of the Scottish Green Bus Fund to encourage bus operators to invest in low emission vehicles, Transport Scotland intends to launch its Ultra-Low Emission Bus Scheme to reduce carbon emissions from buses and improve air quality, particularly in urban environments. Since 2010 bus operators have been able to apply for the Bus Service Operators Grant, a subsidy that encourages the operation of green, environmentally-friendly buses.

A comprehensive piece of legislation now exists with the recently implemented Transport (Scotland) Act 2019. This pursues implementation and management of low emission zones, but importantly offers flexibility in the development and implementation of partnerships between bus operators and local authorities (both local councils and regional transport authorities). It embraces service planning, fares and ticketing, taking advantage of multi-modal smartcard technology and provision of information, along with the option of franchising.

It also allows the opportunity for local authorities to run their own local bus services, if that is considered appropriate to address the travel needs of the community.

INDEX

Note: conclusions, further reading, introductions *and* references are indexed as such; page numbers for figures and tables are in *italics*.